The Politics of Deforestation in Africa

Nadia Rabesahala Horning

The Politics of Deforestation in Africa

Madagascar, Tanzania, and Uganda

Nadia Rabesahala Horning
Department of Political Science
Middlebury College
Middlebury, VT, USA

ISBN 978-3-030-08301-4   ISBN 978-3-319-76828-1 (eBook)
https://doi.org/10.1007/978-3-319-76828-1

© The Editor(s) (if applicable) and The Author(s) 2018
Softcover re-print of the Hardcover 1st edition 2018
This work is subject to copyright. All rights are solely and exclusively licensed by the Publisher, whether the whole or part of the material is concerned, specifically the rights of translation, reprinting, reuse of illustrations, recitation, broadcasting, reproduction on microfilms or in any other physical way, and transmission or information storage and retrieval, electronic adaptation, computer software, or by similar or dissimilar methodology now known or hereafter developed.
The use of general descriptive names, registered names, trademarks, service marks, etc. in this publication does not imply, even in the absence of a specific statement, that such names are exempt from the relevant protective laws and regulations and therefore free for general use.
The publisher, the authors and the editors are safe to assume that the advice and information in this book are believed to be true and accurate at the date of publication. Neither the publisher nor the authors or the editors give a warranty, express or implied, with respect to the material contained herein or for any errors or omissions that may have been made. The publisher remains neutral with regard to jurisdictional claims in published maps and institutional affiliations.

Cover image: Per Bengston/Alamy Stock Photo
Cover design: Thomas Howey

Printed on acid-free paper

This Palgrave Macmillan imprint is published by the registered company Springer International Publishing AG part of Springer Nature
The registered company address is: Gewerbestrasse 11, 6330 Cham, Switzerland

Ho an'i Naina sy Nanja, ary koa ny zanaka aman-jafiny.

Acknowledgements

There is irony in single authorship when one's work depends on so many others' input and support. I am indebted to the many farmers, government officials, NGO workers, scholars, and researchers from whom I learned so much over the course of decades of research. I also owe much to three individuals who helped me navigate variable logistical and cultural environments in Madagascar, Tanzania, and Uganda. Whenever I needed them, Josiane Ravaosolo, Lydia Mbaze, and Mohamed Bukenya were there. Working with them was a joy.

Colleagues from Sokoine University of Agriculture and Makerere University kindly hosted me and supported me anyway they could to make this research possible. A heartfelt thank you goes out to Professors George Kajembe, Seif Madofe, Susan Balaba, and to my wonderful Swhahili teachers, Dr. Waithera Roki and Olais Mungaya.

Away from the field, exceptionally dedicated Middlebury College students were instrumental in helping sift through scholarship, organize data, and conduct statistical analyses. Nandumiso Qwabe, Cullen Edes, and Hannah Stonebraker were veritable heroes, and I will not soon forget their patience and professionalism. Middlebury College, including the Rohatyn Center for Global Affairs, was generous in its support to make it all possible.

My gratitude also goes out to colleagues whose own areas of expertise fall outside my own and yet were generous enough to help me clarify my argument. David Steinhardt, Mark E. Williams, and anonymous reviewers read parts of or the entire manuscript at various stages of its development. Their editorial and substantive suggestions helped me improve this book's content and style. Any remaining shortcomings are mine alone.

At Palgrave Macmillan, Alina Yurova, John Stegner, Velvizhi Mari, and Mary Fata knew just how to balance firmness and flexibility to advance this manuscript through the various stages of production. It was delightful to work with them.

Through years of research, travel across Africa, juggling multiple projects in academia, and raising two sons, Ned Horning was my steady source of stability and comfort. Accomplishments are his as much as they are mine.

To all, misaotra betsaka!

ansanteni sana!

weebale nnyo!

Contents

1 Why Deforestation Persists in Africa: Actors, Interests, and Interest Alignment — 1

2 Seeing Like a Farmer: Resource Politics at the Community Level — 43

3 Executive Branches and Trees: Environmental Politics at the National Level — 89

4 Across the Great Divide: Collaborative Forest Management — 135

5 Epilogue — 165

Index — 177

ABBREVIATIONS

ANAE	*Association Nationale d'Actions Environnementales* (Madagascar)
ANGAP	*Association Nationale pour la Gestion des Aires Protégées* (now MANAPA)
CBFM	Community-Based Forest Management (Tanzania)
CBNRM	Community-Based Natural Resource Management
CCM	*Chama Cha Mapinduzi* (Tanzania)
CFM	Collaborative Forest Management (Tanzania and Uganda)
CFMA	Collaborative Forest Management Agreement
CFR	Central Forest Reserve (Uganda)
CLB or COBA	Communauté Locale de Base
DD	*Direction des Domaines* (Madagascar)
DEA	Directorate of Environmental Affairs (Uganda)
DEF	*Direction des Eaux et Forêts* (Madagascar)
DFS	District Forest Service
FD	Forest Department (Uganda)
FID	Forestry Inspectorate Division (Uganda)
FR	Forest Reserves (Uganda)
FSSD	Forestry Sector Support Department (Uganda)
FTM	*Foiben-Taosarintanin'i Madagasikara* (national geographic institute)
GCF	*Gestion Contractuelle des Forêts* (contract-based forest management, Madagascar)
GELOSE	*Gestion Locale Sécurisée* (secured local [resource] management, Madagascar)

GTZ	*Deutsche Gesellschaft für Technische Zusammenarbeit* (now GIZ for Deutsche Gesellschaft für Internationale Zusammenarbeit)
IFI	International Financial Institution
IFRI	International Forest Resources and Institutions
IUCN	International Union for Conservation of Nature
JFM	Joint Forest Management (Tanzania)
JMA	Joint Management Agreement
KFW	*Kreditanstalt für Wiederaufbau*
LAFR	Local Authority Forest Reserve (Tanzania)
LC	Local Councils (Uganda)
LFR	Local Forest Reserve (Uganda)
LOGA	Local Government Authority (Tanzania)
MAAIF	Ministry of Agriculture, Animal Industry and Fisheries (Uganda)
MANAPA	Madagascar National Parks
ME	Ministry of Environment (Uganda)
MEMD	Ministry of Energy and Mineral Development (Uganda)
MITI	Ministry of Tourism, Trade and Industry (Uganda)
MLG	Ministry of Local Government (Uganda)
MWE	Ministry of Water and Environment (Uganda)
NCAA	Ngorongoro Conservation Area Authority (Tanzania)
NEAP	National Environmental Program
NEMA	National Environment Management Authority (Uganda)
NFA	National Forest Authority (Uganda)
NFR	National Forest Reserve (Tanzania)
NGO	Non-Governmental Organization
ONE	*Office National de l'Environnement* (Madagascar)
PA	Protected Area
PCE	Policy Committee on Environment (Uganda)
PFE	Permanent Forest Estate (Uganda)
PFM	Participatory Forest Management
PRC	People's Republic of China
PRSP	Poverty Reduction Strategy Paper
SAP	Structural Adjustment Program
SFD	Scientific and Forest Department (Uganda)
SMB	*Secrétariat Multi-Bailleurs* (Madagascar)
TANAPA	Tanzania National Parks
TANU	Tanganyika National Union
TAS	Tanzania Assistance Strategy
UNDP	United Nations Development Programme
USAID	United States Agency of International Development
UWA	Uganda Wildlife Authority
VFC	Village Forest Committee

LIST OF FIGURES

Fig. 1.1	Theoretical framework for analyzing forest conservation outcomes	4
Fig. 2.1	Study sites in southern Madagascar	46
Fig. 2.2	Five communities near four forests in Bara land, Madagascar	50
Fig. 3.1	Institutional framework for forest management in Madagascar	104
Fig. 3.2	Institutional framework for forest management in Tanzania	108
Fig. 3.3	Institutional framework for forest management in Uganda	113
Fig. 3.4	Institutional linkages among development sectors: Uganda	118

LIST OF TABLES

Table 1.1	Forest as percentage of land in Madagascar, Tanzania, and Uganda	9
Table 2.1	Rates of compliance with state and community rules around Analavelona, Madagascar (*Source* Author's Madagascar survey)	57
Table 2.2	Self-reported illegal uses of Zombitse forest, Madagascar. Forty-four respondents discussed which rules are enforced and how they are enforced (*Source* Author's Madagascar survey)	63
Table 2.3	Impact of legitimacy and enforcement on rule compliance in Madagascar and Tanzania (combined) (*Source* Author's Madagascar and Tanzania surveys)	76
Table 2.4	What type of leader are you most comfortable with? (*Source* Author's Madagascar and Tanzania surveys)	78
Table 2.5	Ugandan farmers' problems with forest governance (*Source* Uganda IFRI/SANREM)	79
Table 2.6	The relationship between rule enforcers and compliance in Uganda	81
Table 2.7	Relationship between external enforcement and user group compliance in Uganda (*Source* Uganda IFRI/SANREM)	81
Table 3.1	Net ODA as percentage of GNI (1990–2009) (*Source* World Bank (WDI online))	95
Table 4.1	Models of CBNRM for forest management in the three countries	143

CHAPTER 1

Why Deforestation Persists in Africa: Actors, Interests, and Interest Alignment

Since 1990, the government of Madagascar and its development partners have spent an impressive US$700 to preserve the island's exceptional biodiversity.[1] This unprecedented investment in the country's environmental sector put Madagascar on a promising path to sustainable development. But on March 17, 2009, the island experienced something resembling a coup d'état. A group of disgruntled politicians, led by the young neophyte Andry Rajoelina, seized power from twice democratically elected President Marc Ravalomanana. In short order, the African Union and broader international community declared they would not recognize the new government, and the AU threatened to suspend Madagascar's membership. The international donor community swiftly froze non-humanitarian aid and vowed that only the restoration of democratic rule would normalize relations again. This event, along with similar developments elsewhere on the continent, sent shock waves out of Africa and defied the optimism of those who believed in the possibility of democratic rule in Africa.

Meanwhile, far from the capital region, loggers were busily preparing shipments of timber harvested, in defiance of Malagasy law, to overseas markets. For these entrepreneurs, no news could have been better than the new political disorder. The chaos meant a free for all for resource extraction. Within weeks, cargo containers filled with precious hardwoods left the island on French ships headed for Asia. Effectively, this meant that deforestation was back in full swing despite the progress Madagascar had made under the previous administration to stop

© The Author(s) 2018
N. R. Horning, *The Politics of Deforestation in Africa*,
https://doi.org/10.1007/978-3-319-76828-1_1

1

environmental degradation from devastating the country's economy and natural heritage.

To many, this tragic turn of events was just more trouble from Africa, a continent that intrigues onlookers in part because its problems seem so many but also because its promise is so great. The current excitement about the continent's promise is captured in a statement made by US Secretary of State, John Kerry, in the Washington Post on May 2, 2014:

> The best untold story of the last decade may be the story of Africa. Real income has increased more than 30 percent, reversing two decades of decline. Seven of the world's 10 fastest-growing economies are in Africa, and GDP is expected to rise 6 percent per year in the next decade. HIV infections are down nearly 40 percent in sub-Saharan Africa and malaria deaths among children have declined 50 percent. Child mortality rates are falling, and life expectancy is increasing.[2]

For all the enthusiasm these recent developments have generated, many continue to think of Africa as war-torn, disease-ridden, poverty-stricken, or democratically challenged.[3] As of late, environmental problems have joined the continent's growing list of crises. Africa's environmental woes are not a recent phenomenon, but they have garnered more and more attention because they have worsened and taken new forms. Today they include desertification, recurring droughts, air and water pollution, and deforestation. Deforestation is commonly regarded as an issue because of the multiple problems associated with the phenomenon. Prominent among them are habitat loss, soil erosion, carbon emission, loss of biodiversity, decreased agricultural productivity, etc. It bears keeping in mind, however, that deforestation comes with concrete benefits including expansion of agricultural lands for subsistence and commercial farmers, employment and income-generating opportunities for multiple economic operators through timber and other trades, legal and illicit. Additionally, global consumers who gain access to inexpensive commodities that enhance their living standards benefit from deforestation.[4] On balance, however, the costs associated with deforestation far exceed the benefits, even if one looks at the number of winners versus losers. As such, deforestation preoccupies more than it excites.

This book explains why deforestation persists in Sub-Saharan Africa despite concerted efforts to conserve the continent's forests. It analyzes persistent deforestation by examining the workings of three African political systems, Madagascar, Tanzania, and Uganda, with special focus on how decision-making power is negotiated and exercised at two principal levels: the local, where communities make decisions regarding forests on a daily basis, and the national, where environmental policies are negotiated and enacted. Madagascar, Tanzania, and Uganda are good cases to examine the political economy of forest conservation for two important reasons. First, as detailed below, all three countries' forest policy efforts have benefitted from foreign donors' support largely due to their exceptional biodiversity. Second, despite strong support for forest conservation, Madagascar, Tanzania, and Uganda have experienced deforestation above the continental average, albeit to variable degrees. Put differently, the three countries have had variable success with forest conservation even though all three have attracted significant foreign assistance to fight deforestation. For these reasons, these countries help understand the politics of deforestation in Africa.

The book's central claim is that deforestation persists in Africa because conservation policies and projects, which are largely underwritten by foreign donors, consistently ignore the fact that conservation is possible only under limited and specific conditions. These conditions relate to the concurrent alignment of key actors' interests at two critical levels of decision-making: local and national. At the local level, the rules restricting forest access and uses are negotiated among village communities, public officials, and private businesses. Local actors' interests vis-à-vis forest resources entail conservation or exploitation for consumptive purposes (clearing for agriculture, logging, mining, food and medicine extraction, etc.) and nonconsumptive ones (worship, recreation, conservation, shelter for cattle, etc.). Consequently, when actors' interests converge toward forest protection rather than exploitation, the rules devised to restrict forest access raise the prospect of conservation significantly. Conversely, when actors' interests diverge, e.g., the state opts for conservation while private actors opt for exploitation (or vice versa), continued deforestation is likely regardless of whatever rules are devised. Under these conditions, those who make conservation rules develop the capacity and willingness to make such rules "matter." Thus, at the local level, actors' interests must align for conservation to happen.

At the national level, the most powerful actors are the executive-dominated African governments and the foreign donors who finance, wholly or in part, these governments' environmental initiatives. Together, these actors negotiate governments' approaches to development, deciding whether and to what extent they should favor environmental conservation. When donors' and governments' interests align, and conservation-friendly development policies are agreed upon, governments officially commit to conservation, and aid monies flow into African countries to create and expand environmental institutions. Under these conditions, the prospect of protecting Africa's forests is high. By contrast, when interests do not align, African governments refuse to prioritize environmental conservation, and it becomes nearly impossible to control deforestation regardless of institutional investments in the environmental sector. In short, and as is the case at the local level, controlling deforestation is contingent upon the successful alignment of government and donor interests at the national level. Figure 1.1 shows how conservation outcomes are possible under limited and specific conditions relating to the simultaneous alignment of actors' interests at both levels of environmental decision-making.

In arguing that the two levels of environmental decision-making work in tandem rather than interdependently, I do not mean to convey that no interactions exist between them. In fact, as detailed in Chapter 2, the conservation rules that apply at the local level frequently combine formal

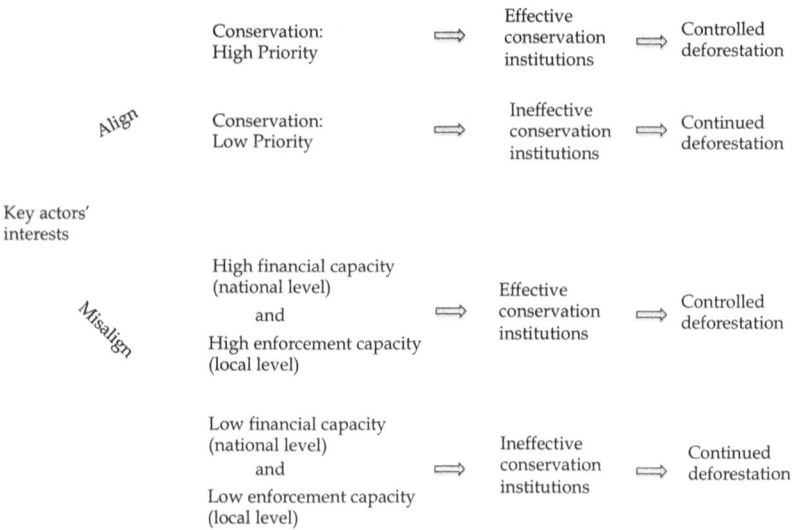

Fig. 1.1 Theoretical framework for analyzing forest conservation outcomes

legislation and community-devised rules. Likewise, as discussed in Chapter 3, deforestation happening at the local level informs interactions between foreign donors and African governments at the national level. Beyond those two domestic levels, deforestation rates deemed "alarming" by conservationists intensify environmental politics on the international scene. Summits on climate change, sustainable development, the Millennium Development Goals (MDGs) and subsequent Sustainable Development Goals (SDGs), and international conventions on various environmental issues, etc. attest to the impact of local-level forest processes on international politics. In turn, international negotiations infiltrate national politics, which percolates to locales where resources targeted for conservation are found. Thus, connections exist between levels of environmental politics. What rarely happens, and I suggest must happen, is the simultaneous alignment of interests at the various levels of environmental decision-making to increase the prospect of forest conservation.

I use the term interest alignment to refer to situations in which actors have shared, compatible, mutually supportive interests, or when one actor's interests do not undermine the others'.[5] Interests align, in the context of this study, when state officials and local communities aim to conserve a particular forest or when donors give aid to conservation-friendly governments. Interests are misaligned when actors have divergent, mutually undermining goals vis-à-vis forest resources.

In principle, aligning interests to achieve conservation should be straightforward. In reality, however, actors hold multiple interests simultaneously, and forest conservation is only one of them. For instance, donors' interests include conservation (in the case of conservation NGOs and the World Bank, for instance), self-promotion (supporting high visibility projects that make donors look good), giving aid and, to the extent that they are instruments of foreign policy, democracy promotion.

African governments, for their part, are often interested in maximizing aid inflows, maintaining and expanding patronage networks, enriching themselves personally by misappropriating aid and other public monies, and "greening" their profiles by committing to conservation friendly policies. This is not to suggest that African governments are never concerned about the environment. Clearly, some are. But there is often a gap between individual politicians' personal convictions and what policy issues they can actually pursue, given the range of problems and political constraints African governments face. Of these multiple interests, powerful actors share only two that support conservation: aid disbursements (giving aid for environmental conservation for donors and receiving it for governments) and image boosting (donors seen as good Samaritans and African government appearing green and progressive).

Clearly, thus, conservation is possible only under the limited and specific conditions at each of the two principal levels of environmental decision-making.

If international and domestic actors drive conservation politics, where are regional actors in the conservation picture? Conspicuously absent from meaningful participation in Africa's forest conservation efforts are regional organizations ostensibly designed to address the continent's common challenges and leverage shared opportunities. Africa enjoys an abundance of regional institutions, some more effective than others.[6] Considering this institutional wealth and also the severity of Africa's environmental problems, some transboundary, one would expect regional actors to play an active role in resource management. The fact is that regional efforts have focused primarily on issues outside of the environmental realm, with the notable exception of water issues confronting Nile River Basin countries and, to a lesser extent, deforestation in the Congo Basin. In reality, regional organizations in Africa have mobilized mostly around agriculture, trade, security and peace, human rights, migration and, to a lesser degree, tourism.[7]

This is not to suggest that no efforts to pool regional resources for environmental conservation have been made, but when it comes to environmental issues in Africa, Western governments, international organizations, and international NGOs have, by and large, been the facilitators, sometimes initiators, of regional cooperation. Regional efforts to conserve the Congo Basin forests in Central Africa illustrate this trend well. In 1999 Cameroon, Equatorial Guinea, the Republic of Congo, Chad, Gabon, and the Central African Republic signed an agreement, the Yaoundé Declaration, to tackle deforestation in the Congo Basin. These six countries formed the Central Africa Forests Commission (COMIFAC), a regional body whose aim is to coordinate and harmonize forest policy to secure the Congo Basin forests' sustainability. Despite demonstrated political will, however, COMIFAC's activities were limited due to lack of funding. In response to the organization's financial weakness, the Congo Basin Forest Fund (CBFF) was created in 2008. Managed by the African Development Bank, the fund is financed by Norway and the UK. Meanwhile, in 2002, the United States' Department of State set up the Congo Basin Forest Partnership Project, or CBFPP, a partnership of seventy stakeholders, including African countries, donor agencies and governments, international organizations, NGOs, scientific institutions and the private sector. As this example from the Congo Basin illustrates, international actors infiltrate conservation politics even when regional bodies form to tackle shared environmental problems. Thus, asymmetries of financial power, coupled with competing regional issues, emasculate regional organizations in the environmental realm.

Nor is it to suggest that there is no future in regional cooperation on the continent. The ongoing efforts to form an effective East African Community made up of Burundi, Kenya, Rwanda, South Sudan, Tanzania, and Uganda is an example of African states pooling their resources to benefit each other. But as Englebert and Dunn (2013) point out, a variety of obstacles have plagued regional groupings' efforts to "coordinate and harmonize policies" so far.[8] These obstacles range from overlapping structures that result in duplication and inefficiencies, disincentives to integrate effectively, intra-regional competition, conflicting regional ambitions and domestic political interests, and related lack of political will to invest in regional efforts. Thinking about the prospects of regional economic integration, Fantu Cheru (2002), like Englebert and Dunn, identifies lack of political will to succeed and he adds some additional hindrances that African countries need to overcome if they are to collaborate meaningfully. According to him, unfavorable legal environments, weak institutions, inadequate transport and communication networks, a shortage of skilled Africans, high commodity dependence, and a chronic colonial complex constitute serious barriers to successful regionalization. Signs of improvement abound in today's Africa, but it remains a reality that overcoming these structural barriers will take concerted effort and time.

Deforestation in the African Context

Deforestation data are notoriously problematic. For one thing, no consensus exists on how to define deforestation.[9] For another, commonly used statistics confine themselves to national-level data, thereby failing to capture variations at the subnational level. Compounding these problems is the fact that deforestation is a dynamic phenomenon, which static data do not capture adequately. With these caveats in mind, comparisons require using consistent data as much as possible.[10] To that end, the United Nations Food and Agriculture Organization (FAO) estimates that 16% of the world's forests are located in Africa.[11] According to some estimates, only about 8% of the continent's original forests remain as large intact natural ecosystems. The Congo Basin rainforest, which is the world's second largest after the Amazon's, is one of those intact ecosystems.

In Africa, the extent of forested land decreased steadily from nearly 70 million hectares to less than 63 million hectares from 1990 to 2007.[12] Average figures for forested land as percentage of the national territory shrank throughout the continent in the same period, going from nearly 24% to less than 23%.[13] In Uganda alone, forest cover diminished from 10.8 million hectares in 1980 to 4.9 million hectares in 1995 and, currently, there are no signs of deforestation abating. Today, half the country's forests have been cleared for agriculture (land and grazing areas), firewood, pit sawing, charcoal making, and industrial development. A review of Uganda's forest sector in the early 2000s estimated that forestry, overall, contributes around 6% of the country's GDP if one takes into account commercial forestry, subsistence uses (wood and non-wood forest products) and the value of ecological services.[14] In terms of ecological value, Uganda's forests and woodlands play a critical role for watershed protection (which in turn affects water supply), soil erosion control, biodiversity conservation (which benefits tourism), and carbon sequestration. Culturally, forests "have also helped to preserve cultures of different communities within the country."[15] This is true for the Buganda kingdom as well as sacred groves throughout the country.[16]

Of course, not all African countries have experienced deforestation to the same extent. In fact, from 1990 to 2005 deforestation rates varied across Africa's eastern-southern, northern-western, and central zones.[17] Of the three zones, annual deforestation rates were highest in eastern-southern Africa and they exceeded average figures for the continent as a whole. Within this region, Madagascar, Tanzania, and Uganda are among biodiversity-rich countries that have yet to control this problem.

FAO data on annual deforestation rates indicate that, overall, from 1980 to 2005 all three countries experienced negative annual change rates in forest cover. Uganda and Tanzania's rates of forest loss, in fact, exceed the average rates for the entire continent for the 1990–2005 period.[18] By contrast, Madagascar experienced a modest improvement in forest conservation during this period. Table 1.1 shows, in fact, that Madagascar lost the least amount of forest from 1990 to 2010 and that forest losses stabilized in the 2005–2010 period.

Looking at these three countries' deforestation statistics, one would think that little has been done about the problem. This is not so. In fact, money can be said to grow on trees in these places: Due to their forests'

Table 1.1 Forest as percentage of land in Madagascar, Tanzania, and Uganda

	1990	2000	2005	2010
Madagascar	24	23	22	22
Tanzania	47	42	40	38
Uganda	24	19	17	15

ecological importance, these countries have been privileged beneficiaries of conservationists' largesse. Madagascar's environmental program alone garnered donor support of at least US$420 from 1991 to 2008.[19] Not surprisingly, the three countries have been the locus of intense conservation politics. Differences in conservation performance, in light of similar opportunities, make Madagascar, Tanzania, and Uganda excellent cases for the study of Africa's conservation politics.

Considering the foreign support that African governments receive to help them control deforestation and associated environmental problems, the larger context of international environmental politics must be kept in mind when assessing conservation efforts in Africa. Due partly to concerns about global warming, deforestation has become an issue of public policy, not just within African polities, but around the globe. Taming the global "bads" that deforestation brings about has compelled an increasing number of key actors including international organizations, governments, civil societies, and farmers at the international, national, and local levels to become involved in managing forest resources in novel ways. Obviously, for those benefitting from deforestation the incentive to govern forest access and uses differently is nonexistent. But for those suffering from deforestation, including champions of environmental conservation and other deforestation victims, change is imperative. As a result, support for conservation has expanded to involve a vast array of actors all over the world. Put differently, the politics of conservation has intensified. International environmental agreements such as the Convention on Biological Diversity (CBD), on the one hand, and multi-stakeholder, multilevel governance initiatives like REDD+ (Reducing Emissions from Deforestation and Forest Degradation) and FLEGT (Forest Law Enforcement, Governance and Trade), on the other hand, are evidence of the intensification of conservation politics since the 1990s. In principle, these global agreements and initiatives are robust tools against the depletion of the world's natural resources, including forests. Their limited success, however, has raised questions about their practicality and even theoretical soundness. Although it is beyond this book's scope to detail the challenges inherent in global environmental governance per se, doing so succinctly offers a valuable theoretical backdrop for the puzzle at hand, namely the persistence of deforestation despite concerted efforts to combat it in Africa. REDD+ is a particularly good initiative to examine since it is explicitly built around the notion of multilevel, multi-stakeholders governance, which is at the core of this book's argument.

A global concern for forest conservation connects the CBD, REDD+, and FLEGT. A quick description of these global programs is needed before discussing why agreed-upon goals and principles have been challenged in practice. Inspired by the international community's commitment to sustainable development, the CBD was introduced at the 1992 United Nations Conference on Environment and Development that took place in Rio de Janeiro. The first international treaty to single out biodiversity protection as a shared goal, with 168 signatories the CBD "represents a dramatic step forward in the conservation of biological diversity, the sustainable use of its component, and the fair and equitable sharing of benefits arising from the use of genetic resources."[20]

With the core goal of reducing net emissions of greenhouse gases through enhanced forest management in developing countries, REDD+ was born as a concept in 2004 and put into motion in 2007 based on the knowledge that tropical deforestation contributes 12–18% of the world's GHG emissions.[21] Conceived as a mechanism developed by Parties to the United Nations Framework Convention on Climate Change (UNFCCC), REDD+ is a framework through which the international community pledges to financially compensate countries that are able and willing to reduce emissions from deforestation and forest degradation. As an international collaborative framework, it binds 64 countries in forest conservation and reforestation agreements across Africa (including Madagascar, Tanzania, and Uganda), Asia-Pacific, Latin America, and the Caribbean.[22] Partnering with the UN-REDD Programme gives signatory countries of the global south access to financial and technical support from the Food and Agriculture Organization of the United Nations (FAO), the United Nations Development Program (UNDP), and the United Nations Environment Program (UNEP). Fundamentally, REDD+ "creates a financial value for the carbon stored in forests by offering incentives for developing countries to reduce emissions from forested lands and invest in low-carbon paths to sustainable development. Developing countries would receive results-based payments for results-based actions."[23] Put differently, REDD+ is a framework for extending financial compensation to communities able and willing to control carbon emissions by conserving forests.

FLEGT, another large program aimed at controlling deforestation, was established in 2003 with the explicit goal of reducing illegal logging by strengthening sustainable and legal forest management as well as improving governance and promoting trade in legally produced timber.[24] Unlike REDD+, which is a UN program, FLEGT was designed as a European Union initiative in response to the fact that the EU is among the largest consumers of the world's timber. FLEGT recognizes that by importing large quantities of timber, EU member states deliberately or inadvertently exacerbate the problem of illegal logging in developing countries. Acknowledging the "devastating impact [of illegal logging] on some of the world's most valuable remaining forests, and on the people who live in them and rely on the resources that forests provide," EU member states introduced the EU Timber Regulation of 2013, and some of these member states have entered into Voluntary Partnership Agreements binding them and timber-producing countries to trade only in legally produced timber.[25]

For all the hope that these global environmental initiatives against climate change produced at the outset, to date they have had limited success, REDD+ being no exception. Analyses of REDD+'s limited success focus on its practical and theoretical flaws. Recall that REDD+ is the framework through which the international community offers financial incentives to countries with the capacity to reduce emissions from deforestation and forest degradation. Some scholars have assessed REDD+'s limitations on the basis of its theoretical premises including the application of an incentive-based model of forest conservation to "fragile" states and the belief that REDD+ projects will generate rents beyond financial gains, among other theoretical flaws. Of particular relevance to this book's argument is the issue of the political environments in which conservation projects are carried out. Seeing as REDD+ projects rely on countries where governance is conducted in ways that differ greatly from credit-needy countries' and also considering the fact that conservation payments are extended to forest-rich countries on the basis of their deforestation reduction performance, some scholars have brought into question the applicability of REDD+ projects in environments where "the failures of the rule of law, weak judiciary systems, and limited government reach are commonly mentioned, along with economic dysfunction and vulnerability to conflict."[26] In such governance conditions, they ask, how can governments realistically prioritize forest conservation over other development options? Additionally, how can such governments effectively include subnational actors to secure compliance with conservation standards?

On the practical side, a 2016 comprehensive review of the REDD+ literature identifies seven clusters that encompass the wide range of topics REDD+ researchers have raised since REDD+ projects' inception. Looking at the 2007–2016 period, the study identifies these clusters as: (1) benefit and opportunity costs; (2) forest cover monitoring; (3) land tenure, local peoples and indigenous communities; (4) ecosystems and biodiversity conservation; (5) safeguards and environmental and social principle; (6) community-based monitoring and land tenure security; and (7) institutional and governance structures.[27] Seeing as REDD+ "promotes the informed and meaningful involvement of all stakeholders, including indigenous peoples and other forest-dependent communities, in national and international REDD+ implementation,"[28] the UN-REDD Programme is a typical global, multi-stakeholder, multi-governance program. As such, and as Smouts (2008) points out, analyzing its limited success to date requires considering the challenges inherent in an international forest regime.[29] Since this study concerns itself with the institutional underpinnings of forest governance, researchers' insights on the seventh cluster of "institutional and governance structures" are worth noting.

> The general argument made by authors in this cluster is that good governance, which is a function of effective institutional arrangements, will play a key role in the success of REDD+. Given that REDD+ is a resource management regime, and given that the inefficiency of resource management regimes ha[s] been linked to governance failure (Pahl-Wostl 2009), the success of REDD+ will depend largely on good governance (and efficient institutions) (p. 147)

In this vein, Thompson et al. (2011) point out that REDD+ "attempts to bring about environmental governance by aligning the interests of a wide range of stakeholders in this process to bring about desired environmental outcomes," adding that "this alignment has thus far been incomplete, suggesting an emerging crisis of governance within REDD+ that will compromise future project and policy goals, and thus the well-being of many stakeholders."[30] In addition to identifying REDD+ projects' failure to align stakeholders' interests, the authors also highlight a critical flaw in the framework's design stating that "[T]hus far, the efforts at aligning the interests of various REDD+ stakeholders remain principally focused on those stakeholders engaged and comfortable with measures and governmental structures common to the Global North."[31]

The idea of REDD+ initiatives being largely exogenous to communities that they target is captured in the notion of discursive institutionalization that den Besten et al. (2014) aptly describe.[32] Their analysis of the REDD+ process from 2004 to 2011 shows how REDD was initiated by actors of the "Global North" with community-level decision makers eventually cast as instruments needed to achieve goals and interests that the latter did not necessarily share with global actors. States' mediation in the process has done little to enable the alignment of global and local actors' interests. Hence REDD+'s lackluster record. Nor is it the case that countries with the largest forests and, therefore, the highest emissions reduction capabilities host the greatest number of REDD+ projects. Mbatu notes, for instance, that Tanzania, which is relatively less forest-rich than its Congo Basin counterparts of Central Africa, has received a great deal of attention only because Norway, one of Tanzania's perennial forest sector donors, targeted Tanzania as soon as REDD+ was established.[33]

The above cursory overview of REDD+ as a framework for controlling global emissions by way of forest conservation and as a series of projects executed in countries of the Global South shows that REDD+ is yet another example of a multi-stakeholder, multilevel, and global initiative poorly conceived. It exemplifies conservation projects' inability to recognize the critical importance of interest alignment *from the local level up* that this book shows as the principal reason for Africa's persistent deforestation. This begs the question: Why is there such resistance to achieving interest alignment from the ground up? Tim Forsyth astutely observes that doing so is time-consuming.[34] Since donor-funded projects demand quick and visible results to sustain themselves, it becomes obvious that expediency must take precedence over the thoughtful management of multi-actor, multilevel forest governance projects.

Deforestation, a Complex Issue

Deforestation is a complex phenomenon. As such, it is not clear what drives it. Geist and Lambin (2002), for instance, find that in the Tropics, no single variable accounts for forest loss. Instead, their study of 152 cases across Africa, Asia, and Latin America leads them to conclude that a combination of proximate and underlying causes must be taken into account when explaining deforestation.[35] Additionally, they suggest, drivers of deforestation vary across geographies and historical contexts. With that in mind, they situate individual decisions within "changing national- to global-scale economic opportunities and/or policies, as mediated by local-scale institutional factors," pointing out that "regionally distinct modes of agricultural expansion, wood extraction, and infrastructure extension" constitute proximate causes.[36] The difficulty of isolating single explanatory variables is compounded by poor-quality data and weak methods that lead to questionable economics models that take into account wrong explanatory factors, the most common of which are discussed below.[37]

Unsurprisingly, no single body of literature suffices to account for Africa's persistent deforestation. Consequently, this analysis builds on insights from three bodies of scholarship, each of which offers explanations for deforestation. The first set of theories comes from the literature on deforestation and, relatedly though separate, forest conservation. In the last two decades research on these topics in developing countries has produced abundant scholarship on the reasons for and possible solutions to tropical deforestation.[38] The most commonly cited culprits are: (1) demographics (population growth, urbanization, the swelling of rural populations, the influx of refugees, other displacements, etc.); (2) poverty (agricultural expansion, subsistence economies, technology, education); (3) the international regime (trade, debt burden, aid dependency and aid ineffectiveness, foreign capital penetration, wars, international environmental agreements, etc.); and (4) institutional flaws and poor governance (uncertain property rights and limited tenure security, restricted rule of law, poor policies, etc.).[39]

As will be shown shortly, empirical evidence from Sub-Saharan Africa reveals that demographics, poverty, international regimes, and levels of aid dependency do not adequately account for variations in deforestation outcomes. From the vast literature on tropical deforestation, however, the role that donors play in influencing development policies becomes clear. Donors have used foreign aid as leverage to encourage African politicians to adopt conservation-friendly policies (or not). This has been the case in Madagascar, Uganda, and Tanzania. Donor influence is thus given prominence in the present analysis.

Tropical Deforestation

Population growth is one of the most commonly cited causes of deforestation in developing countries. Notwithstanding raging debates on the exact relationship between population growth and environmental degradation,[40] a glance at demographic trends shows that African countries with the best and worst deforestation records experienced similar annual population growth rates from the 1970s to the 2000s. On the one hand, Burundi experienced the biggest jump in deforestation from 1990 to 2005 (−3.7 to −9%), but its population was stable. The same is true of neighboring Rwanda.

Comparable demographic trends yielded no change in deforestation rates for the Central African Republic and Cameroon. On the other hand, a marked increase in population growth rates (from −0.71 to 2.6% from the 1970s to the 1990s) barely affected deforestation rates in Equatorial Guinea.

In the three countries under study, both Tanzania and Madagascar's population growth rates increased, but Madagascar's deforestation slowed down while Tanzania's accelerated. Uganda and Kenya's population trends are similar (and fairly stable, although high), but Kenya's deforestation did not worsen like Uganda's did. Based on this cursory examination of population and deforestation trends, in Africa the relationship between population growth and rates of deforestation is, at best, unclear. This observation echoes what several studies have concluded based on a variety of studies conducted in different parts of the non-Western world, which leads Mather and Needle (2000) to conclude that "[o]utright rejection of the notion that forest trends are related to population trends is no more justifiable than an unqualified assertion that population growth is *the* driver of deforestation."[41] Another important cause of deforestation discussed in the scholarship is poverty (broadly defined). If poverty and deforestation were clearly related, one would expect the poorest countries to experience the most deforestation and the richest the least.

While it is true that those countries experiencing the worst deforestation in the 1990–2000 period belong in the World Bank's Low-Income category, these countries' annual deforestation rates cover a wide range, with Burundi experiencing the worst deforestation (−9%) for this decade and The Gambia registering a positive rate of forest cover change (+1%). This variation is also observable in the lower middle-income countries (Cameroon −1%, Angola −0.3%; Republic of Congo −0.1%). Finally, some upper middle-income countries such as Equatorial Guinea and Mauritius experienced more deforestation than low-income countries such as Kenya, Tanzania, and The Gambia. At least in terms of these indicators, therefore, the relationship between poverty and deforestation is tenuous at best.

In the three countries of this study Uganda and Tanzania have worse deforestation records than Madagascar for 1990–2000 and 2000–2010. Yet from 1990 to 2000 and 2000 to 2010, the World Bank reports that Uganda's annual per capita GDP growth rate averaged at 3.3 and 3.5%, respectively, figures for Tanzania are 0.4 and 3.7%, and those for Madagascar are −1.2 and 0.2%.[42] If poverty alone caused deforestation, one would expect Uganda and Tanzania's economic performance to be worse than Madagascar's. Sub-Saharan Africa patterns reflect what Bhattarai and Hammig (2001) discovered through a cross-country analysis of the determinants of tropical deforestation in Africa, Asia, and Latin America.[43] They find that the relationship between income and deforestation varies across continents and that the relationship between levels of wealth and deforestation is anything but straightforward in Africa and elsewhere. Poverty alone thus cannot account for deforestation and one must look to other explanations.

Could it be that the more foreign aid a country receives, the better able it is to fight deforestation? Of the 42 Sub-Saharan countries for which WDI data on aid as percentage of GNI and deforestation data are available for the period 1990–2012, two (Gabon and Seychelles) registered no change in forest cover as percentage of land area; six (Cabo Verde, Côte d'Ivoire, Gambia, Lesotho, Rwanda, and Swaziland) experienced positive change; and the remaining 34 registered forest cover losses ranging from a staggering 82% in Comoros to a low 1.5% in the Republic of Congo. If more development aid (ODA) helped control deforestation, one would expect an inverse relationship between aid as percentage of GNI and deforestation rates. Looking at the eight countries that experience no to positive changes in forest cover from 1990 to 2012, foreign aid figures are variable. Only Cabo Verde and Rwanda confirm the hypothesis that more aid result in less deforestation. The other six countries had relatively low levels of aid as percentage of their GNI (7% or lower), suggesting that development assistance alone is not a reliable predictor of deforestation. Among the larger group of countries that experienced forest cover loss, only five (Angola, Botswana, Cameroon, Namibia, and Nigeria) were in the low aid recipient category (5% of GNI or lower), with all the others in the moderate (6–14%) to high (15% and higher) categories. In the three countries studied, the data also challenge the claim that more development assistance results in controlled deforestation. Tanzania and Uganda are the larger aid recipients, with average rates of 15.4 and 14.3%, respectively. The figure for Madagascar is 11.7%.[44] Foreign aid alone, therefore, cannot fully explain deforestation outcomes.

Correlation, of course, says little about causation, but the above glance at statistical trends helps unveil what various analyses on conditions for successful environmental conservation converge to conclude: (1) since no causal relationships are universal due to variable economic, political, and environmental contexts, each context must be carefully examined; and (2) the effects of conventional factors on deforestation are mitigated by other factors, notably institutions.[45] Agrawal (1995), for instance, finds in the Indian Lesser Himalayas that "[a]t the local and the micro level, a host of social and institutional variables mediate the impact of larger structural variables. Put directly, the level of institutional effectiveness is more important in determining the condition of resources than either population pressure or market forces *per se*."[46] A decade and a half later, Bhattarai and Hammig (2001) conclude something very similar looking at deforestation outcomes across America, Africa, and Asia: "The institutional dimension of the deforestation problem needs to be better scrutinized, especially with respect to the political economy of the EKC [Environmental Kuznets Curve], since democratic institutions also emerge as societal income increases."[47]

In sum, depending on specific ecological, economic, and political contexts, different factors affect deforestation in a variety of ways. Demographic, economic, and structural variables such as aid dependency do impact forests neither universally nor simultaneously across Africa, much less the rest of the world. An important reason for this variability has to do with mitigating factors, institutions being a prominent one.

However defined (rules, norms, property regimes, etc.), these institutions affect the state of forests by creating particular incentives at various levels of environmental decision-making: international, national, and local (or micro).

African Politics

African politics is the second body of scholarship that informs the puzzle at hand. Relative to other parts of the world and owing to its colonial history, Africa is considered a late bloomer in the realms of political and economic development. Upon achieving independence (mostly from the 1960s to the 1980s), African governments aimed for national unity and prosperity. This dual imperative ushered in an era of authoritarian rule ranging from benevolent dictatorships to tyrannies of the worst kind. So long as cold war politics enabled African leaders to centralize and monopolize power (by supporting Africa's "big men"), there was little incentive to move away from authoritarian rule. Arguably, this continued to be the case even after the Berlin Wall came down in 1989. But at that point, Western powers began to pressure African leaders to reform their political and economic systems. Reflecting this evolution, and considering the incidence of strife on the continent since the 1960s, four overarching themes have dominated the scholarship on African politics, namely: authoritarianism,[48] development,[49] democratization,[50] and conflicts.[51] Throughout this seemingly disparate literature, three fundamental concepts make African politics distinct: personal rule,[52] patronage politics,[53, 54] and predatory states.[55] At the heart of it all is the idea that those who have power use public resources such as oil and other minerals,[56] foreign aid,[57] or legal command[58] to achieve or stay in power and secure personal wealth.

Although natural resources such as forests and water are part of the public domain, few scholars have looked at how natural resource management strategies affect African political systems, and vice versa.[59] A few notable exceptions must nonetheless be acknowledged in the scholarly literature. Examining the making of wildlife policy in Zambia, Zimbabwe, and Kenya, Gibson (1999) unveils how interests and institutions, rather than political structure per se, shape power relations and political decisions in Southern Africa. Reno (1998), for his part, shows how oil, diamonds, and other minerals were instrumental in shaping warlord politics in Sierra Leone, the DRC, and Nigeria (in Liberia, timber supplemented minerals). Also connecting mineral wealth and the workings of African politics, Poteete (2009) shows that, in Botswana, broad and stable political coalitions prevented this mineral-rich country from falling into the classic resource curse traps including Dutch disease. Most recently, Nelson (2010) make a compelling case for understanding that "[f]ew matters are more central to the daily lives of African societies than the use and governance of natural resources."[60] Although this volume's focus is decentralized resource governance, it clearly shows how natural resource management is deeply political in the African context. In a similar way, Death (2016) states in the introduction of his book that "many students of African politics still tend to regard the green agenda as well below issues of conflict, security, poverty, development, etc. In contrast, I want to show that environmental politics is central to the production and transformation of states in Africa, and it has been a crucial element of governance and contestation of land, people, economies, and international relations."[61] Africanists concerned with natural resource management have focused primarily on wildlife management,[62] land tenure,[63] and mineral extraction,[64] mainly because these resources play a critical role in African economies and, in the case of minerals, in the global economy.

But forests are just as important a resource in shaping African political systems, and this book fills this knowledge gap. In Africa forest play a critical role in fueling patronage networks involving domestic and international actors; forests have also been central to interest articulation, public goods allocation, and state-society relations in general. During colonial times, forests served as a refuge for farmers eager to evade taxation or otherwise escape the wrath of the state. More recently, forests have provided shelter for rebels in times of civil strife (as was the case in Sierra Leone and Uganda where rebels were known to hide "in the bush"). Forests have also served as leverage for African leaders to attract foreign aid, in some cases enhancing their legitimacy at home and abroad. This three-country comparison shows that key actors from the local, national, and international levels create and manipulate conservation institutions to maximize the benefits derived from exploiting or conserving these forests. At the local level (Chapter 2), this analysis explicates forest users' compliance calculations when facing constraints and opportunities that conservation rules impose on or afford them. At the national level (Chapter 3), the analysis highlights African politicians' responses to donor prescriptions (about development and how public monies should be spent) that typically accompany foreign aid, while also documenting donors' adaptive responses to Africans' behavior. The third empirical chapter (Chapter 4) delves into actual attempts at bridging the gap between national and local decision makers by means of decentralized resource management schemes. Studying each country's forest conservation history, going through the emergence of conservation norms, policies, programs, and projects, makes it abundantly clear that Africa's forests have played, and continue to play, a critical role in shaping African political systems that involve African governments, foreign players, and ordinary Africans.

Global Commons

Finally, and to the extent that Africa's forests are a global commons, this analysis draws on commons management theories, specifically on issues of scale. In particular, it connects various levels of decision-making (local, national, international) that ultimately affect African forests. Largely inspired by the work of Elinor Ostrom (1990), commons scholars have studied commons governance through single-level phenomena. Many have focused on the local (community) level.[65] Some have focused on the national[66] and international levels,[67] sometimes linking these two levels.[68] Yet others have explored the linkages between local and global commons governance[69] and between national and local commons governance.[70] While focusing at one level or the other has generated some important lessons, previous scholars have failed to recognize and demonstrate that these lessons carry consistently *across* levels. This book addresses this theoretical gap by demonstrating how the logic and dynamics of forest conservation that prevail at the community level also apply to the national level.

Of course, politicians, development practitioners, and scholars are aware that realms of decision-making often fail to influence one another. For instance, looking at local communities' relationships with forests in the developing world, Gibson et al. (2000) write that "[i]t is becoming increasingly clear that local communities both filter and ignore the central government's rules. They also add their own rules, generating local institutions—rules-in-use—and patterns of activity that can diverge widely from legislators' and bureaucrats' expectations."[71] Nor is this the first study to place resource users' interests at the heart of resource politics. Two decades ago, Peluso examined the relationships between foresters and peasants in Java, noting that "[w]here the interests of states and peasants clash, we often find environmental deterioration, poverty and ambivalent power relations."[72] Finally, many studies before this one have used institutional analysis to shed light on a wide array of resource management issues.[73] In her seminal work, *Governing the Commons*, Ostrom challenges Hardin's contention that a strong state, private property, and markets are panaceas to the tragedy of the commons. Chief among Ostrom's claims is the idea that communities around the world have shown remarkable capacity to devise institutions, understood as rules and social norms, adapted to their local realities without or even despite strong, central states. Because local institutions are rooted in communities' knowledge of their natural environments, overharvesting and resource degradation have been successfully avoided in many instances. Successful institutions, according to Ostrom, comprise eight design principles that connect resource users ("appropriators"), institutions (i.e., formal and informal rules), and resource systems.[74]

While recognized for the contributions her work has made to the study of institutions, rational choice theory, and environmental governance, Ostrom has not escaped criticism. Ostrom's critics have raised issues ranging from her conflating private partnership arrangements and commons,[75] her formulaic narrative and consequent misguided environmental policy decisions,[76] and her confinement to choice rationalistic models of human behavior.[77] Block and Jankovic (2016) are the harshest among her critics, charging that Ostrom did nothing more than "pillage" the commons by failing to notice that what she calls commons, or collective, governance amounts to private partnership arrangements.[78] As such, the claim that she uncovered an alternative to free markets and central government for resource management is baseless. Nor is Ostrom, they point out, capable of imagining the enforcement of property rights by actors other than governments.[79] For these reasons, rather than recognize Ostrom for her various intellectual contributions, the authors deem it necessary to "drag her through the intellectual mud," which they dutifully do.[80] Other, more credible challenges to Ostrom's work come from a burgeoning school of thought that labels itself Critical Institutionalism. Scholars from this school of thought see her work in Mainstream Institutionalism as rigid due to its reliance on the tenets of new institutional economics whereby individuals' behaviors can be shaped or modified by crafting institutions (rules and norms) that provide incentives to behave in some ways and not in others. The second source of rigidity lies in Mainstream Institutionalists' insensitivity to contexts in which institutions and communities emerge. As a result, the relational factors (i.e., people to nature, people to people in social, cultural, and political contexts) that shape institutions and affect their effectiveness are overlooked.[81] A final point of contention rests in Mainstream Institutionalists' belief in the necessity to use rigorous empiricism (the more cases, the more robust theories are) to construct models of human behavior which, in turn, enable predictions about behavioral outcomes. In the end, Critical Institutionalists bemoan the appeal of Mainstream Institutionalists' "grand theoretical narrative that can be more easily utilized" to design resource management policies and projects. At the same time, they recognize the challenge of "making complexity legible," especially where policy expediency trumps nuanced understandings of why forest users behave the way they do.[82]

In the context of existing debates briefly outlined above, the theory of interest alignment presented in this book is situated in the overlap between the two institutionalist schools of thought. While embracing the idea that individuals respond to incentives that will best serve their interests, the processes of institution formation described in Chapters 2 (community level) and 3 (national level) take into account the historical, political, and cultural contexts in which interests are shaped and institutions negotiated and used to advance or protect a constellation of interests. By describing how institutions come about at the two principal levels of decision-making, the empirical chapters that follow this introduction uncover a process that Cleaver (2012) calls *bricolage*, or "mak[ing] creative and resourceful use of whatever materials are at hand, regardless of their original [intended] purpose"[83] in order to "imbue configurations of rules, traditions, norms and relationships with meaning and authority."[84] In the same vein, and specifically in the African context, Dayo Olopade (2014) uses the term *kanju* to capture African ingenuity in the face of scarcity. What looks like Africans breaking rules is, in her words, "frugal genius."[85] The subsequent chapters of this book show that the scarcity that Africans deal with when it comes to forest conservation politics is scarcity of power. At the national level, Africans trade in sovereignty in exchange for donors' aid. When this happens, Africans regain some agency (in addition to millions of dollars and euros in aid monies), and in the process, they end up "coming up with a totally different game,"[86] which explains why deforestation persists. At the local level, forest users incorporate state rules into existing systems of resource management, which leads to hybrid institutional configurations that influence forest users' behaviors. But Chapter 2 does more than offer detailed descriptions of how institutions emerge in forest management across communities in the three countries included in this book. Instead, it investigates, by means of quantitative analysis and months of field interviews, whether farmers in Madagascar, Tanzania, and Uganda respond similarly to the institutional environments in which they operate.

This study isolates interest alignment at and across various levels of authority to explain the efficacy (or inefficacy) of institutions in taming deforestation. The commons management literature, while mentioning interests repeatedly, does not focus attention on interests, much less interest alignment. This book aims to fill this theoretical gap. It benefits partly from Mancur Olson's insights on collective action. According to Olson, barriers to the provision of public goods, of which forest conservation is an example, can be overcome by creating the proper incentives to discourage free riding. Environmental institutions, it will be shown, create incentives to conserve or degrade forests. What, then, makes certain institutions more effective than others? This book argues that for environmental institutions to be effective, they must result from the proper alignment of key actors' interests at critical levels environmental decision-making. It shows how foreign and domestic actors interact around environmental issues and the ways they articulate and defend their interests through institutional innovation have more explanatory leverage than conventional explanations of deforestation relating to economic, demographic, and political factors. This is not to suggest that interest alignment is a sufficient condition for conservation. Clearly, no single factor explains deforestation. What this book suggests, however, is that interest alignment is a sine qua non for effective forest conservation. For this reason, it is necessary to understand under what circumstances interests are likely to align or misalign.

Why Interest Alignment Matters

Among other things, focusing on interest alignment at multiple levels of authority helps shift our attention from repeatedly asking what the problem is to *who* is behind deforestation. In turn, doing so compels us to think about agents of deforestation and helps us reorient our accusatory gazes away from "poor and desperate" farmers to the less suspected culprits: African governments and foreign partners. In this respect, Kremen and colleagues' analysis of the economic benefits of conserving Masoala

National Park in Madagascar is illuminating. The cost-benefit analysis they carry out reveals a clear example of interest misalignment.[87] Defining interests in economic terms, they find that conservation generated significant benefits at the global and local levels, but not at the national level: Forest exploitation for logging revenues was more lucrative than forest conservation in the short term. The authors conclude that international institutions such as the Kyoto Protocol can and should be used as mechanisms to create international markets of forest protection, thereby altering incentives—in this case of national-level actors—in ways that prevent further forest liquidation.[88] I refer to this redefinition of incentives by means of institutional innovation as interest alignment.

Beyond shedding light on why deforestation continues to vex a wide array of decision makers across the globe, this book accomplishes additional goals. First, it makes evident the paradox of poor forest conservation despite strong support for it. To this effect, the book addresses two important empirical questions. The first is, of course, the book's main question: Why does deforestation persist despite concerted efforts to control it? The second is equally intriguing: Why does support for conservation continue despite discouraging results? Second, it challenges two prevailing and rarely questioned regarding solutions to deforestation. The first is that conservation begins with formal legislation. The second is that foreign aid enables conservation. I will show that formal rules and foreign aid can help but also harm conservation initiatives. Third, the book constitutes the first comparative study of Madagascar, Tanzania, and Uganda's environmental politics. Madagascar is often viewed as unique and different from mainland Africa, mostly because of its non-Bantu cultural foundations and unique flora and fauna (hence the label "the Earth's eighth continent"). This book shows that the nature of Madagascar's politics is similar to the other two countries', as evidenced by shared and similar environmental problems. Recognizing that no two countries are exactly alike, this book nonetheless debunks the myth of Madagascar's exceptionalism. Finally, by showing similarities across seemingly different countries, this book's conclusions can inform processes in other African countries, hopefully encouraging Africans to look to one another—instead of perpetually using the wrong reference points of the West—for solutions to shared problems within Africa. What happens in Africa can also inform solutions in other regions of the world where people are dealing with the nefarious effects of deforestation and other forms of environmental degradation.

Organization

In the subsequent pages, I show that deforestation persists in Madagascar, Tanzania, and Uganda because conservation policies and projects are predicated upon three unexamined assumptions: First, the state can create institutions powerful enough to constrain resource users' behavior. In particular, state-sanctioned rules are a sine qua non for forest conservation. Second, conservation requires foreign aid. The more aid foreign donors pour into conservation, the more conservation is possible. And third, the local and national realms of decision-making are interdependent, i.e., outcomes at one level influence decisions at the other. This view makes no allowance for the possibility that the two realms of politics function in tandem, mostly disconnected, ways. These fundamental misconceptions about what informs people's behavior toward forests lead to a chronic failure to recognize that conservation is possible only under specific and limited conditions. As a result, institutional investments in forest conservation fall short of addressing deforestation effectively, and the problem remains.

To do this, I examine how actors shape environmental politics, based on their multiple interests, at the national and local levels of decision-making to gain a better understanding of why deforestation persists in Africa despite efforts to battle it.

Following this introduction, Chapter 2 examines the causal link between conservation rules and forest users' compliance behavior across village communities of Madagascar, Tanzania, and Uganda. The rules under consideration are rules-in-use, which are hybrids of state legislation and community-devised rules and norms that result from a dynamic relationship among key actors, some from village communities, others associated with the state, who operate according to particular interests in specific, dynamic contexts. Rather than mere tools of administration, local rules serve the purpose of monopolizing resource access on the part of those who devise and enforce them (i.e., key actors such as local representatives of the state—foresters, bureaucrats, law enforcement agents, agricultural extension workers, or state-sanctioned lumber and mining companies, etc.—and community leaders). Compliance with conservation rules is a function of key actors' ability to (1) devise and diffuse rules-in-use that are compatible with local productions systems; (2) monitor compliance and enforce rules; and (3) legitimize their authority and the rules they devise to monopolize forest access.

Chapter 3 details national-level policymaking and highlights the central role that foreign aid plays in the three countries' environmental politics. It provides a brief history of conservation to underscore the executive branch's predominance in development policymaking. It discusses the evolution of aid flows to Africa in the postcolonial era and highlights how foreign donors strive to influence development policies, following trends in vogue, to variable effect. At this level, donors' ability to influence development policies in a pro-conservation direction is contingent upon their capacity to sway the executive, using development aid as leverage. For their part, African presidents use their countries' natural endowments (especially biodiversity) and competition (to extend aid) among donors to maximize aid inflows. Negotiations between national and international actors produce institutions that, if properly aligned with key actors' interests, can lead to conservation-friendly development policies.

Chapter 4 examines the third erroneous assumption discussed above, namely that the two levels of environmental decision-making work in a symbiotic relationship that renders them interdependent. To do this, I describe and analyze concrete attempts made to bridge the gap between local and national environmental decision makers in the three countries. Attempts to connect the two realms of environmental politics were made by way of community-based natural resource management (CBNRM) projects initiated in the 1990s. In Madagascar, *Gestion Locale Sécurisée* (GELOSE, for secured local management) contracts were put in place to turn rural communities and the state into forest co-managers. In Tanzania, Participatory Forest Management (PFM) has been the model for empowering local communities in forest management. In Uganda, the 2003 Forest Sector Governance Reform has been the vehicle for decentralizing resource management, in principle granting decision-making powers to governance units below the national level. This chapter identifies the conditions under which these experiments have had a positive impact on forest conservation. It also analyzes factors behind limited success.

The Epilogue, Chapter 5, revisits the book's main question: Why is deforestation continuing given substantial efforts invested in curbing the problem in Africa? The chapter highlights findings by identifying common trends, opportunities, and constraints across the three African political systems. It also highlights variations in the ways conservation politics are played out across the three countries. Based on lessons learned at both local and national levels, the chapter presents policy recommendations to better connect actors across decision-making levels, on the one hand, and make more effective use of existing institutions and resources, on the other.

Notes

1. Waeber, Patrick O., Lucienne Wilmé, Jean-Roger Mercier, Christian Camara, and Porter P. Lowry II. "How Effective Have Thirty Years of Internationally Driven Conservation and Development Efforts Been in Madagascar?" *PLoS One* 11.8 (2016): e0161115.
2. Kerry, John. "Africa Is on the Rise, and We Need to Help to Make Sure It Continues." http://www.washingtonpost.com/opinions/africa-is-on-the-rise-and-we-need-to-help-make-sure-it-continues/2014/05/02/e9684466-d165-11e3-9e25-188ebe1fa93b_story.html, accessed September 20, 2014.
3. Keim, Curtis A., and Carolyn Somerville. *Mistaking Africa: Curiosities and Inventions of the American Mind*. Hachette, UK, 2017.
4. Rainforest Conservation Fund. Web. http://www.rainforestconservation.org/rainforest-primer/5-who-gains-from-deforestation/, accessed December 1, 2017.
5. The term interest alignment is commonly used in the management and business literatures and less so in political science. A notable exception is Xinyuan Dai's work on the impacts of international institutions on states' compliance with international treaties. In this context, Dai (2002) conceptualizes interest alignment in terms of whether or not states represent and protect the interests of domestic victims of non-compliance: "To the extent that noncompliance victims are protected by their own states, I say that the interests of noncompliance victims and those of their states are aligned" (413).
6. Söderbaum, Fredrik. *Handbook of Regional Organizations in Africa*. Uppsala: Nordiska Afrikainsitutet, 1996, p. 8.
7. Møller, Bjørn. "Africa's Sub-Regional Organisations: Seamless Web or Patchwork?" Danish Institute for International Studies. Working Paper no. 56, 2009.
8. Englebert, Pierre, and Kevin C. Dunn. *Inside African Politics*. Boulder and London: Lynne Rienner, 2013, pp. 322–325. See also Cheru, Fantu. *African Renaissance: Roadmaps to the Challenge of Globalization*. London: Zed Books, 2002, pp. 127–133.

9. Contreras-Hermosilla, Arnoldo. *The Underlying Causes of Forest Decline*. CIFOR Occasional Paper no. 30. CIFOR, Bogor, Indonesia, 2000, pp. 3–4.
10. Ibid., p. 7.
11. Food and Agriculture Organization of the United Nations. *Global Forest Resources Assessment* 2005. Rome: Food and Agriculture Organization of the United Nations, 2007.
12. Food and Agriculture Organization of the United Nations. *Forest Resources Assessment 1990: Global Synthesis*. Rome: Food and Agriculture Organization of the United Nations, 1995; Food and Agriculture Organization of the United Nations. *Global Forest Resources Assessment 2005*. Rome: Food and Agriculture Organization of the United Nations, 2007.
13. World Bank Group. "*WDI Online*" WDI Online. Web. http://www.worldbank.org/wdiquery, accessed October 10, 2010.
14. Government of Uganda. *Forest Sector Review* 2001.
15. Gombya-Ssembajjwe, William S. "Sacred Forests in Modern Ganda Society," *The Uganda Journal* 42 (1995): 34.
16. Banana, Abwoli Y., Joseph Bahati, William Gombya-Ssembajjwe, and Nathan Vogt. "Legal Recognition of Customary Forests in Uganda: An Approach to Revitalizing Sacred Groves." *African Sacred Groves: Ecological Dynamics and Social Change* (2008): 195–206.
17. Food and Agriculture Organization of the United Nations. *Forest Resources Assessment 1990: Global Synthesis*. Rome: Food and Agriculture Organization of the United Nations, 1995; Food and Agriculture Organization of the United Nations. *Global Forest Resources Assessment* 2005. Rome: Food and Agriculture Organization, 2007.
18. Food and Agriculture Organization of the United Nations. *Forest Resources Assessment 1990: Global Synthesis*. Rome: Food and Agriculture Organization of the United Nations, 1995; Food and Agriculture Organization of the United Nations. *Global Forest Resources Assessment 2005*. Rome: Food and Agriculture Organization of the United Nations, 2007.
19. Horning, Nadia Rabesahala. "Strong Support for Weak Performance: Donor Competition in Madagascar." *African Affairs* 107.428 (2008): 405–431.
20. Convention on Biological Diversity. Web. https://www.cbd.int/history/, accessed August 17, 2017.
21. Gregersen, Hans, Hosny El Lakany, Alain Karsenty, and Andy White. "Does the Opportunity Cost Approach Indicate the Real Cost of REDD+? Rights and Realities of Paying for REDD+" (2010), p. 1. The UN-REDD website reports a wider range of 12–29%. See UN-REDD

Programme. Web. http://www.un-redd.org, accessed December 5, 2017.
22. UN-REDD Programme Workspace. Web. http://www.unredd.net/about/what-is-redd-plus.html, accessed December 11, 2017.
23. Ibid.
24. EUFLEGT Facility. Web. http://www.euflegt.efi.int/what-is-flegt, accessed August 3, 2017.
25. Ibid., Web. http://www.euflegt.efi.int/flegt-action-plan, accessed August 15, 2017.
26. Karsenty, Alain, and Symphorien Ongolo. "Can 'Fragile States' Decide to Reduce Their Deforestation? The Inappropriate Use of the Theory of Incentives with Respect to the REDD Mechanism." *Forest Policy and Economics* 18 (2012): 38–45.
27. Mbatu, Richard S. "REDD+ Research: Reviewing the Literature, Limitations and Ways Forward." *Forest Policy and Economics* 73 (2016): 140–152.
28. http://www.un-redd.org, accessed August 15, 2017.
29. Smouts, Marie-Claude. "The Issue of an International Forest Regime." *International Forestry Review* 10.3 (2008): 429–432.
30. Thompson, Mary C., Manali Baruah, and Edward R. Carr. "Seeing REDD+ as a Project of Environmental Governance." *Environmental Science & Policy* 14.2 (2011): 100–110, p. 101.
31. Ibid., p. 108.
32. den Besten, Jan Willem, Bas Arts, and Patrick Verkooijen. "The Evolution of REDD+: An Analysis of Discursive-Institutional Dynamics." *Environmental Science & Policy* 35 (2014): 40–48.
33. Mbatu 2016, p. 149.
34. Forsyth, Tim. *Multilevel, Multiactor Governance in REDD+: Participation, Integration and Coordination*. Center for International Forestry Research (CIFOR), Bogor, Indonesia, 2009.
35. Geist, Helmut J., and Eric F. Lambin. "Proximate Causes and Underlying Driving Forces of Tropical Deforestation: Tropical Forests are Disappearing as the Result of Many Pressures, Both Local and Regional, Acting in Various Combinations in Different Geographical Locations." *BioScience* 52.2 (2002): 143–150.
36. Ibid., p. 150.
37. Angelsen, Arild, and David Kaimowitz. "Rethinking the Causes of Deforestation: Lessons From Economic Models." *The World Bank Research Observer* 14.1 (1999): 73–98.
38. Myers, Norman. *Conversion of Tropical Moist Forests: A Report for the Committee on Research Priorities in Tropical Biology of the National Research Council*. Washington, DC: National Academy of Sciences,

1980; Brown, Katrina and David William Pearce, *The Causes of Tropical Deforestation: The Economic and Statistical Analysis of Factors Giving Rise to the Loss of the Tropical Forests.* Vancouver: University of British Columbia Press, 1994; Burns, Thomas, Edward Kick, and Byron Davis. "Theorizing and Rethinking Linkages Between the Natural Environment and the Modern World-system: Deforestation in the Late 20th Century." *Peace Research Abstracts* 41.5 (2004): 357–390; Jorgenson, Andrew K., and Thomas J. Burns. "Effects of Rural and Urban Population Dynamics and National Development on Deforestation in Less-Developed Countries, 1990–2000." *Sociological Inquiry* 77.3 (2007): 460–482.
39. Otsuka, Keijiro, and Frank Place. *Land Tenure and Natural Resource Management: A Comparative Study of Agrarian Communities in Asia and Africa.* Baltimore and London: Johns Hopkins University Press, 2001.
40. Ehrhardt-Martinez, Karen. "Social Determinants of Deforestation in Developing Countries: A Cross-National Study." *Social Forces* 77.2 (1998): 567; Southgate, D. "The Causes of Tropical Deforestation in Ecuador: A Statistical Analysis." *World Development* 19.9 (1991): 1145–151; Inman, K. "Fueling Expansion in the Third World: Population, Development, Debt, and the Global Decline of Forests." *Society and Natural Resources* 6.1 (1993): 17; Cropper, Maureen, Charles Griffiths, and Muthukumara Mani. "Roads, Population Pressures, and Deforestation in Thailand, 1976–1998." *Land Economics* 75.1 (1999): 58–73; Cincotta, Richard P., Jennifer Wisnewski, and Robert Engelman. "Human Population in the Biodiversity Hotspots." *Nature* 404.6781 (2000): 990–992; Carr, David, Laurel Suter, and Alisson Barbieri. "Population Dynamics and Tropical Deforestation: State of the Debate and Conceptual Challenges." *Population and Environment* 27.1 (2005): 89–113.
41. Mather, A. S., and C. L. Needle. "The Relationships of Population and Forest Trends." *The Geographical Journal* 166.1 (2000): 10.
42. World Bank Group. "WDI Online." *WDI Online.* Web. http://www.worldbank.org/wdiquery, accessed October 10, 2010.
43. Bhattarai, Madhusudan, and Michael Hammig. "Institutions and the Environmental Kuznets Curve for Deforestation: A Crosscountry Analysis for Latin America, Africa and Asia." *World Development* 29.6 (2001): 995–1010.
44. Ibid.
45. See, for instance, Mather and Needle (2000) for the relationships between population and forest trends; Adams et al. (2004) for the link between poverty and biodiversity conservation; see also Fisher on drivers of deforestation in Africa, notably rural-to-urban migration rates;

Schwartzman et al. (2000) on conservation as first and foremost a political process; O'Connor et al. (2003) on the critical importance of governance as a criterion for setting conservation priorities; Smith et al. (2003) and Agrawal et al. (2008) on governance as a condition for effective forest management; and Bhattarai and Hammig (2001) on economic analyses of tropical deforestation, leading the authors to conclude that institutional factors provide a more robust explanation for deforestation than "other frequently cited factors like population and macroeconomic conditions." (p. 1006)

46. Agrawal (1995), *Unasylva* 181: 57.
47. Bhattarai and Hemmig 2001, p. 1004.
48. Kirschke, Linda. "Semipresidentialism and the Perils of Power-Sharing in Neopatrimonial States." *Comparative Political Studies* 40.11 (2007): 1372–1394; Diamond, Larry Jay. "The Rule of Law versus the Big Man." *Journal of Democracy* 19.2.
49. Ake, Claude. *Democracy and Development in Africa*. Washington, DC: Brookings Institution, 1996; Englebert, Pierre. *State Legitimacy and Development in Africa*. Boulder: Lynne Rienner, 2000; Moss, Todd. *African Development: Making Sense of the Issues and Actors*. Boulder: Lynne Rienner, 2007.
50. Van De Walle, Nicolas. "Africa's Range of Regimes." *Journal of Democracy* 13.2 (2002): 66–80; Lindberg, Staffan I. "The Surprising Significance of African Elections." *Journal of Democracy* 17.1 (2006): 139–151; Diamond, Larry Jay, and Marc F., Plattner. *Democratization in Africa: Progress and Retreat*. Baltimore: Johns Hopkins University Press, 2010.
51. Henderson, Errol A. "When States Implode: The Correlates of Africa's Civil Wars, 1950–92." *Studies in Comparative International Development*. 35.2 (2000): 28–47; Azam, Jean-Paul. "On Thugs and Heroes: Why Warlords Victimize Their Own Civilians." *Economics of Governance* 7.1 (2006): 53; Falola, Toyin, and Raphael Chijioke Njoku. *War and Peace in Africa*. Durham: Carolina Academic, 2010.
52. Jackson, Robert H., and Carl G. Rosberg. "Personal Rule: Theory and Practice in Africa." *Comparative Politics* 16.4 (1984): 421–442; Diamond, Larry Jay. "The Rule of Law Versus the Big Man." *Journal of Democracy* 19.2 (2008): 138–149.
53. Clapham, Christopher S. *Private Patronage and Public Power: Political Clientelism in the Modern State*. New York: St. Martin's, 1982; Bratton, Michael, and De Walle, Nicolas, Van. *Democratic Experiments in Africa: Regime Transitions in Comparative Perspective*. Cambridge, UK and New York: Cambridge University Press, 1997, 61–96; Bach, Daniel C. and

Mamoudou Gazibo. *Neopatrimonialism in Africa and Beyond*. New York: Routledge, 2012.
54. Other concepts are used to capture the idea of rent seeking in African politics. They include: Clientelism, neopatrimonialism, prebendalism, etc.
55. Bayart, Jean-François. *The State in Africa: The Politics of the Belly*. Harlow: Longman, 1995; Reno, William, *Warlord Politics and African States*. London: Lynne Rienner, 1998.
56. Reno (1998).
57. Gibson, Clark, Krister Andersson, Elinor Ostrom, and Sujai Shivakumar. The *Samaritan's Dilemma: The Political Economy of Development Aid*. Oxford and New York: Oxford University Press, 2005.
58. Englebert, Pierre. *Africa: Unity, Sovereignty, and Sorrow*. Boulder: Lynne Rienner, 2009.
59. This excludes land distribution policies on which plenty has been written, notably on Zimbabwe (Alexander 2006) and Kenya (Burgess 1975; Klopp 2000).
60. Nelson, Fred. Ed. *Community Rights, Conservation and Contested Land: The Politics of Natural Resource Governance in Africa*. London: Earthscan, 2010, p. 3.
61. Death, Carl. *The Green State in Africa*. Yale University Press, 2016.
62. Gibson, Clark. *Politicians and Poachers: The Political Economy of Wildlife Policy in Africa*. Cambridge, UK and New York: Cambridge University Press, 1999; Duffy, Rosaleen. *Killing for Conservation: Wildlife Policy in Zimbabwe*. London and Bloomington: International African Institute in Association with J. Currey, Oxford; Indiana University Press, 2000. Duffy, Rosaleen. *Nature Crime: How We're Getting Conservation Wrong*. New Haven: Yale University Press, 2010; Brockington, Dan. *Fortress Conservation: The Preservation of the Mkomazi Game Reserve, Tanzania*. Oxford and Bloomington: International African Institute in Association with James Currey; Indiana University Press, 2002.
63. Alexander, Jocelyn. *The Unsettled Land. State-Making & the Politics of Land in Zimbabwe 1983–2003*. Oxford: James Currey; Harare: Weaver Press; Athens: Ohio University Press, 2006; Mwangi, Esther. *Socioeconomic Change and Land Use in Africa: The Transformation of Property Rights in Maasailand*. New York: Palgrave Macmillan, 2007.
64. Reno, William, *Warlord Politics and African States*. London: Lynne Rienner, 1998; Klare, Michael, and Daniel Volman. "The African Oil Rush and US National Security." *Third World Quarterly* 27.4 (2006): 609–28; Poteete, Amy. "Is Development Path Dependent or Political? A Reinterpretation of Mineral-Dependent Development in Botswana." *Journal of Development Studies* 45.4 (2009): 544–571.

65. Bromley, Daniel W., and David Feeny. *Making the Commons Work: Theory, Practice, and Policy*. San Francisco: ICS, 1992; Uphoff, Norman Thomas. *Learning from Gal Oya: Possibilities for Participatory Development and Post-Newtonian Social Science*. Ithaca: Cornell University Press, 1992; Gibson, Clark C., Margaret A. McKean, and Elinor Ostrom, *People and Forests: Communities, Institutions, and Governance*. Cambridge: Massachusetts Institute of Technology Press, 2000; Agrawal, Arun, and Clark C. Gibson. *Communities and the Environment: Ethnicity, Gender, and the State in Community-Based Conservation*. New Brunswick: Rutgers University Press, 2001.
66. Ascher, William. *Why Governments Waste Natural Resources: Policy Failures in Developing Countries*. Baltimore: Johns Hopkins University Press, 1999.
67. Breitmeier, Helmut, Oran R. Young, and Michael Zürn. *Analyzing International Environmental Regimes: From Case Study to Database*. Cambridge: Massachusetts Institute of Technology Press, 2006.
68. Ostrom, Elinor. "A Framework Relating Human 'Driving Forces' and Their Impact on Biodiversity." Bloomington: Workshop in Political Theory and Policy Analysis, 1995.
69. Keohane, Robert O., and Elinor Ostrom. *Local Commons and Global Interdependence: Heterogeneity and Cooperation in Two Domains*. London and Thousand Oaks: Sage Publications, 1995; Young, Oran R. *The Institutional Dimensions of Environmental Change: Fit, Interplay, and Scale*. Cambridge: Massachusetts Institute of Technology, 2002.
70. Agrawal, Arun. *Environmentality: Technologies of Government and the Making of Subjects*. Durham: Duke University Press, 2005.
71. Gibson, Clark C, Margaret A. McKean, and Elinor Ostrom, *People and Forests: Communities, Institutions, and Governance*. Cambridge: Massachusetts Institute of Technology Press, 2000, p. 3.
72. Peluso, Nancy Lee. *Rich Forests, Poor People: Resource Control and Resistance in Java*. Berkeley: University of California, 1992, p. 4.
73. Ostrom, Elinor. *Governing the Commons: The Evolution of Institutions for Collective Action*. Cambridge and New York: Cambridge University Press, 1990; Schlager, Edella, and Elinor Ostrom. "Property-Rights Regimes and Natural Resources: A Conceptual Analysis." *Land Economics* 68.3 (1992): 249–262; Leach, M, R Mearns, and I Scoones. "Environmental Entitlements. Dynamics and Institutions in Community-Based Natural Resource Management." *World Development* 27.2 (1999): 225; Gibson, Clark. *Politicians and Poachers: The Political Economy of Wildlife Policy in Africa*. Cambridge, UK and New York: Cambridge University Press, 1999; Imperial, Mark T. "Institutional Analysis and Ecosystem-Based Management: The Institutional Analysis and Development Framework."

Environmental Management 24.4 (1999): 449–465; Agrawal, Arun. *Greener Pastures: Politics, Markets, and Community among a Migrant Pastoral People.* Durham, NC: Duke University Press, 1999; Matsaert, Harriet. *Institutional analysis in natural resources research.* Socioeconomic Methodologies for Natural Resources Research. Best Practice Guidelines. Chatham, UK: Natural Resources Institute, 2002.

74. Ostrom, Elinor. *Governing the Commons*, pp. 88–102.
75. Block, Walter, and Ivan Jankovic. "Tragedy of the Partnership: A Critique of Elinor Ostrom." *American Journal of Economics and Sociology* 75.2 (2016): 289–318.
76. Hall, Kurt, Frances Cleaver, Tom Franks, and Faustin Maganga. "Capturing Critical Institutionalism: A Synthesis of Key Themes and Debates" *The European Journal of Development Research* 26.1 (2014): 71–86.
77. Forsyth, Tim, and Craig Johnson. "Elinor Ostrom's Legacy: Governing the Commons and the Rational Choice Controversy." *Development and Change* 45.5 (2014): 1093–1110.
78. Block and Jankovic (2016), p. 297.
79. Ibid., p. 300.
80. Ibid., p. 311.
81. Hall et al., p. 80.
82. Ibid., pp. 82–83.
83. Cleaver, Frances. *Development Through Bricolage.* London and New York: Earthscan, 2012: p. 33.
84. Ibid., p. 34.
85. Olopade, Dayo. *The Bright Continent: Breaking Rules and Making Change in Modern Africa.* Houghton Mifflin Harcourt, 2014, p. 23.
86. Ibid., p. 31.
87. Kremen, Clair, John O. Niles, M. G. Dalton, G. C. Daily, P. R. Ehrlich, J. P. Fay, D. Grewal, and R. Phillip Guillery. "Economic Incentives for Rain Forest Conservation Across Scales." *Science* 288.5472 (2000): 1828–1832.
88. Ibid., p. 1831.

Bibliography

Adams, W. M., Aveling, R., Brockington, D., Dickson, B., Elliott, J., Hutton, J., Dilys, R., Bhaskar, V, and W. Wolmer. "Biodiversity Conservation and the Eradication of Poverty" *Science* 306.5699 (2004): 1146–1149.

Agrawal, Arun. "Population Pressure = Forest Degradation: An Oversimplistic Equation?" *Unasylva* 181.46 (1995): 50–58.

———. *Greener Pastures: Politics, Markets, and Community Among a Migrant Pastoral People.* Durham, NC: Duke University Press, 1999.

———. *Environmentality: Technologies of Government and the Making of Subjects.* Durham: Duke University Press, 2005.

Agrawal, Arun, and Clark C., Gibson. *Communities and the Environment: Ethnicity, Gender, and the State in Community-Based Conservation.* New Brunswick: Rutgers University Press, 2001.

Agrawal, Arun, Ashwini Chhatre, and Rebecca Hardin. "Changing Governance of the World's Forests." *Science* 320.5882 (2008): 1460–1462.

Ake, Claude. *Democracy and Development in Africa.* Washington, DC: Brookings Institution, 1996.

Alexander, Jocelyn, 2006. *The Unsettled Land: State-Making & the Politics of Land in Zimbabwe 1983–2003.* Oxford: James Currey; Harare: Weaver Press; Athens: Ohio University Press.

Angelsen, Arild, and David Kaimowitz. "Rethinking the Causes of Deforestation: Lessons from Economic Models." *The World Bank Research Observer* 14.1 (1999): 73–98.

Ascher, William. *Why Governments Waste Natural Resources: Policy Failures in Developing Countries.* Baltimore: Johns Hopkins University Press, 1999.

Azam, Jean-Paul. "On Thugs and Heroes: Why Warlords Victimize Their Own Civilians." *Economics of Governance* 7.1 (2006): 53.

Bach, Daniel C., and Mamoudou Gazibo. *Neopatrimonialism in Africa and Beyond.* New York: Routledge, 2012.

Banana, Abwoli Y. Joseph Bahati, William Gombya-Ssembajjwe, and Nathan Vogt. "Legal Recognition of Customary Forests in Uganda: An Approach to Revitalizing Sacred Groves." *African Sacred Groves: Ecological Dynamics and Social Change* (2008): 195–206.

Bayart, Jean-François. *The State in Africa: The Politics of the Belly.* Harlow: Longman, 1995.

Bhattarai, Madhusudan, and Michael Hammig. "Institutions and the Environmental Kuznets Curve for Deforestation: A Crosscountry Analysis for Latin America, Africa and Asia." *World Development* 29.6 (2001): 995–1010.

Block, Walter, and Ivan Jankovic. "Tragedy of the Partnership: A Critique of Elinor Ostrom." *American Journal of Economics and Sociology* 75.2 (2016): 289–318.

Bratton, Michael, and van de Walle, Nicolas. *Democratic Experiments in Africa: Regime Transitions in Comparative Perspective.* Cambridge, UK and New York: Cambridge University Press, 1997.

Breitmeier, Helmut, Oran R. Young, and Michael Zürn. *Analyzing International Environmental Regimes: From Case Study to Database.* Massachusetts Institute of Technology Press, 2006.

Brockington, Dan. *Fortress Conservation: The Preservation of the Mkomazi Game Reserve, Tanzania.* Oxford and Bloomington: International African Institute in Association with James Currey and Indiana University Press, 2002.

Bromley, Daniel W., and David Feeny. *Making the Commons Work: Theory, Practice, and Policy*. San Francisco: ICS, 1992.
Brown, Katrina, and David William Pearce. *The Causes of Tropical Deforestation: The Economic and Statistical Analysis of Factors Giving Rise to the Loss of the Tropical Forests*. Vancouver: University of British Columbia Press, 1994.
Burgess, Stephen F. *The Politics of Land in Kenya*. The Hague: Institute of Social Studies, 1975.
Burns, Thomas, Edward Kick, and Byron Davis. "Theorizing and Rethinking Linkages Between the Natural Environment and the Modern World-System: Deforestation in the Late 20th Century." *Peace Research Abstracts* 41.5 (2004): 357–90.
Carr, David, Laurel Suter, and Alisson Barbieri. "Population Dynamics and Tropical Deforestation: State of the Debate and Conceptual Challenges." *Population and Environment* 27.1 (2005): 89–113.
Chabal, Patrick, and Jean Pascal Daloz. *Africa Works: Disorder as Political Instrument*. London: International African Institute in Association with James Currey, Oxford.
Cheru, Fantu. *African Renaissance: Roadmaps to the Challenge of Globalization*. London: Zed Books, 2002.
Cincotta, Richard P., Jennifer Wisnewski, and Robert Engelman. "Human Population in the Biodiversity Hotspots." *Nature* 404.6781 (2000): 990–992.
Clapham, Christopher S. *Private Patronage and Public Power: Political Clientelism in the Modern State*. New York: St. Martin's, 1982.
Cleaver, Frances. *Development through Bricolage*. London and New York: Earthscan, 2012.
Contreras-Hermosilla, Arnoldo. *The Underlying Causes of Forest Decline*. CIFOR Occasional Paper no. 30. CIFOR, Bogor, Indonesia, 2000, pp. 3–4.
Convention on Biological Diversity. Web. https://www.cbd.int/history/. Accessed August 17, 2017.
Cropper, Maureen, Charles Griffiths, and Muthukumara Mani. "Roads, Population Pressures, and Deforestation in Thailand, 1976–1989." *Land Economics* 75.1 (1999): 58–73.
Dai, Xinyuan. "Information Systems in Treaty Regimes." *World Politics* 54.4 (2002): 405–436.
Death, Carl. *The Green State in Africa*. Yale University Press, 2016.
den Besten, Jan Willem, Bas Arts, and Patrick Verkooijen. "The Evolution of REDD+: An Analysis of Discursive-Institutional Dynamics." *Environmental Science & Policy* 35 (2014): 40–48.
Diamond, Larry Jay. "The Rule of Law Versus the Big Man." *Journal of Democracy* 19.2 (2008): 138–49.
Diamond, Larry Jay, and Marc F., Plattner. *Democratization in Africa: Progress and Retreat*. Baltimore: Johns Hopkins University Press, 2010.

Duffy, Rosaleen. *Killing for Conservation: Wildlife Policy in Zimbabwe.* London; Bloomington: International African Institute in Association with J. Currey, Oxford; Indiana University Press, 2000.
———. *Nature Crime: How We're Getting Conservation Wrong.* New Haven: Yale University Press, 2010.
Ehrhardt-Martinez, Karen. "Social Determinants of Deforestation in Developing Countries: A Cross-National Study." *Social Forces* 77.2 (1998): 567.
Englebert, Pierre. *State Legitimacy and Development in Africa.* Boulder: Lynne Rienner, 2000.
———. *Africa: Unity, Sovereignty, and Sorrow.* Boulder: Lynne Rienner, 2009.
Englebert, Pierre, and Kevin C. Dunn. *Inside African Politics.* Boulder and London: Lynne Rienner, 2013.
EUFLEGT Facility. Web. http://www.euflegt.efi.int/what-is-flegt. Accessed August 3, 2017.
Falola, Toyin, and Raphael Chijioke Njoku. *War and Peace in Africa.* Durham: Carolina Academic, 2010.
Fisher, Brendan. "African Exception to Drivers of Deforestation." *Nature Geoscience* 3.6 (2010): 375–376.
Food and Agriculture Organization of the United Nations. *Forest Resources Assessment 1990: Global Synthesis.* Rome: FAO, 1995.
———. *Global Forest Resources Assessment 2005.* Rome: FAO, 2007.
Forsyth, Tim. *Multilevel, Multiactor Governance in REDD+: Participation, Integration and Coordination.* Center for International Forestry Research (CIFOR), Bogor, Indonesia, 2009.
Forsyth, Tim, and Craig Johnson. "Elinor Ostrom's Legacy: Governing the Commons and the Rational Choice Controversy." *Development and Change* 45.5 (2014): 1093–1110.
Geist, Helmut J., and Eric F. Lambin. "Proximate Causes and Underlying Driving Forces of Tropical Deforestation: Tropical Forests are Disappearing as the Result of Many Pressures, Both Local and Regional, Acting in Various Combinations in Different Geographical Locations." *BioScience* 52.2 (2002): 143–150.
Gibson, Clark. *Politicians and Poachers: The Political Economy of Wildlife Policy in Africa.* Cambridge, UK and New York: Cambridge University Press, 1999.
Gibson, Clark, Margaret A. McKean, and Elinor Ostrom. *People and Forests: Communities, Institutions, and Governance.* Massachusetts Institute of Technology Press, 2000.
Gibson, Clark, Krister Andersson, Elinor Ostrom, and Sujai Shivakumar. *The Samaritan's Dilemma: The Political Economy of Development Aid.* Oxford and New York: Oxford University Press, 2005.
Gombya-Ssembajjwe, William S. "Sacred Forests in Modern Ganda Society." *The Uganda Journal* 42 (1995): 32–44.

Government of Uganda. *Forest Sector Review 2001*.
Gregersen, Hans, Hosny El Lakany, Alain Karsenty, and Andy White. "Does the Opportunity Cost Approach Indicate the Real Cost of REDD+? Rights and Realities of Paying for REDD+" (2010).
Hall, Kurt, Frances Cleaver, Tom Franks, and Faustin Maganga. "Capturing Critical Institutionalism: A Synthesis of Key Themes and Debates." *The European Journal of Development Research* 26.1 (2014): 71–86.
Henderson, Errol A. "When States Implode: The Correlates of Africa's Civil Wars, 1950–92." *Studies in Comparative International Development* 35.2 (2000): 28–47.
Horning, Nadia Rabesahala. "Strong Support for Weak Performance: Donor Competition in Madagascar." *African Affairs* 107.428 (2008): 405–31.
Imperial, Mark T. "Institutional Analysis and Ecosystem-Based Management: The Institutional Analysis and Development Framework." *Environmental Management* 24.4 (1999): 449–465.
Inman, K. "Fueling Expansion in the Third World: Population, Development, Debt, and the Global Decline of Forests." *Society and Natural Resources* 6.1 (1993): 17.
Jackson, Robert H., and Carl G. Rosberg. "Personal Rule: Theory and Practice in Africa." *Comparative Politics* 16.4 (1984): 421–42.
Jorgenson, Andrew K., and Thomas J. Burns. "Effects of Rural and Urban Population Dynamics and National Development on Deforestation in Less-Developed Countries, 1990–2000." *Sociological Inquiry* 77.3 (2007): 460–82.
Karsenty, Alain, and Symphorien Ongolo. "Can "Fragile States" Decide to Reduce Their Deforestation? The Inappropriate Use of the Theory of Incentives with Respect to the REDD Mechanism." *Forest Policy and Economics* 18 (2012): 38–45.
Keim, Curtis A., and Carolyn Somerville. *Mistaking Africa: Curiosities and Inventions of the American Mind*. Hachette UK, 2017.
Keohane, Robert O., and Elinor Ostrom. *Local Commons and Global Interdependence: Heterogeneity and Cooperation in Two Domains*. London; Thousand Oaks: Sage Publications, 1995.
Kirschke, Linda. "Semipresidentialism and the Perils of Power-Sharing in Neopatrimonial States." *Comparative Political Studies* 40.11 (2007): 1372–394.
Klare, Michael, and Daniel Volman. "The African Oil Rush and US National Security." *Third World Quarterly Third World Quarterly* 27.4 (2006): 609–28.
Klopp, Jacqueline M. "Pilfering the Public: The Problem of Land Grabbing in Contemporary Kenya." *Africa Today* 47.1 (2000): 7–26.

Kremen, Clair, John O. Niles, M. G. Dalton, G. C. Daily, P. R. Ehrlich, J. P. Fay, D. Grewal, and R. Phillip Guillery. "Economic Incentives for Rain Forest Conservation Across Scales." *Science* 288.5472 (2000): 1828–1832.
Leach, M, R Mearns, and I Scoones. "Environmental Entitlements: Dynamics and Institutions in Community-Based Natural Resource Management." *World Development* 27.2 (1999): 225.
Lindberg, Staffan I. "The Surprising Significance of African Elections." *Journal of Democracy* 17.1 (2006): 139–51.
Lund, H. Gyde. "A 'Forest' by Any Other Name..." *Environmental Science & Policy.* 2.2 (1999): 125–133.
Mather, A. S., and C. L. Needle. "The Relationships of Population and Forest Trends." *The Geographical Journal* 166.1 (2000): 2–13.
Matsaert, Harriet. *Institutional Analysis in Natural Resources Research.* Socioeconomic Methodologies for Natural Resources Research. Best Practice Guidelines. Chatham, UK: Natural Resources Institute, 2002.
Mbatu, Richard S. "REDD+ Research: Reviewing the Literature, Limitations and Ways Forward." *Forest Policy and Economics* 73 (2016): 140–152.
Møller, Bjørn. "Africa's Sub-Regional Organisations: Seamless Web or Patchwork?" Danish Institute for International Studies. Working Paper no. 56, 2009.
Moss, Todd. *African Development: Making Sense of the Issues and Actors.* Boulder: Lynne Rienner, 2007.
Mwangi, Esther. *Socioeconomic Change and Land Use in Africa: The Transformation of Property Rights in Maasailand.* New York: Palgrave Macmillan, 2007.
Myers, Norman. *Conversion of Tropical Moist Forests: A Report for the Committee on Research Priorities in Tropical Biology of the National Research Council.* Washington, DC: National Academy of Sciences, 1980.
Nelson, Fred. Ed. *Community Rights, Conservation and Contested Land: The Politics of Natural Resource Governance in Africa.* London and Washington, DC: Earthscan, 2010.
O'Connor, Casey, Michelle Marvier, and Peter Kareiva. "Biological vs. Social, Economic and Political Priority-Setting in Conservation." *Ecology Letters* 6.8 (2003): 706–711.
Olopade, Dayo. *The Bright Continent: Breaking Rules and Making Change in Modern Africa.* Houghton Mifflin Harcourt, 2014.
Ostrom, Elinor. "A Framework Relating Human 'Driving Forces' and Their Impact on Biodiversity." Bloomington: Workshop in Political Theory and Policy Analysis, 1995.
———. *Governing the Commons: The Evolution of Institutions for Collective Action.* Cambridge and New York: Cambridge University Press, 1990.

Otsuka, Keijiro, and Frank Place. *Land Tenure and Natural Resource Management: A Comparative Study of Agrarian Communities in Asia and Africa.* Baltimore and London: Johns Hopkins University Press, 2001.
Pahl-Wostl, Claudia. "A conceptual framework for analysing adaptive capacity and multi-level learning processes in resource governance regimes." *Global Environmental Change* 19.3 (2009): 354–65.
Peluso, Nancy Lee. *Rich Forests, Poor People: Resource Control and Resistance in Java.* Berkeley: University of California, 1992.
Poteete, Amy. "Is Development Path Dependent or Political? A Reinterpretation of Mineral-Dependent Development in Botswana." *Journal of Development Studies* 45.4 (2009): 544–71.
Rainforest Conservation Fund. Web. http://www.rainforestconservation.org/rainforest-primer/5-who-gains-from-deforestation/. Accessed December 1, 2017.
Reno, William. *Warlord Politics and African States.* London: Lynne Rienner, 1998.
Schlager, Edella, and Elinor Ostrom. "Property-Rights Regimes and Natural Resources: A Conceptual Analysis." *Land Economics* 68.3 (1992): 249–262.
Schwartzman, Stephan, Adriana Moreira, and Daniel Nepstad. "Rethinking Tropical Forest Conservation: Perils in Parks." *Conservation Biology* 14.5 (2000): 1351–1357.
Smith, Robert J., R. D. J. Muir, M. J. Walpole, A. Balmford, and N. Leader-Williams. "Governance and the Loss of Biodiversity." *Nature* 426.6962 (2003): 67–70.
Smouts, Marie-Claude. "The Issue of an International Forest Regime." *International Forestry Review* 10.3 (2008): 429–432.
Söderbaum, Fredrik. *Handbook of Regional Organizations in Africa.* Uppsala: Nordiska Afrikainsitutet, 1996.
Southgate, D. "The Causes of Tropical Deforestation in Ecuador: A Statistical Analysis." *World Development* 19.9 (1991): 1145–151.
Thompson, Mary C., Manali Baruah, and Edward R. Carr. "Seeing REDD+ as a Project of Environmental Governance" *Environmental Science & Policy* 14.2 (2011): 100–110.
UN-REDD Programme. Web. http://www.un-redd.org. Accessed December 5, 2017.
UN-REDD Programme Workspace. Web. http://www.unredd.net/about/what-is-redd-plus.html. Accessed December 11, 2017.
Uphoff, Norman Thomas. *Learning from Gal Oya: Possibilities for Participatory Development and Post-Newtonian Social Science.* Ithaca: Cornell University Press, 1992.
U.S. Department of State. "Congo Basin Forest Partnership" Web. http://www.state.gov/e/oes/ecw/cbfp/. Accessed July 22, 2016.

van de Walle, Nicolas. "Africa's Range of Regimes." *Journal of Democracy* 13.2 (2002): 66–80.

Waeber, Patrick O., Lucienne Wilmé, Jean-Roger Mercier, Christian Camara, and Porter P. Lowry II. "How Effective Have Thirty Years of Internationally Driven Conservation and Development Efforts Been in Madagascar?" *PLoS One* 11.8 (2016): e0161115.

World Bank Group. "WDI Online" WDI Online. Web. http://www.worldbank.org/wdiquery. Accessed October 10, 2010.

Young, Oran R. *The Institutional Dimensions of Environmental Change: Fit, Interplay, and Scale*. Cambridge: Massachusetts Institute of Technology, 2002.

CHAPTER 2

Seeing Like a Farmer: Resource Politics at the Community Level

Can states create institutions powerful enough to constrain resource users' behavior at the local level? How effectively does forest legislation protect forests? What rules, other than formal ones, apply at the local level? This chapter addresses these questions by examining how rules-in-use, or rules as applied, emerge and how they affect forest users' compliance choices and forest conditions at the local level.

Through a detailed analysis of rules and compliance choices across five communities in southern Madagascar, this chapter shows that where interests converge toward forest protection, the rules devised to restrict forest access raise the prospect of conservation significantly. Where and when interests converge toward exploiting forests, however, no rules can effectively contain deforestation. Conversely, when actors' interests diverge (e.g., the state opts for conservation while private actors opt for exploitation or vice versa) conservation is possible only where those who enforce forest rules have the capacity to make such rules "stick." The chapter goes beyond the single case of Madagascar, however, and insights from Tanzanian and Ugandan farmers are brought into the analysis to show that, in the three countries, farmers are equally dependent of forests for their livelihoods and welfare, and they face similar constraints and opportunities when it comes to resource access and use.

Due to the magnitude of the problem and its harmful effects, deforestation is viewed as a public bad that requires urgent policy responses

© The Author(s) 2018
N. R. Horning, *The Politics of Deforestation in Africa*,
https://doi.org/10.1007/978-3-319-76828-1_2

across the globe. Until commercial logging was widely identified as an important driver of deforestation, the literature on deforestation in the developing world was littered with language picturing small-scale farmers as agents of deforestation: plagued by poverty, ignorance, and the urge to multiply rapidly, farmers turned to forests for survival, with scarce concern for resources' future. According to this narrative, farmers are trapped in a spiral of environmental destruction.[1] In order to contain the damage that farmers inflict upon the environment, states have historically asserted themselves as guardians of the forests. Using central approaches to policymaking, many have relied on legislation to contain farmers' destructive behavior. Hence, the prevailing notion that state-devised rules are necessary to control deforestation.

That rules can control forest-degrading behavior is, to some extent, reasonable to assume. In fact, rules governing individuals' access to forest resources were present in all communities encountered in this study. However, the rules in question are not necessarily the ones devised by the state. In some cases, in fact, community rules have more regulatory power than formal legislation. It is thus more accurate to say that community rules coexist with state regulations, which means that rules affecting behaviors at the community level are hybrids of formal legislation and community rules and norms. These hybrid rules emerge out of repeated interactions, over time, between village communities, private businesses, and the state, based on these actors' respective interests. These rules-in-use, or rules as they effectively apply, vary across local contexts and, unlike formal legislation, are dynamic since they seek to adapt to an ever changing local context of resource control.

Just as local rules vary, communities' responses to them also vary: high levels of compliance are observed in some communities, whereas rule breaking is common in others. This variation in compliance behavior suggests that the context in which these rules are negotiated and applied, rather than the existence of rules per se, determines the extent to which rules are likely to affect forest conservation. Thus critical but often overlooked questions must be asked: Could rules be more efficacious in some environments than in others? What components of these varied environments, other than the ones evoked in Chapter 1, might affect forest users' behavior? What specific aspects of rules encourage or deter compliance? Do the rules themselves or forest users' reactions and responses to them induce compliance? In other words, under what conditions are rule compliance more or less likely to occur? Answering these questions is important because it can inform how deforestation can be controlled in the varied environments in which it is occurring.

In the next chapter, I will show that, at the national level, foreign and domestic actors interact over the role of environmental conservation in development policies. These national-level interactions give rise to environmental institutions that create opportunities for key actors to protect and advance their interests. The environmental institutions that emerge at the national level are designed to influence government policies and, by extension, alter the behavior of the people who live closest to the resources targeted for protection, namely forest-dependent village communities. Throughout Africa (and the rest of the non-Western world), legislation has been the means of choice to achieve conservation goals. For instance, the designation of areas as protected by law makes it difficult, at least in principle, for villagers to exploit forest resources as they see fit in and around these protected areas. Seldom, however, do proscriptions and prescriptions from above instantly transform behaviors at the local level because, as is the case with the national level, forest rules are negotiated at the local level. This takes time and energy.

At the local level, on which this chapter focuses, the rules restricting forest use are negotiated between village communities, public officials, and private interests that exploit forest resources in some capacity. Forest use entails exploitation for consumptive purposes (clearing for agriculture, logging, mining, food extraction) and nonconsumptive ones (worship, recreation, concealment of cattle for tax evasion purposes, etc.), on the one hand, and conservation, either mandated by local communities or by the state, on the other.

How Community-Level Data Were Collected

This chapter's analysis relies on survey data from the three countries, although the bulk of the chapter discusses Madagascar in greater depth because more extensive fieldwork was conducted in the southern part of the country. These sites were chosen because, while geographically close, the forests included in this study vary in legal status. As such, these forest sites are ideal for examining various rule configurations across sites that combine local rules with forest laws of variable strictness. Two of the five communities live on either side of Analavelona Sacred Forest, two are

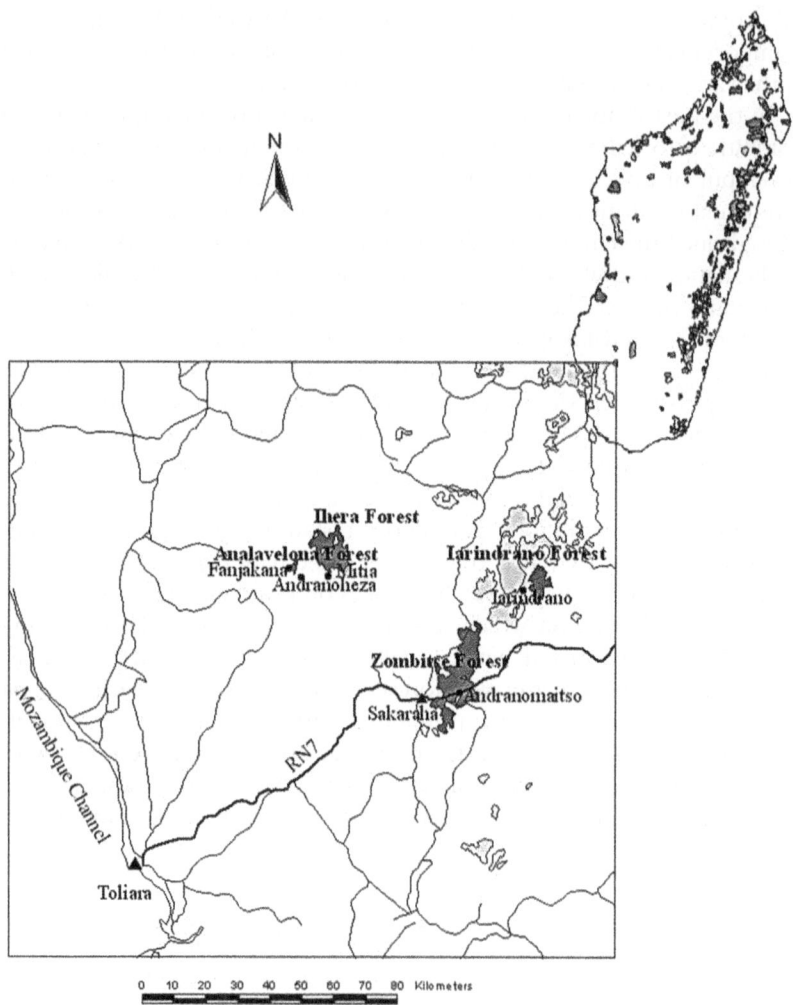

Fig. 2.1 Study sites in southern Madagascar

on the periphery of the Iarindrano and Ihera Classified Forests, and the last one is adjacent to Zombitse National Park (see Fig. 2.1). In southern Madagascar, a questionnaire, rapid appraisal exercises, semi-structured interviews, and visual analysis of remotely sensed data were used to assess village communities' relationships with forests over the course of twelve months from 1998 to 1999. Because it is possible to combine statistical and case study analysis for Madagascar, the results from this country case are more robust than they would be if only one or the other method was used, as is the case for Tanzania and Uganda.

In Tanzania, the questionnaire used in Madagascar (in Malagasy) was translated into Swahili to survey four village communities, one near Nyumba-Nitu Forest Reserve, one near Amani Nature Reserve, and two near Kitulanghalo Forest Reserve. The Tanzania fieldwork was also conducted over the course of twelve months from 2008 to 2009, but fewer village-level in-depths interviews were carried out due to multiple constraints related to Tanzania's research environment. In Uganda, where no village-level, in-depth interviews were possible due to resource constraints, a different but closely related data set from the IFRI/SANREM project[2] serves to assess whether results from Uganda support findings from the other two countries. The total number of respondents from Madagascar, Tanzania, and Uganda are 170, 120, and 585, respectively.

With these methodological caveats in mind, the remainder of this chapter examines the variable effectiveness of rules in constraining users' behavior across forest-dependent communities.

Communities' Forest Dependence

Whether in Madagascar, Tanzania, or Uganda, village communities depend heavily on forests for their subsistence and, for some, for their spiritual wellbeing. Forests are the primary, and sometimes only, source of food and water, shelter, health, and worship. For many communities, forests also perform services such as water supply, shelter for ancestors' spirits, cattle protection from the elements, tax evasion, and concealment of rustled cattle.

Survey results indicate that all respondents from Madagascar use at least one forest product on a regular basis. In Tanzania, more than 95% do. Of the 260 people who answered the question about the number of products taken from the forest in the two countries, 26, 41 and 30% reported that they take one, two, or three products from the forest, respectively. In Madagascar, the principal forest products are: fuelwood (70% of respondents mentioned it the first product), construction timber (56% mentioned it as second product), and food (38% mentioned it as third product). In Tanzania, they are: fuelwood (49% of respondents mentioned it as first product and 23% as second) and charcoal (23% mentioned it as second product and 16% as third). With no distinction made between primary and secondary products in the surveys, the three main forest products are fuelwood, water, and construction timber.

Collectively, thus, the most commonly cited forest products across surveyed communities are fuelwood and construction timber. For other forest products there were variations across communities: in Tanzania and Uganda, survey respondents cited charcoal, which only one community, Andranomaintso, mentioned in Madagascar. There, unlike in Tanzania and Uganda, the forest is an important source of supplementary foods such as honey (which is also used as medicine), tubers, and tenrecs.[3] Some of these products are for users' own consumption but others, notably charcoal and timber, are taken to earn some income. While variations do exist in terms of forest products, the fact remains that the surveyed communities depend heavily on forests for the basic needs of food and shelter.

Village communities are not, however, the sole forest users. States, private businesses, and public officials operating in their private interests also have a stake in either forest conservation or exploitation. In the subsequent pages, I discuss rule making and local reactions and responses to these rules in the context of interactions among these key local actors.

Focusing on situations encountered in the late 1990s in southern Madagascar (see Fig. 2.1), I begin with two situations of interest convergence. The first case, Analavelona sacred forest, is where local communities and the state found it in their best interest to conserve the forest. The second case, Zombitse National Park, is a situation in which communities, public officials, and private businesses share an interest in exploiting the forest. I then move to cases of interest divergence. In the first scenario, village communities aim to protect the forest against state-sanctioned private businesses' intrusions (Ihera community near Iarindrano classified forest); in the second scenario, the state seeks to protect the forest against both private businesses' and communities' exploitation (Mitia community near Ihera classified forest). Figure 2.1 shows where the five village communities are located in relation to the four forests and to one another.

WHERE INTERESTS CONVERGE: ANALAVELONA SACRED FOREST AND ZOMBITSE NATIONAL PARK

Analavelona and Zombitse represent contrasting cases of forest conservation. Around Analavelona sacred forest, communities and the state have a shared goal of conservation, and the result is remarkable forest conservation. In this case, rules play a critical role in controlling users' forest access and uses. By contrast, massive deforestation has occurred in Zombitse forest as the result of interest convergence toward exploitation:

once the state and private actors, including Andranomaintso residents, profited from exploiting this forest, no institutional maneuvering could reverse deforestation.

What is described in the subsequent pages can be summarized as follows: geographic, historical, economic, and social factors partly explain differences in deforestation outcomes around Analavelona and Zombitse forests. While Analavelona communities are isolated, Zombitse is particularly easy to access because a highway was built on this territory. This encouraged in-migrations especially when the government granted a permit to a logging company that proceeded to exploit the forest for six years. Migratory influxes overwhelmed local Bara customs, which prevented the type of social cohesion needed to overcome collective action problems such as deforestation. Meanwhile, Analavelona communities, which are more ethnically homogenous, were largely left to their own devices to come up with effective institutional means to protect the forest.

Ultimately, however, the fundamental difference between the two cases is institutional. The confluence of the factors mentioned above shaped conservation rules and local reactions and responses to them near the two forests. Armed with a strong sense of community commitment to conserve the sacred forest, Analavelona communities were in a situation where conservation rules were compatible with their production systems, where state and community rules were mutually reinforcing, and where monitoring and enforcement capabilities were particularly strong. In this situation, rules were critical and effective in containing deforestation. In contrast, residents of Andranomaintso did not see themselves as one community, did not share a conservation goal, were better off economically exploiting the forest than conserving it in the short term and, consequently, went through a series of institutional experiments that could not contain deforestation due to ineffective enforcement. In that context, rules simply could not resist the forces of economic gain derived from exploiting the forest.

Background on Analavelona and Zombitse

Mount Analavelona, the site of Analavelona sacred forest, is located north of the portion of *Route Nationale* (RN) 7 that links Toliara to Sakaraha, some 25 kilometers (as the crow flies) northwest of the communal town of Mahaboboka.[4] The two survey sites discussed here border the sacred forest: Andranoheza lies southeast and Fanjakana southwest of Analavelona (see Fig. 2.2).

In terms of social organization, these communities are similar and their inhabitants are all members of an ethnic grouping called *Bara Tsienimbalala*. Village territories are organized along the lines of family ties in similar ways, with main settlements, hamlets and cattle camps, and all village communities share a sense of owning the sacred forest. Household sizes are similar, with average figures of 5.1 on the eastern side and 4.8 on the western side.

Both sides consider themselves equally isolated from markets and administrative centers. Yet, traveling to market is necessary to sell produce and purchase household goods, and this involves a 12.3-hour trip for Fanjakana residents and 2.5 hours for Andranoheza residents.

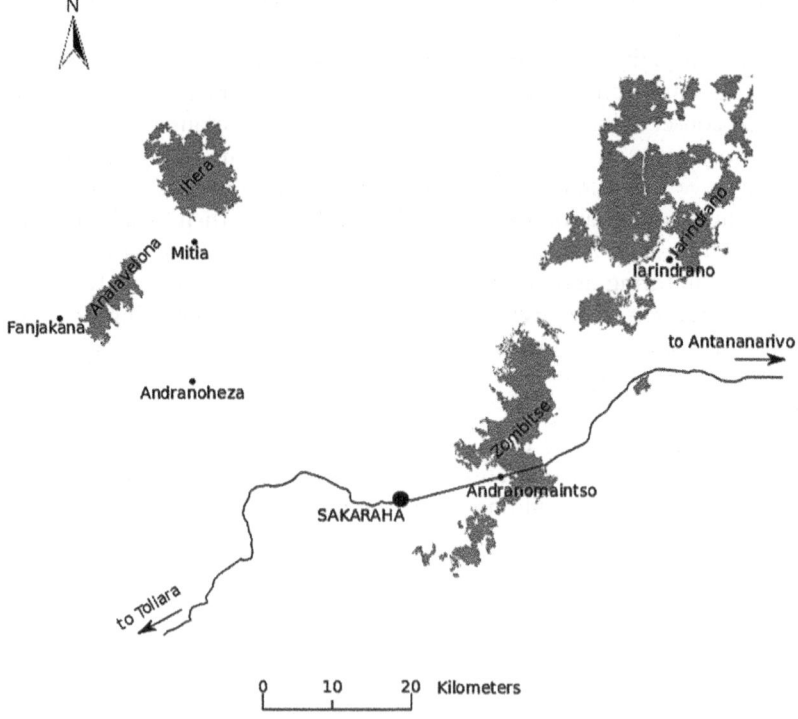

Fig. 2.2 Five communities near four forests in Bara land, Madagascar

Likewise, all administrative matters require a trip to the closest administrative center, and all matters involving the forest administration, such as getting a cutting or burning permit, call for a trip to Sakaraha, which demands a two-day trip, each way, for Fanjakana residents.

Compared to the eastern side, the sacred forest is easier to access on the western side, mostly due to very steep terrain between Andranoheza settlements and the forest. It takes residents of the west about one hour and eastern residents more than three times as long to reach Analavelona sacred forest. Eastern communities, however, have access to alternative forests, while western communities are much more limited and are thus more dependent on Analavelona for a variety of forest products.

On both sides of Analavelona, the forest plays a critical role in villagers' spiritual lives and subsistence. Analavelona is a place of worship, a physical space where people and spirits communicate. As with any place of worship, reverence is expected and disrespectful behavior punished according to a set of community-devised rules (discussed below). In terms of forest products, fuelwood, construction timber, supplementary food, and coffins are equally important forest products on both sides of Analavelona forest. It is also a place of pasture and worship on the eastern side, which it is not on the western portion. For all products, Analavelona itself and surrounding gallery forests are the main sources. For coffins and some pasture, only the sacred forest can accommodate users' needs.[5]

Zombitse forest is located thirteen kilometers east of Sakaraha on RN7. This highway, linking the cities of Toliara, Fianarantsoa, and Antananarivo, cuts through the main settlement of Andranomaintso where the average household size is 5.5. Though no historical demographic data were available at the time of research, one could reasonably assume that the number of Andranomaintso dwellers increased steadily since this settlement formed in 1973.[6] Andranomaintso started off as a Bara zebu camp, but the construction of RN7 and the subsequent arrival of a logging company called *Coopérative* AVOTRA, which operated from 1974 to 1980, dramatically changed the ethnic composition of the settlement's inhabitants as well as land use practices.

Andranomaintso distinguishes itself in the diversity of ethnic groups represented among its inhabitants.[7] Although ethnic diversity does not necessarily preclude a sense of belonging to a community in Andranomaintso ethnicity has polarized people around interests that have not been shared when it comes to Zombitse forest. The necessity to establish social contracts among Andranomaintso residents signifies that competing cultural and other values and interests need to be managed through such contracts.[8]

Andranomaintso inhabitants have easy access to the town of Sakaraha and the regional city of Toliara, which are connected by RN7. Andranomaintso residents go to Sakaraha for the weekly market and to take care of administrative matters when the need arises.[9] On average, it takes them less than two hours to reach Sakaraha, traveling by car or bus and sometimes part way by foot (the distance to cover is about 13 kilometers). They go to the market three Saturdays out of four, and they take care of administrative matters twice a month. When disputes are not resolved locally or at the level of Sakaraha (*commune*), trials take place in the provincial court of Toliara, which is where most cases opposing the forest administration (E&F for *Eaux et Forêts*) or the World Wildlife Fund (WWF) to Andranomaintso residents are heard.

In Andranomaintso, livelihood strategies are intricately linked with the settlement's history and with its location on a major highway that serves at least three major regional markets: Toliara, Fianarantsoa, and Antananarivo. The first occupants, who were Bara herders, needed the forest as a standing forest to care for their cattle. The AVOTRA logging project transformed the relationship between Andranomaintso dwellers and the forest by introducing commercial logging. Once in the area, migrant loggers introduced slash-and-burn maize culture, locally called *hatsaka*. Lucrative as growing maize was, local climatic conditions and decreasing soil fertility eventually made this activity unreliable. Such uncertainties induced farmers to explore other ways of profiting from the forest, which led them to produce charcoal and fuelwood for local and regional markets.[10]

Andranomaintso residents rely on Zombitse and, to a lesser extent, Hazoroa forests for fuelwood (75% of surveyed respondents mentioned this product), construction lumber (48%), supplementary food (25%), medicine (7%), and agricultural parcels also called *hatsaka* (2%). Bara members of this settlement also use Zombitse to harvest coffin wood, but this represents a minority of people. Though Zombitse is easily accessible from the settlement, the fact that it was classified as a National Park in 1997 has made it riskier for men to harvest timber there. For that reason, some revert to the alternative forest of Hazoroa, as E&F regulations require, for construction lumber.

Just as importantly, Andranomaintso is known as a major source of illegal products, including charcoal and fuelwood, for markets serving neighboring small towns (e.g., Sakaraha and Mahaboboka) and larger urban centers such as Toliara and Fianarantsoa. In addition, lumber comes out of Zombitse forest to supply Sakaraha, Toliara, Fianarantsoa, and even Antananarivo woodshops, particularly furniture shops.[11] Finally, maize grown using slash-and-burn techniques has been a highly sought-after commodity regionally and even internationally: the maize is exported for use as animal feed to neighboring Comoros and La Réunion and, especially since the 1980s, metropolitan France.[12]

Forest Rules

Analavelona
A mix of state legislation and community rules applies for forest products in Andranoheza and Fanjakana.[13] State rules dominate for construction timber and grazing areas. Under these rules, villagers are required to apply for a permit prior to burning or cutting trees, for a fee, and that they respect what is specified in the permits in terms of tree size, tree species, timing of harvesting or burning, and containing fires. Overall, state rules are prescriptive (must ... or else) and proscriptive (must/may not ... or else).

Community rules apply to the forest as a sacred site and for harvesting fuelwood and food in particular. Overall, these community-devised rules balance proscriptions, prescriptions, and permissions. As mentioned above, proscriptions focus on unacceptable behavior inside the sacred forest. It is forbidden to kill birds and lemurs, to do "bad" and "dirty" things, such as urinate, defecate, engage in sexual relations, take particular meats (excluding beef since cattle are permitted) and prosper from selling forest products. Permissions include harvesting tenrecs and honey, though strictly for one's consumption, and harvest large trees to make coffins when someone from the community dies.[14] Prescriptions require one to consider what they are wearing, which should not be ostentatious, with whom one is traveling to the forest, a short payer and offerings of honey, rum, and small change to the spirits upon entering the forest.

State rules and community rules overlap in the specific case of construction lumber and lumber for coffins, both of which require cutting trees of a particular size and of specific species. For these products state legislation actually supports community rules, and vice versa, since trees needed for these particular purposes are found exclusively in Analavelona forest.

Zombitse

Because Andranomaintso residents are reputed forest destroyers, one would not suspect that a rich array of rules actually apply to constrain forest access and use in Zombitse. To make sense of Andranomaintso's complex institutional landscape, one must bear in mind the settlement's history, on the one hand, and distinguish legal uses of Zombitse forest from illegal ones, on the other. Like Analavelona, Zombitse was originally a sacred Bara forest with Bara herders as the sole forest users. In 1962, Zombitse became a classified forest, which officially gave the state the authority to manage it. In 1974, *Coopérative* AVOTRA was granted a permit to log Zombitse and, in 1985, RN7 was paved to link southern provincial towns to the capital city. Together these two developments encouraged migrations to the area. In time, the influx of people from various parts of the island overwhelmed Bara customs and rules and deforestation ensued. To contain it, the state upgraded Zombitse's protection status to national park in April 1998. Coincidentally or not, this status upgrade happened at the time sapphires were discovered in the area, further encouraging in-migrations.[15]

For legal uses, fuelwood collection is largely regulated by proscriptions pertaining to entering the national park (proscriptions were cited by 82% of those who discussed rules pertaining to fuelwood collection), selling fuelwood (79%), cutting down trees (52%), and harvesting species specified by the forest administration (45%). While it is true that respondents also discussed three activities that were permitted, the one of most interest here concerns collecting dead wood on the outskirts of Zombitse (cited by 70% of respondents). Unlike fuelwood, prescriptions dominate when it comes to harvesting lumber for construction; respondents who discussed rules on harvesting this product were unanimous about the requirement to obtain a cutting permit from the local branch of the forest department (Eaux & Forêts or E&F) prior to cutting trees for building posts. Proscriptions about entering Zombitse to get timber and selling it are also well acknowledged (90% of respondents cited both these prohibitions). As far as which species to harvest or not to harvest, some species are permitted, which indicates some flexibility on the part of E&F. Overall, men are well aware of E&F's rules regarding this product. As far as collecting supplementary food, half of those who discussed the rules regulating harvesting food mentioned that it is prohibited to enter Zombitse for this purpose (10% specifically said that it is fine to harvest outside of the Park's limits) while 90% said that it was fine to sell supplementary food (10% specifically said that it is not).

The responses for food collection suggest that this product is regulated by E&F regulations, albeit only partly.

Overall, forest legislation, rather than community rules, or even a mix of the two, dominates Andranomaintso's institutional landscape. This is hardly surprising given this settlement's history of constant aggression against Zombitse forest. Additionally, prohibitions are consistently featured among E&F rules regarding the various products that Andranomaintso households need. In fact, prohibitions were by far the most frequently cited. That said, what respondents said about what is permitted indicates that forest legislation seeks, at least to a limited extent, to accommodate people's needs.

Does this mean that no community rules govern this forest's uses and access? By the early 1990s, it became obvious that Zombitse forest had receded due to the steady expansion of agricultural fields. This was the impetus for E&F to officially condemn *hatsaka* and establish rules regulating forest clearing and burning for agriculture. The result was the *Dinan'ny Mpanao Hatsaka* (hereafter DMH) that took final shape in 1995.[16] From the survey it is clear that DMH is a central component of Andranomaintso's institutional landscape and that it is highly proscriptive set of rules-in-use.

Initially, DMH received positive attention in conservation and decentralization circles because it was one of the first and, indeed, rare attempts to effectively transfer resource management control to so-called local communities in Madagascar. Further enhancing DMH's legitimacy, local Bara pastoralists also supported its enactment because, like E&F, this group found it in its interest to contain agricultural expansion given that it was shrinking grazing areas. The 1991 version of DMH specified that "it is strictly forbidden to clear new [forest] parcels... Or else rule-breakers will have to abandon their land to the state and their crops to the community. In addition, they will be fined." In its early phase, weak enforcement rendered the DMH ineffective despite the clarity of its purpose.

In 1994, ANGAP entrusted WWF with managing the Zombitse and Vohibasia forest complex. One of the first actions that WWF took was to reinforce E&F's initiative and update the 1991 DMH. What distinguished the second from the first version was the inclusion of community-based monitors. But problems of enforcement continued to compromise DMH's effectiveness. So, in 1995, having realized that some state actors from Sakaraha were sharecropping (and thus encouraging *hatsaka*) in Andranomaintso, WWF sought to include a wider range of Sakaraha-based monitors. The 1995 version of DMH went along the following lines: "The *dina* [DMH] is maintained, and an effort is explicitly requested for enforcing the rules, which is the responsibility of both community leaders and state authorities. Rule-breakers will be turned in so that state authorities can duly sanction them. A fine will be imposed for infractions." This time, *hatsaka* came under better control, but the fact that WWF decided to place agents in the community of Andranomaintso to reinforce monitors' efforts suggests that results remained inconclusive.

Other than being highly proscriptive, DMH is also a misnomer, since it deals not just with *hatsaka*, as the name suggests, but with a broader range of forest uses. So much so that it is difficult for users to separate DMH from E&F regulations per se. Finally, considering the top-down process through which it emerged, it is difficult to think of DMH as community based.

Deforestation Outcomes

A quick look at the evolution of forest cover for the two areas for the period of 1949–2007, using visual comparisons of 1949 aerial photographs and a series of satellite images, reveals how exceptionally conserved Analavelona sacred forest is.[17] For the eastern side (Andranoheza area), spatial data show evidence of some pasture activities inside the forest. For instance, there is a patch northwest of Andranoheza that was cleared and subsequently burned on a regular basis; however, this patch of about 12.5 acres never expanded. On the western side, changes in forest cover are practically undetectable. The most obvious evidence of clearing appears in the southern tip of Analavelona, where burning for pasture also occurs and where a passage linking the two areas was established over time. The visual aids show that an area of approximately 5–7 acres was cleared between 1949 and 1989.[18] So, although some degradation, most likely due to fires for grazing, is observable on the southeastern and southern edges of the forest, the changes are negligible, especially compared to surrounding forests, not to mention the rest of the country's forests.[19]

In sharp contrast, topographic maps and aerial photographs reveal that between 1949 and 1989, some 1800 hectares of forests were cleared, leaving a big hole in the middle of the northern portion of Zombitse forest.[20] Since the settlement of Andranomaintso appeared in 1973, this clearing took place in less than 20 years! Numerous testimonies indicate that rates of deforestation peaked around 1991. Deforestation around Zombitse continued, albeit at a reduced rate, with approximately 9% loss, between 1994 and 2000. From 2000 to 2007, more deforestation occurred, but the rate of deforestation dropped to 3.6%.[21]

It is counterintuitive that Zombitse, the forest with its national park status, experienced more deforestation than Analavelona, the sacred forest. Why, in fact, did a forest with higher official protection status succumb to deforestation when the forest with lower protection status did not? The answer to this question lies in forest users' reactions and responses to rules governing forest uses. In the subsequent sections, I compare and contrast villagers' responses to these rules to account for differences in deforestation outcomes.

Explaining Different Deforestation Outcomes: Communities' Reactions to Rules

Analavelona Communities

Analavelona forest users' reactions to rules are captured in two facts. First, state rules are more commonly broken than community ones, as survey results make clear: rates of compliance with state rules for construction lumber are 78% in Andranoheza and 40% in Fanjakana, and rates of compliance with community rules for fuelwood and supplementary food are 80 and 91%, respectively (see Table 2.1).

Second, for the three main forest products, rates of compliance are generally higher in Andranoheza than in Fanjakana. In Andranoheza, community rules are neither questioned nor challenged. Only 2 out of 30 informants reported that some community rules had been broken.

Table 2.1 Rates of compliance with state and community rules around Analavelona, Madagascar (*Source* Author's Madagascar survey)

Forest product	Andranoheza (%[a])	Fanjakana (%)	Source of rule
Fuelwood	90	85	Community
Construction lumber	78	40	State
Food	91	80	Community

[a]Rates reflect percentages of respondents who answered "always" to the question of whether community members comply with specific rules.

In one case, someone broke a rule within Analavelona forest and, the story goes, the offender temporarily got lost in the forest. To redeem himself, the rule-breaker sacrificed a zebu, which is a significant expense, at the spot where the infraction had been committed. The second case was of someone who cut trees in Analavelona. He was first reprimanded by community leaders and subsequently became chronically ill. Eventually, one of his children died, which left him without descendants. Although most villagers did not witness these unfortunate events first hand (they "happened a long time ago"), no one seemed to question the veracity of these stories from the past. By contrast, attitudes toward community rules in Fanjakana suggested that harsh sanctions to infractions may be just tales. But there, too, respondents reported that when community members broke rules, offenders became ill and did not get better until a zebu was sacrificed or a diviner performed rituals, for a fee, to remove the curse imposed on rule-breakers. For those who did not respect specific rules about Analavelona, offenders got lost in the forest, some say permanently, others say temporarily.

State rules are another matter. When asked if anyone from the community had ever been caught breaking rules, most of those who answered in the affirmative in Andranoheza reported breaking formal (rather than community) rules. Cutting trees without a permit appears to be a common offense, and setting bush fires comes next. As far as cutting trees for construction is concerned, there are three forms of noncompliance: either the person cuts without a permit; or the person gets a cutting permit after cutting down trees; or the person gets a cutting permit but ignores E&F regulations about tree species, tree size, and expiration date. In Andranoheza, these infractions take place in gallery forests at the edge, not inside Analavelona forest. In Fanjakana, four men reported taking construction lumber, unauthorized, out of Analavelona forest itself. For those who got caught, their hamlets were collectively fined. Likewise, individuals who were caught cutting trees without a permit were heavily fined. Some even served time in jail for five years.

What, then, deters compliance with state rules? Fanjakana and especially Andranoheza residents consider state rules to be an unnecessary nuisance since communities deem their forest protection measures adequate, sufficient, and effective. Besides, in their view, the forest belongs to the community, and so the state should not be responsible for its protection. Additionally, state rules are expressed as absolute prohibitions regardless of the fact that quantities extracted are small and extraction infrequent. Building posts, for instance, are usually required every five to six years for structural repairs on houses. The need for coffin trees is only occasional since deaths do not occur frequently. Moreover, state rules are costly to follow. Not only do they take time, but they also tap into cash savings that Bara men would rather spend on purchasing household items and cattle. From the way some men justify their decisions to break the law, one can infer that the problem has to do more with the costs of compliance than any rejection of the rules' validity or utility. First, one has to travel far to obtain a permit. If one reaches the office of the *Chef de Cantonnement Forestier* in Sakaraha, there is no guarantee that he will be around or that he will be available. Second, when people go by E&F's rules, by the time the paperwork gets done, builders may have passed the best opportunity to harvest in Analavelona and to build when their agricultural activities are not demanding.

Despite all this, state rules are not systematically broken. So, why do people follow them? In a word, people fear the state. Given that the *Chef de Cantonnement*, whose name was Kamosa at the time of research, had not once visited these two remote areas since assuming office in 1991, it is puzzling that villagers should claim that they fear the state's wrath and that they feel bound by state rules.[22] In reality, other state authorities occasionally circulate in the area. On both sides of Mount Analavelona, we were told repeatedly about abuses inflicted on villagers whenever the rural police, or *gendarmes*, and the military tour the area. The *gendarmes* and military come to their villages mainly for two purposes: to look for and arrest zebu rustlers, and to monitor conformance with E&F regulations regarding bush fires and building material permits. More often than not, *gendarmes*' visits result in arbitrary arrests, bribe extractions, verbal abuse, and even physical torture (I saw evidence of this multiple times). As far as E&F regulations are concerned, *gendarmes* assist the *Chef de Cantonnement* when touring the area, which consists of merely glancing at houses and surrounding fields.[23] Constructions in process or new constructions are easy to detect, as are burned or burning areas amid acres of open savanna. In Fanjakana, several respondents commented that people comply with the rule on cutting permits (obtainable at the Mayor's office) simply to protect themselves from the *gendarmes* and from military abuses because, in this case, the "guardians" are simply not guarded. In other words, compliance is motivated by self-protection rather than concerns for deforestation.

If villagers' bad experiences with the armed forces largely contribute to a collective fear of repression, there are nonetheless respondents who stated that state rules were "good" and "necessary" because they reinforce community rules. Twenty-one percent of respondents who answered the question about what they thought of state rules in Fanjakana said that they were in favor of them. This could be indicative of villagers' weakening confidence that community rules are sufficient to protect the forest, a hypothesis I revisit below. Another plausible explanation is that villagers do not mind state rules to the extent that they do not clash with their need for a standing forest in order to sustain their production system and, by extension, their Bara cultural identity.

What about villagers' responses to community rules? Community rules about the sacred forest are no less harsh than state rules. Even though there is some flexibility in terms of what is permitted rather than what is forbidden, judging from the number of permissions that respondents mentioned about collecting fuelwood, honey and tenrecs, the most frequently cited rules were nonetheless prohibitions and prescriptions for these products.[24] Monitoring is also tight: villagers believe that their ancestors, whose spirits dwell in the sacred forest, monitor who enters the forest. This belief has a clear effect on users' decision to comply with community rules every time they interact with the forest. In fact, one incident reported by others, rather than one's own experience, suffices as evidence that spirits will strike in case of noncompliance. This sketchy, unsubstantiated evidence provides sufficient motivation for complying with community rules, the majority of which are passed down within the Bara clan from generation to generation. What is more, sanctions reserved for rule-breakers range from having to sacrifice the most expensive kind of zebu to facing death, possibly leaving no descendants behind. These sanctions are locally seen as terrifying.

Another important reason why community rules are readily complied with is because the size of the resource system subject to community protection is relatively small, and access to the sacred forest is easily monitored. On the western side, anyone entering or exiting the forest is highly visible given the proximity of settlements and the fact that savannas surround the forest. In terms of visible "monitoring agents," herders walking their cattle and occupants of cattle camps at the edge of the forest are well trained to detect human and zebu traffic into and out of the forest. This, and the local belief that the spirits are watching, keeps the probability of detection high, which in turn has a deterrent effect on potential transgressors.

2 SEEING LIKE A FARMER: RESOURCE POLITICS AT THE COMMUNITY LEVEL 61

In sum, these cases suggest several reasons why compliance is higher for community rules than state rules. First, the transaction costs of obtaining a cutting or burning permit exceed the costs of observing community rules. Second, the punishment for breaking community rules is greater–sacrificing a zebu, becoming chronically ill, and losing a loved one–than simply paying a fine or spending time in jail. Finally, it is easier to avoid sanctions for breaking state rules than community rules because negotiating with spirits and avoiding their wrath is more difficult and the outcomes less certain than paying a bribe or a fine to the state. On this last point, cultural values and beliefs matter; people genuinely fear the retribution of spirits, and these beliefs govern their behavior in ways that induce compliance.

Beyond this universal fear of repression, however, compliance is the result of different motivators and circumstances particular to Analavelona: rules are compatible with production systems, rule enforcement is strong because community and state rules are mutually reinforcing, and forest users consider community rules and those who enforce them to be legitimate. On both sides of Mount Analavelona, at least two-thirds of respondents claim to own cattle. Community rules are designed to control entry into the forest because this is where the Bara keeps their cattle. Also, food crops require no forest destruction. Additionally, to the extent that most locals' livelihoods depend on harvesting forest products, controlling current consumption, by means of access and harvest rules, secures future supplies of these products. Finally, local cultural practices, such Bara funerals and other rituals, require the forest to exist. Community rules are therefore backed by a collective concern for economic, social, and cultural survival. For this important reason, they make sense (*mitombina*), they are regarded as acceptable and, on the basis of their legitimacy, they are followed.

The opposite is true of state rules. In Andranoheza, over half of respondents who discussed how they felt about forest rules expressed dissatisfaction with forest legislation. Though this rate is lower in Fanjakana (18%), it is fair to say that villagers think of state rules as superfluous. For those who actually gave reasons for disliking or not accepting state rules, they stated that state rules are either not fair (*tsy ara-drariny*) or they just do not make sense (*tsy mitombina*). In the words of two Andranoheza men, "Even if the state did not protect the forest, our community would do so effectively." Another added: "Anyone wishing to go into the forest, if not stopped by the state, would still be prevented by the community from doing so." That state rules are neither needed nor acceptable captures how locals view forest legislation.

In particular, villagers unequivocally dislike E&F's requirement for cutting permits for a fee prior to harvesting trees for construction. Most respondents in Andranoheza said that they did not mind the permit requirement itself, but that paying for a cutting permit reduces their ability to purchase cattle and enhance their social status locally. In short, villagers resent the financial cost of obeying and breaking the law. This resentment is exacerbated by the Bara's extreme suspicion of *vazaha*, the generic term locals use to refer to anyone alien to the community, whether educated, city dwelling, or foreigner. To the Bara representatives of the state are quintessential *vazaha* and, as such, they cannot be trusted. This local resentment and suspicion of state authorities are compounded by the low probability of detection and the possibility of avoiding sanction in case of noncompliance.

Communities' geographic isolation are the final reason for noncompliance with state rules. Very few outsiders make it to the western side of Analavelona forest, and E&F agents are no exception. Sakaraha-based Kamosa had not once been to Andranoheza or Fanjakana at the time of research. According to him, he had no means to travel to these remote areas, hence his occasional reliance on WWF agents and state law enforcement agents to do his job. To add to his material constraints, he was troubled, in his own words, by "the size of [his] big belly." His lack of physical fitness was thus another impediment to proper rule enforcement, as reaching these remote areas is physically demanding.[25]

Andranomaintso Residents

The people of Andranomaintso are reputed rule-breakers: in defiance of the law, they make and sell charcoal, firewood, and they clear the forest to expand their agricultural fields. Although deforestation showed signs of abating in 1991, in the Andranomaintso portion of the forest, a question remains: Why have concerted efforts involving E&F, WWF, community leaders, and even community members, failed to control noncompliance with DMH? If legal uses captured the extent of residents' forest dependence, the story would be relatively simple. However, legal uses (firewood for household consumption, construction lumber, supplementary food, medicine, coffins, and clearing for agriculture) represent only a fraction of residents' claims to the forest. E&F rules seem to have accommodated these legitimate needs fairly reasonably. But the aforementioned illegal uses of Zombitse, detailed in Table 2.2, complicate the issue. With 70% of respondents reporting making and selling charcoal,

Table 2.2 Self-reported illegal uses of Zombitse forest, Madagascar. Forty-four respondents discussed which rules are enforced and how they are enforced (*Source* Author's Madagascar survey)

Uses affecting forests	Frequency (N = 44)	Percentage (N = 44)
Making charcoal	31	70
Collecting firewood to sell	16	36
Forest clearing	14	32
Hunting animals (lemurs, tenrecs)	4	9
Cutting timber without a permit	4	9
Introducing machete into Zombitse	1	2
Entering Zombitse without a permit	1	2

and roughly a third reporting selling firewood and clearing forest for agriculture, explaining the persistence of deforestation originating in Andranomaintso requires focusing on these illegal activities and communities' reactions to E&F regulations.

Andranomaintso residents are well aware of the rules governing Zombitse access and use. In general, locals think of these rules as clear and strict in the sense that they are more prohibitive and prescriptive than they are permissive.[26] The consequences of breaking the rules are also well known to users, and they are perceived by a few as being "moderately" harsh and by most as "extremely" harsh. Warnings are not common, and fines range from *Ariary* 20,000, roughly the equivalent of US$10, to five times as much.[27] Jail time is always a possibility but not necessarily a reality, judging from the number of times this sanction was mentioned: 23 out of 36 of respondents mentioned jail as a possible sanction.

This would lead one to think that these tough rules stand a good chance of being complied with because, logically, potential violators should fear sanctions. However, the weakness of monitoring and enforcement contributes a great deal to diminishing the effectiveness of these rules. For instance, the credibility of incarceration as a deterrent has been undermined by higher state authorities' failure to enforce court rulings.[28] The visibility of such institutional flaws aggravates the state's lack of credibility: individuals sentenced to serve jail time have come back home from Toliara, often on the same bus as E&F or WWF agents! Over time, this inconsistency can only have reduced the rules' credibility and efficacy.

Despite such irregularities, however, there is a clear sense that rules do apply and that the forest cannot be treated as an open-access resource: forty-one out of 44 respondents said that rules are enforced in the community. According to them, before DMH applied, rule enforcement was the sole responsibility of state authorities, mainly the E&F *Chef de Cantonnement*, whose visits were sporadic and enforcement decisions inconsistent. Once DMH became operational, outside authorities continued to intervene frequently, but the enforcement playing field was somewhat leveled by giving local residents some monitoring responsibilities.

Although attempts were made to give rules more traction, problems relating to enforcement have persisted. It is a known fact, for instance, that E&F agents have not systematically and consistently punished rule-breakers. Some villagers, in fact, allegedly received advice from E&F agents on how best to smuggle products out of the forest at night so as to reduce the chances of being seen. Likewise, logging companies have openly violated forest legislation by exploiting beyond areas officially approved by E&F without being reported by local officials, let alone prosecuted by state officials.[29]

With the integration of *fokonolona* members into the decision-making process, village ethnic leaders ended up sharing monitoring and enforcement responsibilities with E&F. It so happens that these local leaders manipulated the new monitoring process to encourage infractions so as to support Andranomaintso's defiance to outside authority. For instance, one of the ethnic leaders was also *président de fokontany* in 1999, and his strategy was one of playing E&F against WWF to draw attention to Andranomaintso with the hope of getting personal favors from either institution and also to attract resources, mostly in the form of public services such as a water pump, school, etc., to the village. Thus giving power to local leaders did not circumvent the problem of predatory behavior. On the contrary, it extended corrupt practices into local communities where infractions were not discouraged because rule breaking helped select individuals maintain economic and political power locally.

In addition, rule-breakers were not equally and consistently sanctioned. Bribe solicitation has been detrimental to effective rule enforcement, a problem pervasive throughout Madagascar's administration. E&F is no exception. When asked if there were ways out of punishment once caught, 11 out of 44 respondents said yes, 17 refrained from answering, and 16 specifically said that there was no such thing.

Even though 11 hardly constitute a majority of respondents in this case, the fact that 25% of respondents acknowledged that they could pay their way out of sanctions suggests that rules are not properly enforced. Also, the facial expressions of some of those who refrained from answering strongly suggested that corruption was, indeed, pervasive.

To make matters worse, little community spirit is to be found in Andranomaintso to solve collective action problems. In fact, only in Andranomaintso is it the case that people do not clearly distinguish *fokonolona* (socially organized) from *fokontany* (state-mandated) affairs. The unique way this settlement came into being may explain its social deficiencies. The fact that migrants arrived in the area in successive migration waves is not so unusual for this region, but what makes Andranomaintso different from surrounding "communities" is immigrants' failure to adhere to Bara customs in Bara territory. The clearest indicator of this is what one could term the victory of agriculture over pastoralism. This seemingly symbolic conversion has had serious implications for forest conservation since forests had to be cut to make room for agricultural land.

Another clear sign of Bara defeat is seen in the introduction of goats and sheep, which is strictly forbidden in Bara culture, to this settlement: 18% of surveyed households raise sheep, and 7% have goats in the village. This indicates that either the Bara may be more accepting or that they are simply powerless in the face of outside intrusions.

The group of local ethnic leaders has had a difficult time keeping the members of their respective ethnic group out of Zombitse because local institutions, including that of *Ray aman-dReny*, or community elders, have eroded. This, in turn, has perpetuated and even accentuated socio-ethnic divisions in Andranomaintso. Local leaders' inability and unwillingness to restrain aggressors of the forest has been exacerbated by the settlement's proximity to markets (for forest products, such as charcoal, firewood, and lumber) as well as alternative dispute resolution institutions such as the Toliara regional court. Thus, the power of economic gain must be taken into account in this particular context.

With all of F&F and, subsequently, WWF's efforts to contain deforestation, a clear break was achieved in 1998–1999, shortly after sapphires were discovered in the area. While WWF project documents warn against the threat of more deforestation due to sapphire mining (Zombitse-Vohibasia National Park Management Plan 1998), it appears that, lured by the prospect of quick and immense wealth, most males turned away from illegally exploiting Zombitse to mining sapphires. This shift shows that Andranomaintso residents are very receptive to alternative economic activities deemed promising in terms economic (and therefore) social gains. It is ironic, indeed, that by illegally exploiting Zombitse, they are taking risks only to find out that they are not the primary beneficiaries. More often than not, their gains merely allow them to survive, not prosper (had they prospered, most would have left the area to return home). The lack of economic alternatives to growing food and produce, using *hatsaka*, and to exploiting Zombitse illegally significantly reduces the chances that rules will ever produce resource-conserving behavior.[30] In order for rules to achieve the purpose for which they are designed, i.e., forest conservation, there would need to be a shared sense of commitment to conserving, not to deriving maximum economic gain, from the forest. Without such a collective conservation goal, the legitimacy and thus efficacy of conservation rules is compromised.

We learn from the Andranomaintso case that the absence of a sense of shared responsibility and willingness to maintain the forest largely helps explain the extent of noncompliance around Zombitse. The problem is compounded by lack of accountability among both forest users, who break rules with impunity, and state officials who simply do not do their job properly.[31] In a case like this one, rules are largely irrelevant. In spite of a relatively abundant institutional supply, with conservation roles given to community members, WWF agents, and E&F representatives, the fact that E&F, other state officials, and most Andranomaintso residents were interested in gaining from exploiting the forest did little to help WWF meet its conservation goals. In other words, too many key actors found it in their interest to exploit the forest, while at the same time local capacities to enforce rules were too weak to resist the forces of economic gain. As a result, deforestation persisted.

Where Interests Diverge: Iarindrano vs. Ihera Classified Forests

Unlike Analavelona and Zombitse, Iarindrano and Ihera forests have a lot in common beyond their legal status of *forêt classée*. The village communities of Iarindrano and Mitia (Ihera forest) are both small, with between three hundred and five hundred inhabitants. The ethnic majority for both communities is Bara. Dependence on the forest for livelihood is equally heavy, with 94 and 100% of households surveyed, respectively,

2 SEEING LIKE A FARMER: RESOURCE POLITICS AT THE COMMUNITY LEVEL 67

claiming to use forest products for fuel, food, medicine, fodder, pasture and, most importantly, construction. For both communities, the forest is easily accessible, with travel time from settlements to forest of less than one hour. The same is true of ease of access to markets, which villagers can reach in about three hours from each settlement. Both communities share the experience of logging companies coming into their territory and selectively harvesting under the legal protection of state-sanctioned permits. However, in the case of Iarindrano, the loggers did not stay as long as they did in Ihera because of some disagreement on the authority in charge of approving logging activities.

Very similar rules apply at the level of these communities for the main forest products: state regulations apply almost exclusively for construction lumber and bush fires, whereas community rules are used to regulate the collection of fuelwood and foods, such as game, tubers, and honey.[32] Finally, local users' reactions to rules-in-use are similar, at least with regard to their perceptions of rules' legitimacy. In both communities, people are almost equally divided on the question of whether or not they consider some rules objectionable. They are also similarly divided on existence of rules they refuse to accept.[33] Beyond these two points of similarity, opinions on rules diverge, which I discuss below.

Despite similarities in forest dependency, ethnic makeup, and reactions to forest rules, deforestation outcomes differ between the two forests: virtually no forest cover change was detectable in Iarindrano forest from 1989 to 2000 while some deforestation occurred in the same period in Ihera where deforestation rates were 0.13% for the 1989–1994 period and 0.07% for 1994–2000 around the study site of Mitia village.[34] To account for different deforestation outcomes between the two communities, the remainder of this section asks: what are the outstanding differences between the two communities, and how do these differences explain the differential effectiveness of rules-in-use in producing compliance vs. noncompliance behavior?

First, livelihood strategies are different in each community. In Mitia, about half of the people who spoke with us cultivate irrigated rice, while nearly everyone did in Iarindrano. At the same time, 40% of Mitia's informants said that they depended on "other activities" for livelihood, while none did in Iarindrano. Mitia's situation is reminiscent of Andranomaintso, where residents exploit the forest, illegally producing charcoal and selling timber, to boost their incomes. In the case of Mitia, there is no charcoal production, but timber is produced illegally.

In Ihera, what drives the illegal uses of the forest to make money is the social pressure to flaunt one's wealth.

Why are livelihood strategies different in otherwise similar communities? First, the opportunities for marketing timber are better around Ihera than Iarindrano, which is partly why logging has continued in Ihera, albeit at a slower pace. Market penetration is obvious in Mitia: trucks drive to Ihera forest to collect timber on a regular basis. This is not the case in Iarindrano. Second, Iarindrano territory is endowed with fertile land particularly favorable for irrigated rice more so than Mitia. Immigrants residing in Iarindrano grow rice and have been successful enough to prosper through sharecropping with their Bara landlords. Although immigrants murdered a prominent member of the Bara Zafimañely, this family of land owners chose not to expel all immigrants from the territory they control. Instead, they relocated immigrant rice cultivators to a nearby hamlet, which strongly suggests that the Bara Zafimañely have more to gain from accommodating immigrant rice farmers than expulsing them. This settlement arrangement has afforded the Bara the luxury of tending to their zebus exclusively, leaving agricultural tasks to outsiders.

Social cohesion is the second differentiating factor. Although one could argue that some form of mutual isolation exists in both communities, there is no outright animosity among Iarindrano residents, whereas the tension is high in Mitia where the social fabric has eroded over time. This has encouraged economic stratification, with little restraint on making money, flaunting one's wealth, and showing little concern for the less privileged.[35] Christian values have also been embraced, challenging Bara values now relegated to the realm of "ignorant superstitions." A defiant Christian couple went as far as to mention that *Mampisaraka*, the quintessential marker of Bara identity (i.e., if you are Bara, you do not burn this tree species), was excellent firewood. By contrast, Iarindrano residents are socially cohesive. As an indicator of their commitment to stand as one unit, respondents were surprised and even offended by the question of economic stratification, which implies that people in this community might not look out for each other. We were told in no uncertain terms that there was no such thing as poverty in Iarindrano because "everyone makes sure that nobody's needs go unmet."

The system of monitoring and enforcement in place for formal rules constitutes the third differentiating factor between the two communities. As mentioned previously, monitoring and enforcement can be labeled "direct" in Mitia since E&F representatives intervene and perform these tasks on site. By contrast, E&F largely relies on Iarindrano residents to monitor activities taking place in and around the forest. Only in one extreme case did E&F show up to sanction rule-breakers in Iarindrano. It has done so repeatedly in Mitia.

This difference in direct versus indirect resource governance is likely the main reason behind the final distinction between the two communities, namely local users' reactions to rules. If one looks at the extent to which people feel bound by rules-in-use, one can clearly see that Mitia residents feel more constrained than their Iarindrano counterparts, none of whom claimed to feel "really constrained" by fuelwood, construction wood, and food rules. By contrast, Mitia informants claimed to be "really bound" by the same rules, indicating that they feel more tightly controlled by the rules. Given the differences in monitoring and enforcement systems mentioned above, it is hardly a surprise that Mitia residents should feel less free than Iarindrano people, hence their more radical positions on getting rid of rules vs. modifying them. More people in Mitia seem eager to get rid of rules instead of modifying them. The reverse is true in Iarindrano, where there is more interest in rule modification than rule suppression. In addition, the majority of people with whom we spoke in Iarindrano saw a clear connection between a situation of open access (*res nullius*) and resource degradation. In Mitia, fewer people acknowledged the possibility of resource degradation, with an equal proportion of respondents suggesting such a possibility would improve people's welfare!

This begs the question: Why is E&F more present in Mitia than in Iarindrano, especially given Iarindrano's proximity to Vohibasia National Park? At least two explanations are plausible. First, to E&F officials, the financial stakes in controlling forest access are lower in Iarindrano than in Ihera where, recall, logging activities persist. Under these circumstances, select local residents have sought to enhance their economic power by collaborating with loggers, for instance storing illegal lumber in their homes. The loggers, for their part, collaborate with state agents to exploit Ihera at minimal cost by offering alternative payments to actual logging permits. Informants did not know for sure whether loggers actually had permits, some of them benefitting from "assuming" that they do. E&F officials, on the other hand, benefit from concentrating on cutting permits for construction and house repairs while pretending not to notice, as a carpenter mentioned, other visible logging activities: there are logging trails, evidence of recent cutting, and collection posts all around Ihera forest. Thus, Mitia is a clear case of interest convergence toward forest exploitation.

Second, Iarindrano's local leaders (the seven Bara Zafimañely siblings) enjoy favorable conditions for forest conservation, which is in their best interest as pastoralists. In that sense, local guardians of the forest and the state have converging interests in preserving the forest. In addition, since the logging business that tried to exploit Iarindrano ended its exploitation abruptly, market penetration has not advanced there as much as it has in Ihera. As a result and, one can argue, in the absence of state intervention or state interest, community rule enforcement capabilities are sufficient for controlling users' behavior. In spite of easy access to the forest from the settlements, compliance with rules is high because access is tightly controlled and behavior within the forest closely monitored by the Bara landlords. The state can thus rely on the local community to monitor consumption of wood for construction and coffins because it is the Bara Zafimañely's interest to protect the standing forest without which their zebus and, therefore, their economic status and their cultural identity would suffer. In this regard, Iarindrano's situation is reminiscent of Analavelona's.

In Mitia, noncompliance with state rules about timber results not from lack of enforcement per se, but from lack of predictable enforcement despite E&F's pronounced presence. Even though E&F is actually present in Mitia, its ability to monitor what is happening in and around Ihera forest does not measure up to Iarindrano's simply because, unlike the Bara Zafimañely of Iarindrano, E&F is not permanently onsite.

Other than mere physical presence, does anything prevent E&F from being a more effective guardian of the forest? The next section identifies the main impediments to more effective rule enforcement on E&F's part.

Eaux et Forêts' Limitations

While Bara communities generally do not differentiate among E&F personnel, the *gendarmes*, and agents from conservation projects (where applicable), all of whom are *vazaha* representing "the state" (*fanjakana*) in one capacity or another, E&F officials present themselves as well-intentioned forest guardians deprived of the means to defend forest regulations. Interviews with different foresters make this lament clear. Material limitations are the first limitation E&F agents face. When WWF arrived in the area in 1994, part of its mandate was to support its efforts to conserve the area's protected areas (Zombitse and Vohibasia).

As things stood in 1998, however, WWF's material means were far superior to E&F's, as was its ability to reach out to the most remote areas of the region. Support staff, transportation, office supplies, and maps were virtually nonexistent at E&F. Sakaraha's *Chef de Cantonnement* barely had more than an office room (renovated with WWF funds), a desk, a chair, a bench, a map of the area from the 1960s, and a binder with a 1997 compilation of all applicable forestry laws at his disposal. Other structural impediments include the simple fact that one man, who happens to be physically unfit, cannot realistically cover almost 8900 square kilometers encompassing more than eight forests located in over 71 *fokontany* throughout 11 *communes*. Lack of personnel–a solitary forest agent for all of Sakaraha–is the main reason why E&F has to delegate monitoring and enforcement responsibilities to the 30 *gendarmes*.

If there is merit to the argument that lack of personnel and transportation severely limit E&F's ability to patrol and enforce its laws, it is also hasty to conclude that increased means would lead to more effective enforcement. According to WWF project personnel, infractions increased rather than decreased when the project gave Kamosa, the *Chef de Cantonnement*, a motorcycle to tour the area. Seizing the opportunity to make money to supplement his salary, he proceeded to use his newfound mobility to distribute permits generously and collect bribes that protected rule-breakers against reprisals.

Indeed, there are many allegations that, contrary to what Kamosa may claim, he has prospered greatly from negotiating the law with forest users (especially the people around Zombitse). He owns real estate in Sakaraha, he and his family live in a large house provided by his employer, he has plenty of access to food (judging from his physique) and, as rumor has it, to women as well.

E&F's own institutional constraints add to its agents' material limitations. Various factors, some political, some cultural, others personal, combine to inform individual foresters' rule-enforcement strategies. E&F agents are required to monitor compliance and enforce forest legislation by going to the field and writing tickets (*procès verbaux*) when they uncover infractions. Depending on the gravity of the infraction, rule-breakers are given the option to avoid a lawsuit either by paying a fine or by doing labor that improves forest conditions (called a *transaction avant jugement*). If the rule-breaker refuses to settle the matter onsite, then the *Chef de Cantonnoment* refers the matter to the *Circonscription des Eaux et Forêts* (CIREF) in Toliara. At this level, E&F makes a recommendation to the prosecution on what penalty should apply in court.

For trials that have actually happened, results have been variable and unpredictable. According to E&F informants, some judges are "pro-environment" and others are "indifferent." The former can impose sentences harsher than recommended by E&F and, of course, the latter are lenient. Besides judges' personal inclinations, politics infiltrate the legal process and compromise judges' impartiality. As one E&F agent put it, politicians are only "pro-vote" and so, they find ways to stop judges from imposing harsh sentences on constituents who have the means to bribe them. According to Kamosa, corruption has led to dire results: only two out of twenty-four convicted felons received jail sentences of up to six months from 1983 to 1998, hardly a sign of commitment to upholding the law.

Well-established political and social networks further complicate the picture, not just at the village level, but at the provincial level as well. In Toliara, for instance, there is a political network made up of three ethnic groups known as *Tokobetelo*. Extremely influential in Toliara politics, members of this group have little interest in forest conservation. Under these conditions E&F officials wonder how forest legislation can be effective, especially when said legislation is based on French legal principles.

Various other factors make it difficult for E&F to apply its laws. Given the constraints and context described above, E&F agents have little incentive to do their job. In fact, what little financial incentive there was to uphold the law has vanished. For instance, what was called a *prime de procès verbaux*, or bonus payment for issuing citations, is no longer offered. Additionally, some E&F agents see flaws in the current texts. Not only, they say, do the core of forest laws date back to the 1930s, updates are slow to become legislation. Consequently, the general feeling among foresters is that forest legislation is more conceptual than practical.

Personal factors come into play as well: In some cases, compassionate E&F agents have found it morally challenging to apply the law when they know that some local users break rules to grow food and for pasture. Finally, E&F agents reach a plateau in their career: their "severity curve" settles in a middle position after shooting up in the initial years of their careers. In other words, they soften over time.

To recap, despite similar community profiles, Mitia and Iarindrano reached starkly different social and conservation outcomes. In the first case, rules-in-use did not prevent the degradation of Ihera forest. In fact, it was the manipulation of these rules that led to tree species loss. By contrast, in Iarindrano forest conservation rested on these rules, precisely. Mitia local key actors gave personal financial gain precedence over community cohesion and welfare, finding ways to tap into lucrative logging activities to advance personal interests.[36] Iarindrano leaders, by contrast, reclaimed control over their territory and forest resources as soon as the opportunity presented itself. Although they do not claim they had anything to do with the logging company's expulsion from their territory, which is probably true, they used the fact that they had land titles to the family territory to keep outsiders from exploiting the forest by offering them the opportunity to cultivate rice on a territory where soil conditions were good. In doing so, the Bara Zafimañely of Iarindrano successfully preserved their pastoral activities and cultural identity.

Ultimately, they took advantage of discords among state actors (E&F vs. loggers), state rules (land titles), and local soil conditions to monopolize access to the forest. Once they demonstrated that they were in control of forest resources, E&F entrusted them with rule enforcement, thereby empowering them to become *de facto* forest guards. In this way Iarindrano's enforcement and legitimation capabilities were superior to Mitia's, which largely explains the former's better forest conservation performance.

Lessons from Madagascar

What do the cases of interest convergence and divergence from southern Madagascar tell us about the impact of rules on forest users' behaviors? The case of Analavelona forest shows that where interests converge toward forest protection, the rules devised to restrict forest access raise the prospect of conservation significantly. Where and when interests converge toward exploiting forests, however, no rules can effectively contain deforestation, with Zombitse standing as a powerful example. Conversely, when actors' interests diverge (e.g., the state opts for conservation while private actors opt for exploitation, or vice versa) conservation is possible only where those who enforce forest rules have the capacity to make such rules stick. This is what the cases of Iarindrano and Mitia near Ihera forest demonstrate.

Beyond this, the four situations examined in this chapter highlight the importance of forest users' responses to rules *rather than the rules per se*. These responses have three motivational components: (1) the perceived legitimacy of rules and rule enforcers, (2) the quality of rule enforcement, and (3) the extent of social cohesion as measured by local leaders' legitimacy.

If this is true in Madagascar, is it also true in Tanzania and Uganda? In the following section, I answer this important question in two steps. First, using statistical data, I compare forest users' reactions to rules to explain variance in compliance behaviors across forest-dependent communities in Madagascar and Tanzania, where I conducted identical survey research. I then turn to Ugandan communities, using IFRI/SANREM data, based on similar questions regarding forest governance.[37]

DO FARMERS THINK ALIKE? COMPARING MALAGASY, TANZANIAN, AND UGANDAN FARMERS

On Rule Legitimacy

To assess rule legitimacy among farmers they were asked whether there were particular rules regarding the forest products that they used that they did not accept and what they would do if they had the opportunity to change existing rules.

Although two-thirds of respondents said that they could not think of rules that they would reject outright, about one out of five did answer yes to the question of whether some rules were not acceptable. This was true among men in both countries but only among Malagasy women. Regarding what respondents would do if they could change the rules, more respondents were interested in modifying rules rather than getting rid of them altogether. These results are consistent with farmers' awareness that without rules controlling forest access and uses, resources would be depleted.

That said, Tanzanian farmers did not express as strong opinions about rules as Malagasy farmers did, suggesting that perhaps rules are seen as more legitimate in Tanzania than in Madagascar. Considering that forest legislation is more frequently evoked than community rules among Malagasy farmers, the latter's rejection of rules expresses their rejection of state authority over forest governance. This is not surprising since most farmers think that forests are theirs to manage and use.

The impact of the perceived legitimacy of rules on farmers' compliance behavior is made even clearer in the statistical regressions presented in Table 2.3. Supporting the hypothesis that forest users are more likely to comply with the rules that they consider legitimate, respondents who claim to "accept" conservation rules are 38% less likely to report noncompliance than those who are "dissatisfied" with the rules in the Rule Legitimacy Model and 12% less likely in the Comprehensive model.[38]

On Rule Enforcement and Rule Enforcers

To assess the legitimacy of rule enforcers and quality of rule enforcement, farmers were asked whether agents from within or without their communities were in charge of rule enforcement, whether rules were enforced in consistent and predictable ways, and whether they were ways out of punishment in case of nonconformance.

On the question of whether rules are actually enforced, most farmers answered yes in the two countries, although the percentage of yes answers were much higher in Madagascar than in Tanzania. There, a significant percentage of respondents said that they did not know whether rules were actually enforced. Finally, on whether there were ways out of punishment, more Malagasy than Tanzanian farmers said yes and more Tanzanian than Malagasy male respondents said no. Although one could infer that corruption is more pervasive in Madagascar, such a conclusion is questionable considering that the countries had the same corruption perceptions index (CPI) score of 3 and shared the same world ranking of 100 (out of 182 countries) in 2011.[39]

Who are the rule enforcers? In Madagascar, rule enforcement is perceived to be the dominion of outside authorities, whereas in Tanzania respondents replied that they did not know whether outsiders were brought into the community to sanction rule-breakers. This is because, as noted above, Tanzanians do not readily distinguish between "state" and "community." In fact, only a negligible percentage replied yes to the question. By contrast, the majority of Malagasy respondents were divided between yes and no, with only a few answering that they did not know.

The statistical regression results in Table 2.3 clearly demonstrate the impact of enforcement, by both internal and external agents, on rule compliance. Internal enforcement is statistically significant in both comprehensive and enforcement models, whereas external enforcement

Table 2.3 Impact of legitimacy and enforcement on rule compliance in Madagascar and Tanzania (combined) (*Source* Author's Madagascar and Tanzania surveys)

Compliance logistic regression models, (Robust Standard Errors), Marginal effects at the mean

	Comprehensive model	Rule legitimacy	Leader legitimacy	Enforcement
Observations	74	144	157	88
Pseudo R2	.7156	.0653	.0481	.419
Rule acceptance	−.46	−1.67**	–	–
	(1.28)	(.98)		
	−11.55%	−37.57%		
Rule modification	5.86	−.23	–	–
	(6.55)	(.8)		
	29.64%	−5.07%		
Collective tasks: Some	3.91**	–	.7*	–
	(1.81)		(.39)	
	75.05%		17.09%	
Collective tasks: Few	.5	–	−.12	–
	(1.92)		(.46)	
	7.36%		−.03%	
Rules applied	.52	–	–	.36
	(.99)			(1.04)
	12.7%			9%
Enforcement: External	3.99**	–	–	1.3
	(1.85)			(.92)
	97.28%			32.54%
Enforcement: Internal	9.36***	–	–	3.28***
	(2.76)			(.88)
	228.85%			81.7%
Leader type: Imposes limits	14.02***	–	–	–
	(2.36)			
Leader type: Community chosen	15.6***	–	–	–
	(2.01)			
Leader type: State designated	14.12***	–	–	–
	(2.17)			
Household size	.07	−.14**	−.12*	−.08
	(.12)	(.06)	(.06)	(.09)
Gender	3.45**	.24	.26	1.48
	(1.09)	(.37)	(.37)	(.9)
Country	−4.99	−.4	−.47	−3.12**
	(2.08)	(.38)	(.48)	(1.28)
Constant	−40.13***	1.58*	−.02	−5.02*
	(10.35)	(.83)	(.74)	(2.91)

Significance * = .1, ** = .05, *** = .01

is statistically significant in the comprehensive model only. At the same time, the degree to which internal rule enforcement affects forest users' compliance is much greater than that of external enforcement. The comprehensive model predicts that, relative to communities with external enforcement, those without external agents present in the community are 97% more likely to report noncompliance in their communities. The same model predicts that, relative to communities with internal enforcement agents, communities without internal enforcement are 229% more likely to report noncompliance in their community (the rate is 82% in the enforcement model, which contains more observations). These statistical results confirm that rule enforcement is a critical variable affecting compliance. Additionally, they suggest that, relative to external monitors, internal monitoring agents are more likely to secure rule compliance across village communities.

On Leaders' Legitimacy and Social Cohesion

To assess the legitimacy of community leaders, respondents were asked about the extent of participation in collective tasks organized by their leaders and about the individual qualities they sought in leaders. In this context collective tasks are state-mandated and include road maintenance, informational meetings, construction of public buildings such as schools, etc. Survey results are starkly different in Madagascar and Tanzania: in Madagascar the majority of respondents (more than 70%, combining male and female responses) report that "few" and "some" participate in collective tasks. In Tanzania, the overwhelming majority of respondents reported that "all" and "some" participate and a minority (about 10%, combining male and female respondents) reported that only "few" do. These results support the idea that in Madagascar the state suffers from low legitimacy, which may, in turn, explain why state regulations are more frequently challenged than community rules and norms.

Another interpretation relates to social cohesion: if it is difficult for Malagasy farmers to follow their community leaders' orders for state-mandated tasks, it could mean that these communities, on the whole, choose social cohesion when it serves their collective interests and social disunity when their shared goal is to defy the state. In other words, Malagasy farmers clearly distinguish between two realms of collective action, community and state, and they change their cohesion profile depending on the source of collective action. By contrast, Tanzanians do not. This makes sense if one considers how the two countries' rural communities came into being historically: whereas Malagasy village communities emerged spontaneously as the result of migratory waves, in Tanzania, they were planned when Nyerere's government embarked on its version of collectivization, a policy called *ujamaa*, in the early to mid-1970s. When the state engineers local communities, it becomes extremely difficult to separate the two realms of local governance.

These differences notwithstanding, statistical regression results from Table 2.3 strongly suggest that farmers' perceptions of leaders' legitimacy affect compliance behavior. Specifically, relative to respondents who live in communities where people "always" participate in collective tasks (i.e., where people follow leaders' orders), those who live in communities where only "some" people participate are 75% more likely to report noncompliance with conservation rules. These results indicate that where leaders' legitimacy does not warrant participation, i.e., where leaders are not legitimate, noncompliance with rules is more likely.

As for leaders' qualities, overall, communities prefer leaders of their own choosing (see Table 2.4). Malagasy farmers prefer leaders of their own choosing, other attributes mattering less, since this affords them a great deal of autonomy vis-à-vis the state. By contrast, Tanzanians prefer leaders who, by descending order of preference, can effectively impose limits, are of their own choosing, and are flexible. These differences aside, in both countries leaders designated by the state are the least legitimate in farmers' eyes. Thus another explanation for Malagasy farmers' tendency to reject state rules may lie in their determination to remain autonomous from the state.

Table 2.4 What type of leader are you most comfortable with? (*Source* Author's Madagascar and Tanzania surveys)

	Madagascar		Tanzania	
	Men	Women	Men	Women
Flexible	3	5	12	11
Imposes limits	1	1	45	39
I chose	71	60	26	30
State designates	6	4	2	13

What About Ugandan Farmers?

In discussing problems relating to forest management, Ugandan respondents identify "wildlife destroying crops" as the first issue: 39 and 22% acknowledge this as the first and second problem, respectively. Past this, however, issues relating to forest governance constitute the bulk of farmers' concerns. With governance, two sets of problems appear: the first relates to losing access to forest products including fuelwood, fodder, water, medicinal plants, and food; the second is specifically about government officials entrusted with forest management. Table 2.5 shows that one out of three respondents mentioned NFA and UWA officials and forest boundary extension as their first and second problems. Of note are two comments to the effect that the "community fights with forest officials" and that the "community has no control over the forest." Although infrequently made, these two comments indicate that people do not approve of government officials' authority over forest management. Based on this, one can infer that NFA and UWA officials' legitimacy is in question.

Table 2.5 Ugandan farmers' problems with forest governance (*Source* Uganda IFRI/SANREM)

Problem 1 (N = 538)	Frequency	Percentage
Wildlife destroys crops	209	39
Agricultural land shortage	72	13
Fuelwood shortage	49	9
NFA officials	36	7
UWA officials	36	7
Limited forest access	33	6
Forests pests diseases	12	2
Forest dependence	11	2
Wildlife attacks domestic animals	6	1
Forest boundary extension	5	1
Deforestation	4	1
Branches injuries	4	1
Forest use community disagreement	4	1
Forests insecurity	3	1
Poaching	2	0
Wildlife bites people	2	0
None	50	9

(continued)

Table 2.5 (continued)

Problem 2 (N = 142)	Frequency	Percentage
Wildlife destroys crops	31	22
Agricultural land shortage	19	
Fuelwood shortage	9	6
UWA officials	8	6
Limited forest access	4	3
Forests pests diseases	11	
Wildlife attacks domestic animals	3	
Forest boundary extension	3	
Branches injuries	3	
Forests insecurity	3	
Wildlife bites people	11	
None	9	
Land deprivation by forest authorities	1	1
Poverty and lack of alternatives	3	
Fodder shortage	2	1
Water shortage	1	1
Food shortage	6	4
Medicinal plants shortage	1	1
Lower supplies of bamboo and mushrooms	1	1
Excessive rain destroys crops	2	
Building poles shortage	1	
No benefits from forests	1	1
Foresters let timber fall and rot	1	1
Local community has no control over the forest	1	1
Forest burning	1	1
Forest rule breaking	1	1
Local people's resistance to protecting forests	1	1
Illegal tree cutting in National Park	1	1
Private ownership of forests	1	1
Community fights with forest officials	1	1
Ignorance of forest uses	1	1

In terms of rule enforcement, results from Uganda confirm what transpires in Madagascar and Tanzania: compliance rates are significantly higher when rule enforcers are from within the community than when external officials appointed by the government are in charge (Table 2.6).

At the stage of imposing penalties, compliance rates are yet again higher when no external, state-appointed, officials are called in (Table 2.7). As in the case of Madagascar and Tanzania, these results challenge the pervasive assumption that the state is indispensable to forest protection.

Table 2.6 The relationship between rule enforcers and compliance in Uganda

Enforcer of rules created by organization	Compliance with rules			
	No	Yes	No	Yes
	Frequency		Percentage	
Members of the organization itself	16	44	20	60
Members of the use group	10		13	
External officials appointed by the government	8	7	10	10
Other ways specified	45	22	57	30
Total	79	73	100	100

Table 2.7 Relationship between external enforcement and user group compliance in Uganda (*Source* Uganda IFRI/SANREM)

Do different user groups follow the rules?	Have external government officials been called to enforce penalties?	
	No	Yes
No	13	1
Yes	22	2

Conclusion

Whether in Madagascar, Tanzania, or Uganda the prevailing assumption behind conservation policies and projects can be summarized as follows: without rules there can be no conservation. Based on this assumption, policies and projects have encouraged the enactment or tightening of existing forest legislation, rarely questioning how laws actually translate into compliance behavior and, by extension, forest conservation. While not entirely unfounded, the idea that it takes rules to constrain forest users' behavior nonetheless overlooks the fact that rules that apply at the local level reflect a process of adapting forest legislation to local realities. As such, rules-in-use are hybrids that combine formal legislation with local rules and norms. Since these hybrid rules are designed to adapt to local circumstances, they vary across communities, as do local users' reactions and responses to them. Thus, to understand the relationship between rules and compliance choices, one must first understand how the rules that apply come into being, what informs users' compliance choices, and how these choices help conserve forests or not.

As is the case at the national level (discussed in Chapter 3), local institutions emerge from interactions among key actors whose purposes vis-à-vis forest resources are well defined and shape the institutions they put in place to defend and advance those interests. In this regard, the cases from southern Madagascar are illuminating. In a first scenario, interests converged toward forest protection, and the rules devised to restrict forest access raised the prospect of conservation significantly. This was the case near Analavelona sacred forest and Iarindrano classified forest. In both cases, the key actors shaping and controlling forest institutions were community actors and state officials. In Iarindrano, logging companies were tolerated so long as the state authorized them to harvest, but they were not permitted to extend their activities beyond the period they were legally present. In the two cases both forests were well preserved mainly because state and community actors had a common interest in conservation. As a result, state and community rules were mutually supportive and, equipped with strong enforcement capabilities, communities effectively protected the forest.

A second scenario emerged where interests converge toward forest exploitation. In this case, no rules could effectively contain deforestation. This was evident in Mitia near Ihera classified forest. In Mitia, once logging was permitted, local actors learned to personally benefit from clearing the forest. When the logging company ceased its activities, instead of building conservation-friendly institutions to constrain forest access and uses, select local actors pursued their personal interests and continued to illicitly log the forest. The social context made this possible: unlike in Iarindrano (and Analavelona), Bara actors failed to preserve Bara cultural values that favor forest conservation.

A third scenario transpired where actors' interests diverged, with the state officially standing for conservation and private actors eager to exploit the forest. In Andranomaintso, near Zombitse National Park, circumstances surrounding rule creation and enforcement, rather than the rules per se, determined the effectiveness of conservation rules. Easy access to important markets for forest products, such as timber, charcoal, and maize fostered a forest-for-cash mentality that conservation rules could not discourage, especially in light of sporadic and inconsistent monitoring and enforcement. When E&F allowed a logging company to operate in southern Zombitse, this business brought about fundamental changes in terms of demographic composition, economic opportunities, and social cohesion. By attracting various ethnic groups to the area, the logging business transformed livelihood strategies, allowing agriculture to supersede pastoralism and introducing slash-and-burn agriculture. Like in Ihera, environment-friendly Bara values of harmony between humans and spirits eroded, giving economic gain relatively more influence. Rules that were supposedly community-devised were developed and implemented to stop forest clearing, but the very absence of a community identity, with a sense of shared goals, norms, history, and institutions, prevented these rules from curtailing deforestation.

Thus interest alignment is a crucial condition for getting the rules right at the local level. Beyond this, particular aspects of rules actually inform users' compliance choices. The three-country comparison makes it possible to generalize beyond Madagascar and identify three factors, namely, (1) local users' perceptions of whether or not rules are legitimate, (2) their assessment of the quality of enforcement and legitimacy of rule enforcers, and (3) their assessment of local leaders' legitimacy, as determinants of compliance. Across communities, where people see conservation rules as needed, proper, and fair, the likelihood of compliance increases.

In particular, the complementarity of state and community rules raises the prospects of conservation. It also matters who monitors compliance and enforces rules, the main distinction being between internal and external enforcers. In most cases, internal monitors have the upper hand simply because they are motivated to make rules stick and because the costs of monitoring and enforcement are lower for them than for outsiders. Finally, recognition of local leaders' authority, measured by their ability to organize collective action, affects forest users' compliance choices. Where local leaders are capable of obtaining participation with state-mandated collective tasks, compliance with rules is likely. This, of course, begs the question: how do local communities determine their leaders' legitimacy? The answer to this question is universal: people prefer leaders whom they choose. Rarely are these designated by the state.

Notes

1. Jarosz, Lucy. "Defining Tropical Deforestation: Shifting Cultivation and Population Growth in Colonial Madagascar." *Economic Geography* 69.4: 366.
2. International Forestry Resources and Institutions (IFRI) is a research program that examines the impacts of forest governance on forest outcomes. It is made up of Collaborative Research Centers (CRCs) from around the

world. The SANREM Project is hosted at Makerere University's UFRIC (Uganda's Forestry Resources and Institutions Center) in Kampala. See http://www.ifriresearch.net/about-us/collaborating-research-centers/uganda/, accessed August 1, 2016.
3. Tenrecs are mammals that resemble hedgehogs. They are an important source of protein fat for villagers.
4. Under the 1992 constitution of Madagascar, the national territory is divided into the following administrative units: 22 regions, 112 departments, 1395 *communes*, and 17,454 *fokontany*. The town of Mahaboboka is one of the 1395 *communes*.
5. The distinction between the sacred forest located on Mount Analavelona and the surrounding gallery forests is important, especially in terms of rules, because the two forests' structures and legal statuses differ. In the local jargon, *ala* refers to Mount Analavelona, *monto* to surrounding savanna, and *sakasaka* to gallery forests found alongside of rivers just outside the main forest.
6. According to Randriatavy (1994), 436 people lived in Andranomaintso in 1994. According to WWF (1998), 650 people occupied the village in 1997. In 1999, the total number of inhabitants was approximately 800.
7. Of all sites included in our study in Bara land, this is the only community where the Bara are a not an ethnic majority. Eleven ethnic groups are present in Andranomaintso, though some groups (Antandroy, Mahafaly, and Betsileo) are more numerous than others (Masikoro, Antesaka, Tanala, Vezo, Bara, Tanosy, Tanalalana, and Merina).
8. These social contracts are mechanisms by which individuals or groups of individuals of, say, two ethnic clans, swear to always help and never betray each other and their common interests.
9. Most survey respondents (95%) stated that they go the Sakaraha market to sell and buy produce, and purchase small food items and necessities (salt, sugar, coffee, soap, batteries, etc.).
10. All of the 44 respondents included in the survey said that they grow maize (some farmers also grow sweet potatoes and peanuts), 80% claim to use the forest, 70% said that they raise poultry, and as many as 40% rely on nonagricultural activities such as sapphire mining (since late 1998), small commerce, administrative work, and mechanics to make a living. Finally, 40% of male and female respondents (70% of interviewed men, which is probably a better indicator given the patriarchal system of cattle ownership in the area) claim to own cattle. Overall, the majority of people surveyed (65%) considered their production to be sufficient to feed their families year-round, which leaves one-third food deficient.
11. Rahaingosolo, Zanabao. *L'Exploitation Commerciale des Forêts de Zombitse et de Vohibasia, Sakaraha*. World Wide Fund for Nature, 1996.

12. Fauroux, Sylvain. "Instabilité des Cours de Maïs et Incertitude en Milieu Rural: le Cas de la Déforestation dans la Région de Tuléar (Madagascar)." *Revue Tiers Monde* 41.164 (2000): 815–40.
13. Forest rules are discussed in detail in Horning, Nadia Rabesahala. "The Limits of Rules: When Rules Promote Forest Conservation and When They Do Not: Insights from Bara Country, Madagascar." PhD Diss., Cornell University, 2004.
14. Ibid.
15. Duffy, Rosaleen. "Global Environmental Governance and the Challenge of Shadow States: The Impact of Illicit Sapphire Mining in Madagascar." *Development and Change* 36.5 (2005): 825–43; DeLeon, Sarah Wade Dickinson. "Jewels of Responsibility from Mines to Markets: Comparative Case Analysis from Burma, Madagascar, and Colombia." MS Thesis, University of Vermont, 2008. Web. 3 June 2012: 94–96.
16. Before 1995 other attempts to "get the rules right" had been made. These efforts began in the early 1990s, i.e., when the concept of community-based natural resource management reached Madagascar's environmental and legislative circles.
17. Unfortunately, this method does not allow the detection of changes in forest structure and species composition.
18. Horning, Ned. Personal Interviews 2004.
19. Horning, Ned. Personal Interviews 2004.
20. Horning, Ned. Personal Interviews 2003.
21. Horning, Ned. Personal Interviews June 26, 2012.
22. Comparing the two sets of rules, in Fanjakana 97 and 87% of respondents said they felt "tightly bound" by state and community rules, respectively. In Andranoheza, the figures are 76 and 59%, also respectively.
23. Under Malagasy law, forest agents may grant law enforcement agents the power to sanction rule-breakers.
24. There is one outstanding exception: for firewood collection, 88 and 100% of respondents who answered the question in Andranoheza and Fanjakana, respectively, said that nothing, in particular, was obligatory.
25. I traveled through Bara country with a research assistant. Our efforts to reach Fanjakana, Mikoboka area, should illustrate this point: it took us more than eleven hours to get there, going on foot from Mitia, a village located northeast of Analavelona and reachable only by four-wheel drive vehicle. After two failed attempts to reach the Fanjakana by car, and after hiking in for over ten hours, we were convinced that there was some truth to the claim or legend that Mikoboka people are shielded by a protective spell that guards them against outsiders!
26. Andranomaintso residents become familiar with rules through two principal channels. According to locals, WWF, E&F or the state work with clan heads to inform residents at least once a year. So, villagers become aware of rules

from outside authorities, or they hear of them through community leaders. At any rate, they consider it easy to become familiar with rules. Though informants did not explicitly state so, being part of the decision-making process for the fate of rule violators is actually another way that residents become familiar with rules and regulations. For instance, when someone gets caught carrying out illegal activities in and out of the forest, the *fokonolona* deliberates what sanction should apply, as specified in the DMH. On numerous occasions, the *fokonolona* apparently punished charcoal makers, firewood sellers, and forest clearers. In conjunction with the *fokonolona*, outside authorities (WWF, E&F, and *gendarmes*) have intervened to apprehend rule-breakers who refused to comply with *fokonolona* sanctions.

27. This represents a significant percentage of residents' average income.
28. Kamosa. Personal Interview. July 27, 1999.
29. Association Hevitra Maro. *Réalisation d'une Étude Socio-Économique et Forestière des Zones Zombiste-Vohibasia: Rapport Définitif*, Antananarivo, 1994: 82.
30. Association Hevitra Maro. *Réalisation d'une Étude Socio-Économique et Forestière des Zones Zombiste-Vohibasia: Rapport Définitif*, Antananarivo, 1994: 98.
31. Randriatavy, *L'Occupation de l'Espace et l'Organisation Sociale à Beba Manamboay et à Andranomaintso*. Sakaraha: World Wide Fund for Nature, 1994: 22.
32. Horning, Nadia Rabesahala. "The Limits of Rules: When Rules Promote Forest Conservation and When They Do Not: Insights from Bara Country, Madagascar." PhD Diss., Cornell University, 2004: 214–21.
33. Ibid., pp. 224–26.
34. Horning, Nadia Rabesahala. "The Limits of Rules: When Rules Promote Forest Conservation and When They Do Not: Insights from Bara Country, Madagascar." PhD Diss., Cornell University, 2004.
35. In addition to the classic herd size indicator, Western-style tombs have been erected and are very visible from the settlements.
36. This case, incidentally, challenges the usefulness of pitting state actors against community actors since the competition has effectively gone from state versus community (when the loggers first arrived) to community versus community. This is a case where key community actors have come to collaborate with state actors to share with them the benefits of exploiting Ihera forest.
37. In order to test the three hypotheses developed in the previous section, I estimate a comprehensive regression model with all relevant independent variables. Given the decreased number of observations in the comprehensive model, I estimate independent regression equations for each hypothesis (Rule Legitimacy, Leader Legitimacy, and Enforcement). In all models, the dependent variable is other community members' compliance

with rules (do people in this community comply with forest rules?). This variable is coded as "0" if other community members obey local forest rules and "1" if they do not. Categories where respondents reported "do not know," "no answer," or "missing," are dropped for all independent and control variables, except for Rule Acceptance and Rule Modification. Standard errors are robust and marginal effects are reported at mean values of other control and independent variables. As a robustness check, marginal effects are calculated at median values (this calculation does not significantly impact the regression results). Psuedo R^2 values are calculated using McFadden's R^2. Household size, gender, and country are included as control variables in the four models. Leader type is added as a control variable in the comprehensive model as a potentially omitted variable. However, given the difficulty of quantifying different leaders' qualities, inference drawn from Leader Type regression coefficients would be unreliable.

38. Here respondents reported on others' compliance behavior rather than their own.
39. Transparency International. "Corruption Perceptions Index 2011." 2011. http://cpi.transparency.org/cpi2011/results/, accessed May 29, 2012.

Bibliography

Association Hevitra Maro. Réalisation d'une Étude Socio-Économique et Forestière des Zones Zombiste-Vohibasia: Rapport Définitif. Antananarivo, 1994.

DeLeon, Sarah Wade Dickinson. "Jewels of Responsibility from Mines to Markets: Comparative Case Analysis in Burma, Madagascar, and Colombia." MS Thesis, University of Vermont, 2008. Web. Accessed June 3, 2012.

Duffy, Rosaleen. "Global Environmental Governance and the Challenge of Shadow States: The Impact of Illicit Sapphire Mining in Madagascar." *Development and Change* 36.5 (2005): 825–43.

Fauroux, Sylvain. "Instabilité des Cours de Maïs et Incertitude en Milieu Rural: le Cas de la Déforestation dans la Région de Tuléar (Madagascar)." *Revue Tiers Monde* 41.164 (2000): 815–40.

Horning, Nadia Rabesahala. "The Limits of Rules: When Rules Promote Forest Conservation and When They Do Not: Insights from Bara Country, Madagascar." PhD Diss., Cornell University, 2004.

Horning, Ned. Personal Interviews. 2003, 2004.

International Forestry Resources and Institutions. "Uganda." Web. http://www.ifriresearch.net/about-us/collaborating-research-centers/uganda/. Accessed August 1, 2016.

Jarosz, Lucy. "Defining Tropical Deforestation: Shifting Cultivation and Population Growth in Colonial Madagascar." *Economic Geography* 69.4: 366–79.

Kamosa. Personal Interview. July 27, 1999.

Rahaingosolo, Zanabao. *L'Exploitation Commerciale des Forêts de Zombitse et de Vohibasia, Sakaraha.* World Wide Fund for Nature, 1996.

Randriatavy, *L'Occupation de l'Espace et l'Organisation Sociale à Beba Manamboay et à Andranomaintso.* Sakaraha: World Wide Fund for Nature, 1994.

SANREM Data. International Forestry Resources and Institutions. Uganda Collaborative Resource Center.

Transparency International. "Corruption Perceptions Index 2011." 2011. http://cpi.transparency.org/cpi2011/results/. Accessed May 29, 2012.

World Wide Fund for Nature. *Zombitse-Vohibasia National Park Management Plan.* Draft, 1998.

CHAPTER 3

Executive Branches and Trees: Environmental Politics at the National Level

LIST OF ACRONYMS

SAP	Structural Adjustment Program
PRSP	Poverty Reduction Strategy Paper
NGO	Non-Governmental Organization
IFI	International Financial Institution
PRC	People's Republic of China
GTZ	*Deutsche Gesellschaft für Technische Zusammenarbeit* (now GIZ for *Deutsche Gesellschaft für Internationale Zusammenarbeit*)
KFW	*Kreditanstalt für Wiederaufbau*
USAID	United States Agency of International Development
TAS	Tanzania Assistance Strategy
IUCN	International Union for Conservation of Nature
NEAP	National Environmental Program
DEF	*Direction des Eaux et Forêts* (Madagascar)
DD	*Direction des Domaines* (Madagascar)
FTM	*Foiben-Taosarintanin'i Madagasikara* (national geographic institute)
ANAE	*Association Nationale d'Actions Environnementales* (Madagascar)
ANGAP	*Association Nationale pour la Gestion des Aires Protégées* (now MANAPA)

© The Author(s) 2018
N. R. Horning, *The Politics of Deforestation in Africa*,
https://doi.org/10.1007/978-3-319-76828-1_3

MANAPA	Madagascar National Parks
ONE	*Office National de l'Environnement* (Madagascar)
SMB	*Secrétariat Multi-Bailleurs* (Madagascar)
TANU	Tanganyika National Union
CCM	*Chama Cha Mapinduzi* (Tanzania)
NFR	National Forest Reserve (Tanzania)
LAFR	Local Authority Forest Reserve (Tanzania)
TANAPA	Tanzania National Parks
NCAA	Ngorongoro Conservation Area Authority (Tanzania)
LOGA	Local Government Authority (Tanzania)
UNDP	United Nations Development Programme
SFD	Scientific and Forest Department (Uganda)
FD	Forest Department (Uganda)
FR	Forest Reserves (Uganda)
PFE	Permanent Forest Estate (Uganda)
PA	Protected Area
CFR	Central Forest Reserve (Uganda)
LFR	Local Forest Reserve (Uganda)
UWA	Uganda Wildlife Authority
ME	Ministry of Environment (Uganda)
NFA	National Forest Authority (Uganda)
NEMA	National Environment Management Authority (Uganda)
PCE	Policy Committee on Environment (Uganda)
MITI	Ministry of Tourism, Trade and Industry (Uganda)
MEMD	Ministry of Energy and Mineral Development (Uganda)
MLG	Ministry of Local Government (Uganda)
LC	Local Councils (Uganda)
MAAIF	Ministry of Agriculture, Animal Industry and Fisheries (Uganda)
MWE	Ministry of Water and Environment (Uganda)
DEA	Directorate of Environmental Affairs (Uganda)
FID	Forestry Inspectorate Division (Uganda)
FSSD	Forestry Sector Support Department (Uganda)

3 EXECUTIVE BRANCHES AND TREES   91

This chapter explores how environmental policies are negotiated, enacted, and executed in three African contexts. It highlights the central role that foreign aid plays in the making of development policies, some more conservation-friendly than others. It also underscores the executive branch's predominance and foreign donors' role in environmental policymaking. Chapter 2 discussed how local-level actors interact to protect their interests vis-à-vis forest resources. These interactions result in rules-in-use that combine, in various configurations, formal legislation, and local rules. Ultimately, local users' compliance decisions determine whether or not, and to what extent, deforestation is controlled. These rules are most effective in controlling deforestation where and when they emerge from the proper alignment of local actors' interests. Conversely, where interests do not align, they cannot help deforestation. Thus, the mere existence of rules does not guarantee forest conservation.

A similar process takes place at the national level, where the primary actors driving environmental policy are African governments, dominated by the executive office, and foreign donors who use aid to sway governments' development policies. At this level, donors' ability to persuade African governments to commit to conservation-friendly development policies rests on a specific and limited condition: The executive's and foreign interests must align and be consistent with conservation norms. When this is the case, institutional investments, manifest in institutional proliferation, raise the prospect of forest conservation considerably. When interests do not align, however, institutional proliferation reflects not so much conservation commitments on the part of African leaders as it does their eagerness to convert foreign aid into patronage opportunities that serve them politically. This reality, I argue, explains the gap between institutional investments and environmental outcomes. And it challenges the prevailing notion that aid is inherently good for conservation.

Thus, as is the case at the local level, interest alignment is a key condition for successful conservation policies. Though not sufficient (because interests must concurrently align at the local level), this condition is necessary for local institutions to yield conservation at the local level. Understanding this helps us appreciate why forest conservation is extraordinarily difficult to achieve and why deforestation persists even when efforts are invested in conserving particular countries' natural wealth. It also helps target conservation efforts where and when they are most likely to be fruitful, thereby avoiding waste. Stating this, however, is to assume—rather naively—that conservation aid is good for conservation when it is not, at least not always. It has been argued that aid is an instrument of statecraft, a means through which those who extend aid use their power to sway aid recipients' decisions in ways that serve donors', not recipients', interests. Going farther, I have argued that donors continue to extend aid even when recipients do not reach said aid's putative goals (such as conservation) because development gains are peripheral, not central, to the aid game. This reality explains donors' tolerance for poor performance.[1] In this manner, rules-in-use govern negotiations at the national level just as they do at the local level because the actual rules (and norms) of engagement assume one thing, i.e., aid will be extended to states capable of bettering citizens' lives, thereby making development gains, and achieve other things, i.e., more poverty and inequality, because these rules are subject to manipulation where and when they are applied. In light of this, Africa's sorry development record despite billions of development dollars poured into the continent for the past several decades cannot come as a surprise.

How, in the first place, did these national-level dynamics come about? Achieving national prosperity through sound development policies has long preoccupied African governments, and Madagascar, Tanzania, and Uganda are no exception. Consequently, development has been a key feature of the countries' politics. Given the costs of financing development initiatives and considering African governments' inability or reluctance to cover such costs, foreign donors have carved a niche of influence for themselves. One of the ways donors have sought to sway African governments' decisions is in answering a key question: Is rapid economic growth the best means to achieve prosperity, or is good resource stewardship, dubbed sustainable development, a better way to reach this goal? African responses have been mixed: Some African leaders have embraced the sustainable development model, per donors' preference since the 1980s, while others have resisted it.

This chapter details how responses to donor prescriptions have varied across the three countries under study by examining processes of negotiation at critical points of environmental policy development in each of the countries. From 2002 to 2009 Marc Ravalomanana of Madagascar showed remarkable willingness to cooperate with donors eager to protect the island's impressive biodiversity. In Tanzania, throughout the 1960s and 1970s, Julius Nyerere allowed donors to shape his country's conservation policies to protect its extraordinary wildlife. By contrast, Yoweri Museveni of Uganda, in power since 1986, was not readily receptive to the idea that development rests primarily on good natural resource stewardship. Instead, Museveni believes in "processing," i.e., converting natural resources into goods and services that are good for the economy. In examining how conservation policies were made at critical historical junctures in Madagascar, Tanzania, and Uganda, this chapter seeks to explain why Madagascar has been more successful in battling deforestation than its mainland counterparts.

Prior to delving into the details of these countries' environmental politics, however, it helps to understand the broader historical context of African governments–donors relations since the politics of conservation aid is a microcosm of the politics of development aid.

The Urge to Aid Africa

Aid has been integral to Africa's economic and political development since independence.[2] Aid was extended post-independence to help African governments initiate the process of modernization (often understood as industrialization) and bring them into the world economy as competitive partners, after which they would be self-sufficient and prosperous. In contrast to their East Asian counterparts, however, African countries did not follow the path that aid intended to put them on. Instead, most African countries sank into aid dependency after two decades or less of independent rule. With a few exceptions (e.g., Botswana) and despite a drop in the 1990s, aid inflows went up rather than down for the whole continent[3] such that, by the 1980s, the majority of African governments had accumulated debts that they could not easily (if at all) service, much less repay. In fact, by the early 1990s, some countries had to borrow more money to honor their debt obligations. In other cases, the debt (or large portions of it) was forgiven altogether.[4,5]

Why Africa Has Received Aid

At independence, donors were motivated to aid African countries, first because it was in former colonizers' interest to maintain cultural, commercial, diplomatic, and security ties with their former colonies. Schraeder reports that from 1884 to 1989 France—one of the major colonial powers in Africa "maintained and expanded its presence throughout the continent, most notably in what is still referred to as 'francophone Africa'," an area comprising nearly half of all African countries.[6] Second, because African countries became independent during the Cold War (the only exceptions being South Africa, Eritrea, and South Sudan), Western states viewed the continent as an ideological battlefield in their anti-communist struggles. Western donors had an additional motive to offer aid to African leaders sympathetic to their ideological views.

At the end of the Cold War, aid calculations shifted. Since donors no longer needed to give aid in exchange for ideological support, they began using aid to encourage reforms in countries they considered economically inefficient and politically undemocratic. By 1990, the push to liberalize economic and political systems, known as the "Washington Consensus," shaped donor–recipient relations, causing most recipients to subscribe to structural adjustment programs (SAPs).[7] In this context, countries that toed the "Washington Consensus" line attracted considerable development assistance, with mixed results on both economic and political fronts. Most recently, aid has been allocated to governments that show willingness to adopt national anti-poverty policies and strategies (PRSP).

Madagascar, Uganda, and Tanzania follow this historical pattern. Table 3.1 shows that since 1990, the three countries' share of aid to GNI has consistently exceeded 7%, the threshold Knack and Rahman use to distinguish highly aid-dependent countries from the less dependent ones.[8] Aid statistics show the three countries are aid dependent to comparable degrees, with average aid as percentage of GNI figures of 13, 16.7, and 15, respectively, from 1990 to 2008. This is because, since independence, each country has presented a unique set of opportunities for donors to work with successive governments. Uganda's example illustrates this point.

Table 3.1 Net ODA as percentage of GNI (1990–2009) (*Source* World Bank (WDI online))

Year	90	91	92	93	94	95	96	97	98	99	00	01	02	03	04	05	06	07	08	09
Madagascar	13	18	13	11	10	10	9	24	13	10	8	8	9	10	29	18	14	12	9	5
Tanzania	29	22	30	23	22	17	14	12	12	12	12	14	13	17	16	11	13	17	11	14
Uganda	16	20	26	19	19	15	11	13	10	10	14	14	12	16	15	14	16	15	12	11

Called the "darling of the West,"[9] Museveni has been a veritable aid magnet. In 2005, Uganda's finance ministry reported that donors had extended more than US$11 billion of development assistance to the Government of Uganda.[10,11] Uganda has attracted so much foreign aid from so many donors that 50 to 65% of its budget has been underwritten by aid and the government of Uganda is now in a position to reject some of the aid.[12] A few reasons for this deserve mention. Donors have rushed to Uganda because Museveni was the only East African leader to embrace neo-liberal reforms at a time his counterparts resisted such reforms; additionally, the country's economic performance drastically improved shortly after reforms were instituted; finally, Museveni had a clear vision of where he wanted to take the country (and the rest of Africa) and Uganda made impressive progress on many fronts in a short span of time. Donors looked at Museveni as a shining example of what was possible in a troubled continent plagued by bad leaders and poor governance. Museveni's personality also has much to do with his success in attracting aid: He is sharp, focused, aggressive, charismatic, and, most importantly, he has a vision of development in Africa.

The twenty-first century is marked by yet another shift in motivations for giving aid to African countries. Africa's strategic importance has increased in two principal ways. First, the continent's proximity to the Middle East makes Africans important security players, especially in the fight against terrorism. Second, because Africa as a whole possesses natural resources on which old and new industrial countries rely, and given the increasing difficulty of accessing these resources in other parts of the world (notably the Middle East), the continent has become the last frontier for resources such as oil, natural gas, iron ore, copper, uranium, and timber.[13] In this new context, aid is used to secure access to Africa's resources, especially given the emergence of new resource seekers like China and India. Africa's increasing importance has spawned growing competition among donors that seek to influence African states' development policies.

Aid Competition

What does donor competition entail? Donors need to justify their entry into recipient countries compels them to compete over what constitutes the best and most innovative approaches to development (broadly defined). At the heart of this competition is not the privilege of assisting a developing country but, rather, the opportunity to influence that country's development model and conservation policies. The rise in donor competition has attracted scholarly attention and generated multiple ways of conceptualizing it.[14] I define donor competition as the multiplication and diversification of donors seeking to advance their respective interests by establishing privileged relationships with recipient countries' decision makers, using aid as an incentive to align governments' interests with donors' interests. Donor multiplication entails the diversification of donor types, ranging from bilateral and multilateral agencies to international NGOs, as well as an increase in the number of such donors. Typically, such multiplication and diversification results in a greater number of development projects across and within sectors (agriculture, infrastructure, health, education, environment, etc.). It also entails a greater number of foreign "experts," including conservationists, present in recipient countries.[15]

Tanzania illustrates this phenomenon well. As with most countries, at independence in 1961, the primary donor was Tanzania's former colonial master, England. Because President Nyerere's model of development (dubbed African socialism) resonated with Europe's social democrats, Scandinavian countries like Norway, Sweden, and Denmark joined England in extending aid to Tanzania. By the 1980s, IFIs also began to assist the country's development efforts as a way of encouraging neo-liberal reforms. Shortly thereafter, the number of international NGO interventions soared across Tanzania's various development sectors. Mercer reports that 25 NGOs were registered in Tanzania in the mid- to late-1980s.[16] By the early 1990s, the number spiked to over 600. By the early 2000s it exceeded 1800 (including registered and non-registered organizations), and between 2001 and 2003 Tanzania had more than 1500 aid commitments.[17] Currently, Tanzania receives aid from about 50 multilateral and bilateral agencies, and dozens of registered international NGOs.[18] Table 3.1 shows donors' relative aid contributions in the early 2000s in Tanzania.

Donor proliferation necessitates donor coordination to achieve shared goals and presents a united front to recipient governments, especially when the latter resist their policy prescriptions. This is because their proliferation has created problems of duplication and unnecessary waste, lack of coordination, and confusion among themselves and on the part of recipient governments. In some cases, the flurry of donor activities distracts government officials and prevents them from focusing on their tasks. On this particular issue, President Museveni was quoted as saying the following to the Commonwealth delegates on August 6, 2002:

> I work well with Western countries but they interfere too much [...] If we are partners, you shouldn't interfere. *These donors can cause you to make mistakes.* We should be unanimous in rejecting these conditionalities, and we can reject it if we unite.[19]

Tanzanians became so overwhelmed with the multiplicity of donor approaches, projects, reporting requirements, and meetings that, in 2002, the Tanzanian government issued a Tanzania Assistance Strategy (TAS), which outlined a framework to manage Tanzania's aid resources, and restore the government's "ownership and leadership in the design and implementation of aid funded development programmes."[20] The government's concern for owning and leading Tanzania's development initiatives speaks directly to the competition between African governments and donors over controlling development agendas.

Donors also try to convince governments to accept their aid through terms or conditions for loans. In select African countries, China has entered the aid business by offering an alternative model of development assistance (the "Beijing Consensus") that stands in contrast with Westerners' conditional and tied aid. The Chinese model is particularly attractive to African leaders because it imposes fewer political and economic constraints than its Western counterpart.[21] In fact, the People's Republic of China is often criticized for giving aid to countries with poor human rights records such as Sudan. The PRC also offers aid in the form of concrete projects such as infrastructure.

A third way donors seek to enhance the attractiveness of their aid is through disbursement modalities. For example, Germany's *Deutsche Gesellschaft für Internationale Zusammenarbeit* or GIZ (formerly GTZ for *Deutsche Gesellschaft für Technische Zusammenarbeit*) and KFW (*Kreditanstalt für Wiederaufbau*) are willing to give direct budget support to governments (i.e., funds are "injected" into various ministries, which then manage them), whereas the United States Agency for International Development (USAID) channels its assistance through its own local agencies, development experts, and projects (tied aid).

Once in country, donors compete among themselves for high visibility projects that show immediate positive impact. If successful, this secures donors the continued support of their respective governments (in the case of bilateral aid) and contributors (in the case of NGOs). Donors also compete for qualified nationals as collaborators to staff or run their projects. These nationals include individuals employed in both the private sector and government.[22] Finally, donors compete to get the attention of policy makers (elected officials and other influential elites). More often than not, key individuals representing donor interests compete for access to and influence over the president himself, since executive dominance over other political institutions characterizes African political systems.

While it is useful to know how and why donors compete among themselves, it is just as important to note another aspect of competition: Once donors enter a country, they and recipient governments sometimes compete over policy priorities or development approaches. This analysis focuses on this aspect of aid-induced competition, which entails donors exerting power over African governments lacking either a clear vision for achieving development or the financial means and expertise to implement whatever vision they might have. It also involves Africans using their authority and sovereignty to fight for their own ideas of what should be prioritized. An example of this phenomenon is found in Uganda where, in the days of SAPs, the World Bank negotiated loans with the government over whether or not education should be given funding priority over infrastructure development (roads, in particular). The World Bank reasoned that educating people would boost the country's social indicators of development, whereas the Ugandan government considered better roads the key to development. This tension precipitated a series of high-level negotiations involving President Museveni and the World Bank president himself.[23] This battle of wills is powerfully captured in Africa's conservation politics.

The Urge to Protect Africa's Natural Wealth: Interests, Commitments, and Institutional Investments

I stated at the beginning of this chapter that environmental policymaking entails negotiations between African leaders and foreign donors on the place of nature conservation in development. By and large, Western donors have entered these negotiations with a clear interest in protecting

Africa's fauna, flora, and biodiversity, and they have pursued this interest by encouraging African governments to enact conservation-friendly development policies. African politicians, for their part, have reacted to donor prescriptions with an eye on their own interests, political or other. This section describes how donor and government interests aligned in Madagascar under President Ravalomanana and in Tanzania under President Nyerere because complying with donors' visions of development served these two leaders' political interests well. This interest alignment resulted in formal commitments to prioritize nature conservation, which precipitated aid flows into the two countries. I assess conservation commitments by looking at (1) whether the official discourse treats nature conservation as a matter of national interest; (2) the extent to which protected areas are expanded or if the status of existing protected areas is changed to become more restrictive and exclusive; and (3) whether existing environmental institutions are reformed and new ones created to meet environmental challenges. Madagascar and Tanzania invested the aid in environmental institutions to support conservation goals. By contrast, Museveni did not need to comply with donor prescriptions to attract abundant development aid due to Uganda's unique circumstances mentioned above. As a result, he came across as defiant. Curiously, this did not prevent Uganda's environmental programs from being largely underwritten by foreign aid. The result was institutional proliferation that failed to curb deforestation because, I will show, environmental institutions served rent-seeking purposes more than they did forest conservation goals.

Madagascar

Madagascar is known for its extraordinary biodiversity, its high number of endemic and animal species, and similarly high levels of genetic information per unit area (possibly the highest on earth), with discoveries still being made. Consequently, the island is at the top of the world's conservation priority list.[24] In a sense, biodiversity is a global common: Humanity stands to benefit from conserving it or suffer the consequences of destroying it. As a result, protecting Madagascar's natural heritage has been the affair of the international community (represented by western donors) and not just of a sovereign state. Among Western donors, "Anglo-Saxon," or English-speaking countries have emerged as the main force behind Madagascar's conservation initiatives.[25]

While it is undeniable that the Anglo-Saxon conservationists have carved a policy niche for themselves, it would be mistaken to assume that the Malagasy state has never concerned itself with environmental protection. In fact, as early as the late 1700s, the state was presenting itself as a fierce guardian of the forest.[26] To this day, all forests are state property (*domaine de l'État*), which gives the state, at least in principle, sole jurisdiction over forest resources. This has allowed the state to hold tremendous power over forest users, including forest-dependent rural communities and logging and mining companies. However, the state has not generated sufficient human and financial resources to perform the formidable task of protecting Madagascar's forest, especially since gaining independence in 1960. Because of its limited capacity to devise, carry out, and finance its own environmental policies, foreign donors were able to exert considerable influence over the state regarding environmental issues. Consequently, conservation is largely a donor-driven enterprise that involves foreign donors working with the Malagasy state to advance mostly donors' agendas.

Donors' interest in protecting Madagascar's biological wealth has matched Malagasy decision makers' interest in maximizing the benefits they can derive from interacting with foreigners on environmental issues. Interest in and funding for biodiversity conservation has allowed the state to set up institutions with a specific conservation mandate (discussed below), pay its civil servants' salaries and offer them unprecedented benefits (professional development, overseas travels, office equipment, *per diem* allowances that supplement salaries, etc.). It has also raised the state's profile vis-à-vis the international community, placing Madagascar among countries safe for environmental investments. Likewise, some rural communities have been able to gain better access to basic health services, primary education, agricultural techniques, etc., since working with conservation projects on the ground. Finally, a cadre of Malagasy professionals has found steady employment in the conservation sector. These professional opportunities were not available before the environmental sector boom of the 1990s.

But to fully appreciate the extent of donor-state interest alignment in Madagascar, President Marc Ravalomanana's own interests must be considered. His political calculations were critical to aligning his government's interests with those of foreign donors as soon as he came to power in 2002. A self-made small farmer turned agro-industrialist and media mogul, Ravalomanana campaigned for the presidency on a rapid economic growth platform. During this campaign, he pledged to improve Madagascar's economy rapidly, the way he had turned Antananarivo around as the capital's mayor from 1999 to 2001. Five months into his presidency, however, Ravalomanana replaced the term "rapid economic growth" with "sustainable development" in his public speeches. Far from being a coincidence, this change in rhetoric signaled his compliance with donors' prescription that Madagascar's development should not compromise its natural wealth.[27] In doing this, Ravalomanana gained politically. First, he secured foreign aid from countries where conservation was receiving positive public attention, particularly the United States. A happy consequence of Ravalomanana's ability to draw aid from a wider variety of sources was a boost in his political legitimacy domestically and abroad. At home, Ravalomanana came across as capable of attracting the funding necessary to finance visible improvements across sectors of development, notably primary education and infrastructure. Abroad, and especially in the eyes of IFIs and the Anglo-Saxons, Ravalomanana was seen as a progressive leader eager to leave old ways and embrace new ones. In particular, unlike his predecessors, Ravalomanana did not readily bow to France's power and will. Instead, he strengthened the country's ties with the Anglophone world and diversified sources of foreign investments and assistance by bringing in the United States, Germany, and others.

Ravalomanana's commitment to green development policies was manifest in three concrete ways: His government pledged to triple the extent of protected areas barely a year into his presidency, his public speeches made explicit reference to environmental protection and, as I elaborate below, institutional investments favored the environment. In 2003, Ravalomanana made conservation history at the World Parks Congress, held in Durban, South Africa, when he announced his government's pledge (a presidential decree, actually) to triple the surface of the island's protected areas, thereby reaching 11.5% of the national territory, by 2008. This, of course, was no random move. Tripling protected area coverage would allow Madagascar to reach the International Union for Conservation of Nature (IUCN)'s 10% of national territory requirement, thereby satisfying the demand of the most powerful global conservation players.[28]

As it turns out, Ravalomanana's Durban speech was written by Western conservationists and given to the president on his way to Durban.[29] Less than two years later, Ravalomanana unveiled his "*Madagascar, Naturellement!*"[30] policy at an international conference on the science and governance of biodiversity held in Paris. On this occasion, the president publicly stated that fostering economic growth without destroying the country's natural heritage was an expensive and "difficult challenge for which we [Madagascar] *need the support of the international community.*" (emphasis added)[31]

A presidential commitment to adopt conservation-friendly policies, coupled with a plea for foreign assistance, was a welcome development among donors, especially the Anglo-Saxons, who eagerly continued to fund Madagascar's conservation programs. In fact, relative to other African countries, Madagascar's conservation programs were the most generously funded in the 1990s. As of 2006, the environment received the most donor and government support (agriculture was second). In fact, over the National Environmental Action Plan (NEAP)'s lifespan, funding increased steadily, going from US$100 million in Environmental Program 1 (EP1) to US$170 million in the final phase. As an indication of donors' enthusiasm for paying for Madagascar's nature conservation, the maximum share of funding required from state revenues never exceeded 30% of the total budget throughout NEAP's implementation. What is more, in the final of NEAP's three phases, which ran from 2003 to 2008, 70% of donor-generated funds were granted, not loaned, to Madagascar.[32]

With all the foreign support it could wish for, Madagascar built an impressive array of institutions to carry out its environmental policies. Most of these institutions were set up in the 1990s upon adoption of the country's NEAP.[33] While DEF (waters and forests division of the Ministry of Agriculture), DD (land division of the Ministry of Agriculture), and FTM (national geographic institute) predated NEAP, their mandates were resource management, not protection per se. At NEAP's inception these state institutions, like their mainland counterparts, were notoriously inefficient, corrupt, understaffed (particularly the first two), underfunded, and obsolete. Consequently, one of the two main objectives of EP1 was to build institutions for environmental protection and strengthen existing ones. For example, FTM's mapping and aerial photograph production capabilities were improved with technological upgrades, purchases of aerial photographs and satellite imagery, and technical assistance by means of professional training in country and abroad.

Creating and updating environmental institutions in the early 1990s, passing new legislation simultaneously, and establishing new protected areas after 2003 were concrete steps that Madagascar took to reform its environmental sector under NEAP. As pictured in Fig. 3.1, new institutions included the *Association Nationale d'Actions Environnementales*, or ANAE (for environmental activities focused on soil conservation), the *Association Nationale pour la Gestion des Aires Protégées*, or ANGAP (for protected area management and biodiversity conservation, now Madagascar National Parks), and the *Office National de l'Environnement*, or ONE (for policy formulation, regulatory framework improvements, and environmental awareness building). Not only was a new Ministry of the Environment created, legislation was also passed to create foundations and trust funds such as *Tany Meva* for sustainable funding, for forest protection and management, and for decentralized resource management (*Loi* GELOSE). Finally, a Multi-Donor Secretariat (SMB) was created in the early 1990s to coordinate multiple environment-related activities, given the multiplication and duplication of such activities among donors.[34] Ravalomanana's government came into power at the beginning of EP3 and built upon revamped environmental institutions to control deforestation and associated environmental degradation. This is the phase that received the most foreign assistance. It is also the phase in which 70% of this foreign assistance was granted, not loaned to Madagascar.

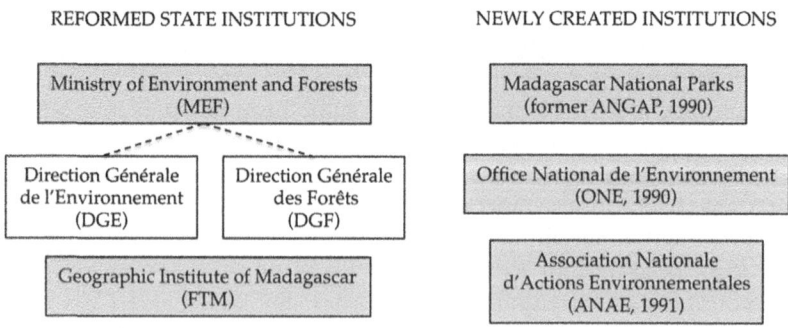

Fig. 3.1 Institutional framework for forest management in Madagascar

Tanzania

In many respects, Tanzania's conservation history is similar to Madagascar's, three differences notwithstanding: Strong government commitment to environmental conservation developed in the 1960s in Tanzania and the 2000s in Madagascar; Tanzania's former colonial power was England, Madagascar's was France; finally, wildlife conservation was initially the primary focus of environmental policy negotiations in Tanzania, and biodiversity conservation by way of forest conservation was the main preoccupation in Madagascar.[35]

Julius Nyerere's stance on wildlife conservation was, to say the least, the product of strategic thinking. Nash (1982) quotes the leader as having said the following:

> I personally am not interested in animals. I do not want to spend my holidays watching crocodiles. Nevertheless, I am entirely in favor of their survival. I believe that after diamonds and sisal, wild animals will provide Tanganyika with its greatest source of income. (342)

When he became president in 1964, Nyerere embarked on an ambitious and expensive socialist program called *ujamaa*.[36] In order to finance his government's socialist programs, Nyerere relied on both internal revenues and foreign aid. With wildlife tourism's great potential for generating foreign exchange earnings, Nyerere found it to his advantage to support wildlife conservation. To do this, he built upon German and British colonial conservation initiatives and even extended national parks and game reserves despite the political risks such initiatives represented.[37,38] In the first few years of Nyerere's presidency, "the new government promised to grant high priority to wildlife conservation and to continue the efforts begun in colonial times, *calling specifically on outside agencies to aid in this task*" (1046, emphasis added).

Relative to wildlife, forestry was neglected in this initial period. According to Hurst (2003), foresters failed early on to demonstrate the sector's ability to contribute to Nyerere's unabashedly pro-peasant, pro-agriculture development policies whose goal was self-reliance. Under the circumstances, forestry simply could not compete with agriculture in the eyes of TANU (Tanganyika African National Union, now CCM for *Chama Cha Mapinduzi*) politicians, and forested areas were considered a constraint to agricultural expansion. Worse yet, conservation initiatives were construed as a vestige of colonialism, and this popular perception made it difficult for Nyerere to push forest conservation despite the fact that he saw merit in protecting forests. Forestry's fortunes changed when Scandinavian aid agencies began to fund the forest sector at the end of the 1960s[39] and, thereafter, forestry became "more central to the political and economic development needs of the country."[40] Thus, the Tanzanian state committed to protecting forests as well as wildlife.

By the 1980s, still under Nyerere's rule, conservation and development agencies merged their agendas and pooled their resources to further strengthen their pro-conservation position vis-à-vis the Tanzanian government. The convergence of donors' interests and visions materialized in conservation and development projects initiated, funded, and implemented by donors.[41] From that point on, the Tanzanian state could not escape from a pro-conservation stance.

The first indicator of the Tanzanian state's commitment to conservation is a statistic: Roughly one-third of the national territory is protected by the state. According to Alden Wily, forests in Tanzania cover 33 million hectares, 14 million of which are set aside for conservation.[42] As early as 1961, to signal his government's commitment to conservation, Nyerere, who was then Tanganyika's prime minister, declared:

> In accepting the trusteeship of our wildlife we solemnly declare that we will do everything in our power to make sure that our children's grandchildren will be able to enjoy this rich and precious inheritance. ... The conservation of wildlife and wild places calls for specialist knowledge, trained manpower, *and money and we look to other nations to cooperate in this important task.*[43]

As was the case with Ravalomanana four decades later, Nyerere's commitment to conservation came with a plea for foreign support. Also similar to what happened with Ravalomanana's Durban declaration, the above portion of Nyerere's speech was written by members of the Western conservation lobby.[44]

Nyerere's tactics paid off because, since he appeared docile, IUCN readily pledged to help the government manage Tanzania's national parks and conservation programs. Subsequently, state-sanctioned wildlife tourism, national parks, and other protected areas received financial, technical, and institutional support from a variety of donors, ranging from international conservation NGOs and development agencies as well as IFIs (mostly the World Bank). Beginning in the late 1960s, Scandinavian governments also funded a significant number of conservation programs, emphasizing the forestry sector.[45] The Swedish government alone disbursed a total of US$240 million for Tanzania's forestry sector from 1969 to 2002.[46] From 1994 to 2006, the Norwegian government financed US$60 million of Tanzania's Management of Natural Resources Program (MRNP), which supported the forestry sector.[47]

Overall, steady foreign assistance for conservation made it possible for Tanzania to build its environmental institutions. By the mid-1970s, Swedish aid alone provided 90% of the Forest and Beekeeping Division (FBD), Tanzania's principal government forestry agency.[48] Swedish aid came in the form of budgetary support to the forestry sector, with FBD in charge of managing the budget, and technical assistance: Swedish foresters worked as Tanzanian government employees paid by the Swedish aid agency.[49]

Tanzania's forest institutions are more complex than Madagascar's. Protected forest, comprising National Forest Reserves (NFRs) and Local Authority Forest Reserves (LAFRs) is owned and managed by central and local governments, respectively.[50] Three parallel structures manage these forest reserves (see Fig. 3.2). The first is the Ministry of Natural Resources and Tourism, the second comprises TANAPA (Tanzania National Parks) and the Ngorongoro Conservation Area Authority (NCAA), and the third structure is the Local Government Authority (LOGA). At least in principle, decentralized resource management happens through LOGA by devolving forest management authority to district councils, ward councils, and, at the lowest administrative level, village councils. TANAPA and NCAA, although part of the overall structure, are semi-autonomous agencies that generate their own revenues and maintain national parks, including Serengeti, Mount Kilimanjaro, and Tarangire, and conservation areas such as the Ngorongoro Crater. All economic activities that can impact the environment fall under the coordinating authority of the Vice President's Office whose Division of Environment is tasked, in principle, with ensuring that economic operators' activities conform with the National Environmental Policy's guidelines.[51]

Figure 3.2 is a simplified representation of Tanzania's institutional framework for forest management. A more complete depiction would include myriad specialized agencies and committees in charge of various

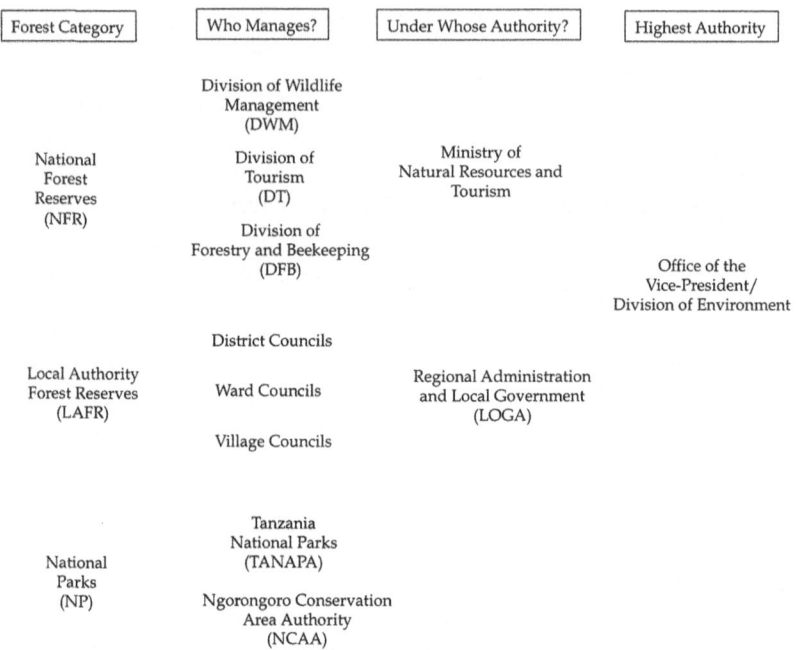

Fig. 3.2 Institutional framework for forest management in Tanzania

aspects of forest governance at multiple administrative levels. In short, Tanzania's forest conservation institutions expanded dramatically as foreign aid for conservation poured into the country. In fact, environmental institutions multiplied to the point where, by the early 2000s, "[m]ultiple actors at both the central and local levels" confronted the need to "act together to form new cooperation and partnerships…[and] ensure a more systematic approach towards conservation and sustainable utilization of natural resources."[52,53] A decade later, analysts continued to point to "inter-ministerial fragmentation in forest governance"[54] whereby institutional proliferation blurs the lines of accountability not only among various ministries (e.g., Finance versus Natural Resources and Tourism, in the case of logging), but between national and sub-national levels of decision-making. This institutional fragmentation has seriously weakened the fight against deforestation in Tanzania.

Uganda

In early 2007, riots broke out in Kampala following the announcement that President Museveni had approved about 25% of Mabira forest to be converted into a foreign-owned sugarcane plantation. The public outcry that this decision provoked was symptomatic of growing tensions between the government of Uganda and the public on the issue of land acquisition by way of forest clearing. Museveni's decision "to give away Mabira forest" signaled to Ugandans that he cared more about his and foreigners' business interests than about his constituents' basic needs.[55] Museveni's response to the initial protests was unequivocal: "I shall not be deterred by people who don't see where the future of Africa lies."[56] To many Ugandans, especially foresters, Museveni's attitude signaled his lack of interest in protecting Uganda's forests.[57]

What explains Museveni's apparent resistance to forest conservation? When he came to power in 1986, the challenge of developing Uganda was particularly great because the country needed to emerge from the ruins of devastating civil wars. Additionally, the government of Uganda was invested in securing its multiple borders, being a landlocked country surrounded by warring Sudan, Rwanda, Democratic Republic of Congo, etc. Because Museveni had to act swiftly on multiple fronts, the environment received little policy attention even though Uganda's natural and biological wealth is arguably comparable to that of Tanzania and Madagascar and despite the fact that environmental degradation is reaching alarming levels there. Ugandan conservationists, especially foresters, commonly express exasperation with the president's lack of appreciation for the importance of sound resource management. When asked about Museveni's commitment to forest conservation, many shrug and some even say that the president is "useless."[58] To many, the 2007 Mabira forest incident epitomizes Museveni's contempt for things environmental.[59] Alternatively, it is a sign of his commitment to "repositioning Africa from backward, agriculturally focused to industrial societies."[60]

With such an outlook on development, conservation can receive Museveni's attention only if it supports tourism as a lucrative industry. In the 1960s tourism was the fastest growing sector in the Ugandan economy. The two decades of political turmoil severely damaged this industry (and the rest of the economy). It cost Uganda its reputation as a natural and safe wonder (the "pearl of Africa," as Churchill famously called it) and pushed its "charismatic megafauna," including the famous mountain gorillas, close to extinction due to uncontrolled poaching during the civil wars. Since regaining stability in 1986, however, the Ugandan government has sought to restore the country's tourism industry and has managed to donor's commitment (World Bank, African Development Bank, UNDP, USAID, and the European Union) to fund a number of initiatives supporting conservation.[61]

Although a weak governmental commitment to environmental conservation is not unique to Uganda,[62] a specific mix of social, historical, and political factors makes Uganda distinct. According to some, Uganda's current leaders are trapped in "cheap business thinking," the kind that favors aggressive industrialization over securing the country's resource base in the long run.[63] Moreover, protecting Ugandan forests can be politically costly. In fact, many politicians view foresters as a threat to their political survival because, in their view, restricting access to forests deprives voters of resources (such as land) they claim to need.[64] Onyango puts it clearly: "Trees don't vote. People do."[65] To protect their political interests, therefore, decision makers tend to favor sectors of development that offer concrete and visible results such as roads, bridges, schools, clinics, and small industrial complexes. Relative to forest protection, improvements in these sectors better guarantee popularity, legitimacy, and thus political support. As such they offer a comparative advantage and so, politicians are reticent to take a strong pro-environment stance.

Additionally, Oloka-Onyango offers that the "national psyche" has not evolved since the days Uganda was an oasis of resource abundance and green, luscious landscapes. Environmental degradation is thus due, in part, to the Ugandan public and politicians' failure to appreciate the extent of the country's environmental plight: Although reality has changed in the past four decades, many have failed to notice.[66] The Mabira forest crisis, however, suggests that elements of Ugandan society recognize and have even become willing to denounce environmental recklessness, largely blaming politicians' eagerness to protect business interests. According to Thomas Kisawuzi, political patronage has much to do with such behavior. Driven by the desire to make money quickly, politicians distribute forests to businessmen who reward their largesse handsomely. Unsurprisingly, politicians view Ugandan "environmentalists" as a hindrance to the pursuit of Uganda's development goals. In other words, they are seen as being bad for business[67] and as enemies of progress.[68]

Despite Museveni's noncommitment to sustainable development policies, the donor community has funded nearly 90% of Uganda's environmental budget in the last decade. This extends a long history of foreign funding for Uganda's environmental initiatives.[69] Foreign donors had much to do with reviving and reforming Uganda's environmental institutions because of one major constraint to Museveni's independence: Faced with the daunting task of rebuilding the country, the government of Uganda had little choice but to turn to IFIs for support at the outset.[70] As they did in other parts of Africa the Bretton Woods institutions responded by imposing sweeping neo-liberal reforms. In the context of the country's SAP, donors recommended that deforestation and other forms of environmental degradation be controlled. To comply, the Ugandan government designated 30,000 hectares of tropical forest reserves as protected areas, and Mt. Elgon, Kibale, Bwindi, Rwenzori, and Mgahinga national parks were given a higher protection status in the early 1990s. As discussed below, the government also undertook a series of reforms in the forest sector, enacted new legislation, restructured old institutions, and set up new ones to improve forest management. At present, 27% of Uganda's territory is set aside for conservation.[71]

Given Museveni's apparent disregard for forest conservation, one would expect limited institutional investment in forest management since his ascent to power in 1986. In reality, Uganda possesses an array of environmental legislation and institutions that have emerged since Museveni took power. Prior to colonization, Uganda's forest resources were subject to a set of indigenous rules and norms such as those found in the Buganda Kingdom.[72] As was the case in neighboring Tanzania, the British colonial government established formal institutions to regulate the use and access of state-owned forests.[73]

In 1898, the Scientific and Forest Department (SFD) was established with a mandate to carry out research and manage forest resources. In 1917, the SFD became the Forest Department (FD) and its mandate was expanded to include forest exploitation for profit, which entailed timber production and the establishment of plantation forests.[74] Beginning in the 1920s, forests became "gazetted," i.e., delimited and formally placed under state management. By the time Uganda gained its independence in 1962, 30% of Uganda's forests were formally designated as forest reserves (FRs). Today, gazetted forests, also referred to as protected areas (PAs), constitute the Permanent Forest Estate (PFE).[75] The PFE is divided into three categories: (1) forest reserves (central and local) make up half of the PFE, while (2) national parks and (3) wildlife reserves comprise the other half. In principle, forest designations determine which agencies are in charge of managing different forests. Initially, FD managed central FRs (CFRs), local districts managed local forest reserves (LFRs), and the Ugandan Wildlife Authority (UWA) managed national parks and wildlife reserves. As is common in Africa, the forest department inherited from colonial days became a weak state institution staffed with foresters lacking technical and management skills and deprived of the means and motivation to do their jobs properly at independence.

FD's capabilities declined markedly in 1972 with Idi Amin's "africanization" policy that aimed to redistribute the means of production, including agricultural land, supposedly to benefit all Ugandans. The 1975 Land Reform Decree declared all lands public, vesting them in the Ugandan Land Commission. Intended to drastically increase Uganda's agricultural production, and working toward "doubling agricultural productivity"[76] as a tool for "economic war" (against imperial powers) Amin's policy severely undermined foresters' authority and crippled FD by encouraging massive forest clearings. At that time, even private forest reserves were encroached upon, using the pretext that guerrilla activities were being organized in these forests.[77] After Amin was deposed in 1979, deforestation continued in many government forests, notably during the guerrilla war led by Yoweri Museveni (1981–1986).

By the time Uganda's SAP took effect in the 1980s, FD was all but incapacitated and deforestation was rampant. The problem received substantial donor and government attention beginning in 1987 when a Ministry of Environment (ME) was created to reform the environmental sector.[78] In collaboration with other ministries, ME moved swiftly, updating legislation and adopting new environmental policies. The adoption of a new Constitution in 1995 created a favorable environment to reform the environmental sector further. Examples of institutional innovation include the 1995 Wetlands Policy, the 1996 Wildlife Policy, the 1998 Land Act, the 2001 Forest Policy, and the 2003 Forest Act that led to the creation of the National Forest Authority (NFA), a parastatal agency tasked with protecting CFRs.[79] Additionally, under the 1995 National Environment Statute, the National Environment Management Authority (NEMA) was created. As a government advisory body, NEMA's charge is to monitor environmental trends, draft environmental regulations (to be approved by the Policy Committee on Environment, or PCE), make policy recommendations, ensure that national planning takes into account environmental concerns, and supervise sectoral

3 EXECUTIVE BRANCHES AND TREES   113

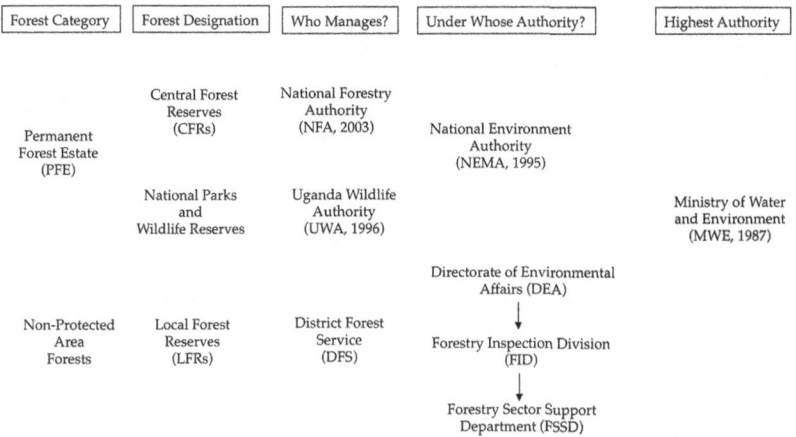

Fig. 3.3   Institutional framework for forest management in Uganda

departments (such as NFA for CFRs and UWA for wildlife reserves and national parks) at both central and district levels.[80] Figure 3.3 presents the institutional framework that resulted from Uganda's forest sector reform. It shows that multiple agencies are charged with managing the country's forests, a situation similar to Tanzania's.

That new and reformed institutions did not effectively address Uganda's deforestation problems is an understatement. In the post-reform period, forested areas (as a percentage of national territory) declined from 25% in 1990 to 18% in 2007 (World Bank Group). According to Kisawuzi, Uganda was leading the world in terms of forest destruction in 2006 with 2% of total land area deforested per year, against the world average of 0.06% per year.[81]

In short, in Madagascar, Tanzania, and Uganda, foreign aid influxes resulted in institutional proliferation and apparent conservation commitments on the part of these countries' presidents.

Why Institutional Proliferation Has Not Helped Deforestation

Looking at these three country cases and the alphabet soup of acronyms enumerated above, one must note that investments in environmental institutions have resulted in institutional proliferation. As soon as governments agreed to conservation-friendly policies, either due to genuine interest or because they simply had to, donors gave them the financial and technical means to reform existing institutions and create new ones in compliance with their visions of sound development policies. These institutional investments could be interpreted as evidence of government commitment to protecting the environment. I argue, however, that such interpretation is misguided. A more accurate understanding is that African governments sanctioned the creation of these institutions to feign compliance with donor prescriptions, attract foreign aid, and, as I discuss below, maintain domestic and international patronage networks. Thus, the real motivation behind institutional investments was not so much taming deforestation as it was pursuing the interests of powerful international and domestic actors. This is largely why these institutions have failed to halt deforestation.

How does one explain these countries' overall disappointing results? The main explanation is that donors and African decision makers have operated under the erroneous assumption that creating new institutions and reforming old ones, using foreign aid, *boosts* institutional capacity.[82] Capacity building is, however, about improving institutional quality, not quantity. Few cases better illustrate this point than Uganda, the country that stands out for the paradoxical combination of institutional proliferation and deforestation. What changed when NFA was created in 2003? First, the number of employees dropped from FD's 1100 to NFA's 350. Efficiency gains may have been realized, but this attrition did not rid the new agency of unequal means between the Kampala office, which was nicely equipped (buildings, computers, vehicles, etc.) when I visited it in 2006, and "the field" where 7 rangers were in charge of 506 CFRs scattered throughout 21 sectors.[83] Second, creating NFA as a way of revamping FD left only 30% of Uganda's forests under NFA's control, while 70% were still managed by farmers, private owners and local governments who lacked personnel and logistical support, to say nothing about a long-term vision of sustainable resource use. This is a major flaw because the actors controlling 70% of the country's forests, by and large, are motivated by short-term economic gain.[84] Third, replacing FD with NFA merely put a new coat of paint on a faulty structure. By 2006, three years after its creation, NFA was generating revenues for the country, notably through its tree-planting activities on public land. Leasing degraded forestland to private plantations was by far the easiest and quickest way to make money.[85] This accomplished two things: NFA overcame the marginalization that had afflicted FD, and donors were reassured that it could sustain itself beyond the initial four years of full donor support.

One perverse effect of such success, however, was that NFA inadvertently attracted the wrong kind of attention: When politicians and other public officials took note of new opportunities to enrich themselves through land deals, they used NFA to advance their private economic interests.[86] Aware of similar practices when FD was in charge, donors tried to protect NFA from such abuses by requiring that its executive director be an expatriate. Donors hoped this stipulation would secure them some control over NFA's budget, agenda, and practices. But, as discussed below, this stipulation could not control rent-seeking behavior, especially in forestry. With a double mandate of protection and production, NFA quickly found itself trapped in "production," which is lucrative for those able to convert forests into agricultural land or turn natural forests into forest plantations. Given the ease of making money through resource exploitation, NFA was unable to prevent abuses or fulfill its protection mandate. Nor did it necessarily want to. Some NFA officials allegedly cleared natural forests to lease degraded land to private tree growers, usually pocketing lease fees kept artificially low.[87]

NFA's conservation mission also faced greater challenges from private businesses which, ironically, the government approved and supported. In 2005, two years before the Mabira planned giveaway angered parliamentarians and Ugandan citizens, Museveni commissioned a palm oil company, BIDCO Oil Palm Uganda Ltd., to convert over 6000 hectares of Buggala Island's tropical forests into a palm tree plantation in Kalangala District. Responding to Museveni's directive, the district council passed a resolution to declassify this forest reserve in 2006. In 2008, the *Daily Monitor* reported that palm growers had cleared over 9500 hectares of natural forests in this island district.[88] NFA officials denounced and condemned the government's legal manipulations, but the Attorney General pressured NFA's Board of Directors, whose members are all presidential appointees, to sanction the president's decision. In protest, the chairman of the board resigned, as did three of the seven other board members. Four members stayed on, determined to carry out NFA's conservation mission. Once the board was reconstituted, its new members turned out to be political allies of the president. At that point, the remaining members of the former board resigned after being pressured and even humiliated by the new chairman in front of the president. Next, NFA's Executive Director, a Norwegian national, was pressured to resign, thus completing the purge intended to eliminate resistance to lucrative business deals that entailed forest conversions.

NFA faced another challenge from a different source: democracy. That democracy has been detrimental to forest conservation is a prominent sentiment among Ugandan foresters. As practiced in Uganda, democracy has empowered the people (i.e., voters) to lay claim on natural resources, especially land. As was the case under Amin's rule, those in search of agricultural land have encroached on forest reserves to grow crops. Known as "squatters," these illegal forest occupants have often enjoyed the protection of politicians, including President Museveni himself, especially around elections. In fact, an executive order against squatter evictions was passed in 2006. During such times, NFA foresters are said to "disturb votes." Another way democratic governance has worked against forest protection is in the influence the electorate can exercise over budgetary allocation decisions at the local (district and sub-district) level. According to foresters at the national and local levels, people rarely think of forest protection, much less afforestation, as priorities. Instead, they view protection as anti-peasant and anti-development, and tree planting as work lacking rapid payoffs. Foresters, squeezed between those who need votes and those who give them, become incapacitated and, whether the regime is autocratic or democratic, forests suffer.

Institutional proliferation has also led to inconsistent, sometimes contradictory decisions among environmental decision makers. The result has been confusion. The overlap between NFA and UWA's responsibilities illustrates this point. Recall that both agencies have protection and production mandates over Uganda's PFE. When, in the early 1990s, the government expanded its network of protected areas and upgraded the status of Mt. Elgon, Kibale, Bwindi, Rwenzori, and Mgahinga national parks, it made it illegal for surrounding communities to extract forest products from these forests.[89, 90] This represented a drastic change of rules for people living on the periphery of these areas. For instance, prior to the status change, Mt. Elgon National Park was managed primarily as a water catchment forest, which allowed limited exploitation of timber resources. In accordance with forestry regulation, the local people had the right to extract minor forest and non-timber forest products for their own consumption without being subject to harvesting fees. But, in the recent past, UWA issued logging rights and authorized tree planting in Mt. Elgon and Kibale national parks to receive carbon funds. These inconsistencies not only confused local forest users, it also created tensions and open conflicts, among NFA and UWA officials.[91]

Redundancy is yet another issue. NFA's production mandate duplicates NFA's and private actors' afforestation efforts such as the Sawlog Production Grant Scheme (SPGS)'s tree-planting project that sells seedlings and provides technical advice to private tree growers.[92] As they did for NFA, donors provided the startup funds for SPGS, which officially started in 2004 with US$2 million. SPGS aid is explicitly for profit, which partly explains its phenomenal success, judging by the fact that planted surfaces have increased, demand for seedlings exceeds supply, and donors have continued funding the project beyond the initial phase (2004–2006).[93] NFA, for its part, has also been successful despite challenges in educating people about the benefits of reforestation. A visit to the National Tree Seed Center, in 2006, made it clear that the center was thriving and trying to expand its seedling operation given the demand for timber and fruit tree seedlings, in particular. The existence of two afforestation operations, one public, the other private, is not necessarily a problem. However, because both were donor initiated and donor funded, their competition for funding makes it difficult for them to collaborate. Second, and in addition to the challenge of evicting forest encroachers mentioned above, NFA officials confront legislation that effectively encourages deforestation: By law, once forest land is degraded, NFA can lease it to private investors for rehabilitation (reforestation) purposes. Because it is in NFA's interest to secure lease revenues, agency officials have no incentive to prevent deforestation.

The problem of institutional proliferation is compounded by the fact that forests cannot be managed independently of other natural resources. For instance, fertile land, wildlife, and water are important resources whose supply depends on the conservation of forest habitats. Because cross-sectoral linkages are integral to development, the relationships among different sectors of development (including forestry) further complicate the institutional picture. As mentioned above, NFA and UWA share management responsibilities for the PFE. Their decisions and activities, however, impact or are impacted by the decisions and activities of other state agencies. Figure 3.4 shows the relationships between forestry and other development sectors and institutions in Uganda.

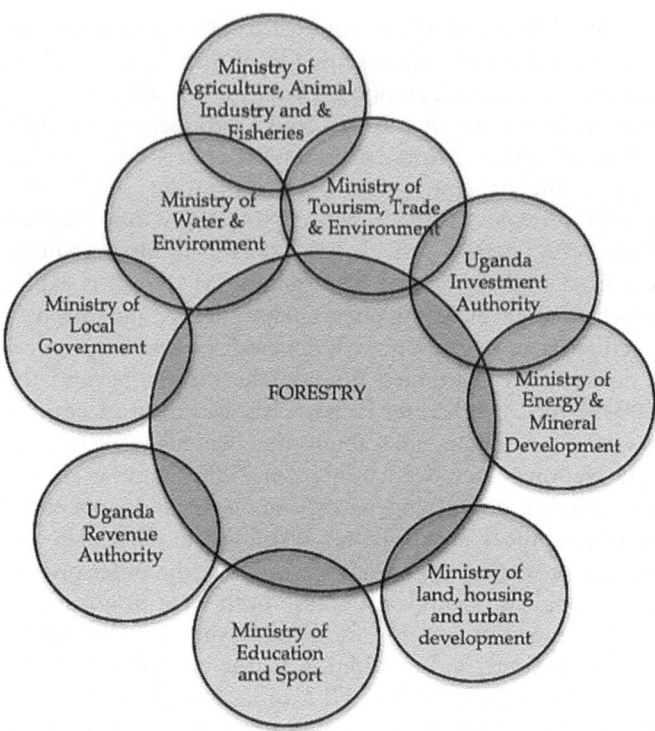

Fig. 3.4 Institutional linkages among development sectors: Uganda

The Ministry of Tourism, Trade and Industry (MITI) is the parent ministry for UWA because of the central role that wildlife plays in tourism. The Ministry of Energy and Mineral Development (MEMD) develops policies and strategies for biomass energy utilization. Success in reducing pressure on forests is, therefore, potentially affected by the decisions of this ministry. In an ongoing search for Uganda's mineral treasures, gold mining in the southwest Albertine region of Kasyoha-Kitomi forest reserve is threatening the stability of important forest ecosystems. NFA and the Ministry of Energy are jointly pursuing mining in Kasyoha-Kitomi.[94] The Ministry of Local Government (MLG) oversees the activities of local governments at district, sub-county, and village levels where people in charge are called Local Councils (LCs). At the district level, DFS is responsible for managing LFRs, including private forests. DFS raises revenues from forest exploitation and the funds are sent to the district treasury for reallocation by the district council. The Ministry of Agriculture, Animal Industry and Fisheries (MAAIF) determines agricultural policy and oversees extension services. Its activities have a direct impact on rural livelihoods, which largely depend on forest resource use. If one considers the fact that each of the ministries has various directorates, divisions, and departments, the burden of coordination becomes evident. For instance, within the Ministry of Water and Environment (MWE) alone, forest management falls under multiple subunits: Below the MWE is the Directorate of Environmental Affairs (DEA), which oversees the Forestry Inspectorate Division (FID). Under FID is the Forestry Sector Support Department (FSSD), which is charged with planning and guidelines across regions.

Finally, decentralizing forest governance has not yielded support for forest conservation. As discussed in Chapter 4, resource management was decentralized throughout sub-Saharan Africa as a logical extension of democracy promotion in the early 1990s. Despite the wealth that Uganda's forests generate at the local level, where trees and non-timber forest products are harvested, public funds have not been invested in environmental conservation. Instead, health, agriculture, industry, mining and energy, and education have taken budgetary precedence over nature conservation at both the national and district levels.[95] This neglect makes little sense, given that Uganda has a well-developed forest industry capable of generating significant revenues. The government's budgetary decisions strongly suggest its interest in quick gains from immediate forest exploitation rather than long-term sustainable management. Given African politicians' habit of "eating" while in power,[96] the notion of sustainability could only have limited appeal to them. In this context, the short-term gains from exploiting forests are simply irresistible. Nor do local people, i.e., the empowered electorate, show much interest in prioritizing forest conservation when it comes to public spending.[97]

The case of Uganda highlights how, far from solving deforestation problems, institutional proliferation can exacerbate them. Undeniably, Uganda possesses an arsenal of environmental institutions. However, these institutions have not prevented Ugandan politicians from engaging in practices detrimental to forest conservation. As mentioned above, there have even been cases where the president gave away forest reserves to investors for industrial development, as was the case in Buggala

Island. Additional examples of executive largesse include Namanve[98] CFR in January 1997, Bugala forests[99] with NEMA's rubber stamp and Butamira.[100,101] While it is true that abuses also take place in Madagascar and Tanzania, arguably the executive has not shown open and blatant disregard for forest conservation the way Museveni has in Uganda.[102]

A final factor that accounts for disappointing forest conservation by way of institutional innovation is that creating new institutions for forest management often amounts to little more than reforming patronage networks. The ease with which multiple environmental institutions emerged in the 1990s suggests that building them was beneficial to domestic and international actors by creating new opportunities for professional and personal advancement. For domestic actors, the material perks that came with donor-funded institutions were unprecedented. ANGAP's example from Madagascar illustrates this point. When it was created, the protected area management agency's personnel enjoyed opportunities that the forestry department's employees could hardly have aspired to. They included new computers, software, transportation (for employees) or personal vehicles (for top administrators), facilities in prime real estate locations, training opportunities in country and overseas, good salaries, and, importantly, clout.

These benefits were simply not available to those working for the Malagasy government, including DEF employees. It is no coincidence, therefore, that many ANGAP employees left DEF to access such benefits. In fact, the first ANGAP director was a former DEF employee. His selection was motivated not by his competence and experience but by donors' need to soften the blow vis-à-vis DEF whose notoriously corrupt personnel could only be threatened by the creation of an environmental watch dog such as ANGAP. Having a familiar colleague at the head of this new institution could serve to appease irritated and nervous members of DEF rent-seekers. By selecting this DEF employee, USAID, the donor, could show good faith to the government while at the same time eroding DEF's power to control access to the island's protected areas.

For international actors, the ability to influence African governments' agendas was also unprecedented. Scholars of African politics tend to focus discussions of patron–client relations in the domestic arena: Those in power buy their legitimacy and secure support by doling out favors through all layers of society. It bears remembering, however, that foreign actors do the same. To the extent that foreign governments need their African counterparts' support to advance their own interests, they have used aid repeatedly to align African politicians' interests with their interests, be they ideological, diplomatic, or commercial.[103] By distributing aid favors to African policy makers, donors have secured these powerful individuals' support for neo-liberalism. This dynamic has affected all facets of politics in Africa, and resource management is no exception. Whether facing highly compliant (Ravalomanana), tolerant (Nyerere), or defiant (Museveni) presidents, foreigners have managed to infiltrate tight policymaking circles, thus influencing Africa's development policies. If one considers this larger picture, it is not unreasonable to suggest that, in the end, reformed environmental institutions do little to break old habits, which explains their inefficacy when it comes to controlling deforestation.

Conclusion

This chapter has examined the politics of policymaking at critical junctures in Madagascar, Tanzania, and Uganda's environmental histories. The three-country comparison reveals that environmental policymaking engages national decision makers and foreign actors over where environmental conservation fits in the pursuit of development. In all three countries conservation is largely underwritten by foreign aid in the form of financial and technical assistance secured from bilateral and multilateral donors. This is because conservation models are predicated upon the assumption that environmental conservation necessitates institutional investments that African states can ill afford. As a result, donors exert considerable influence over African governments and they steer development policies in directions that favor environmental conservation. Conservation nonetheless remains a challenge, as indicated by persistent deforestation. To understand this paradox one must look into the power struggle embedded in policy negotiations.

Outside support for conservation has been invested in environmental institutions. Considerable effort was spent reforming existing institutions and creating new ones. In the three countries, especially in Uganda and Madagascar, this resulted in institutional proliferation, as indicated by the maze and array of agencies, parastatals, positions, and responsibilities discussed in this chapter. The fact that these governments sanctioned such institutional proliferation cannot be interpreted to mean that they are committed to environmental conservation. Rather, the multiplication of environmental institutions has created new opportunities for foreign and domestic patrons to secure the support of those whose approval they need to protect and advance their own interests. This, I argue, is an important explanation for why efforts to protect Africa's forests have been disappointing.

Comparing the three countries, it is clear that donors' conservation interests do not always align with the executive's vision of progress. Such is the case in Uganda under Museveni, and it is in stark contrast to the situation in Madagascar under Ravalomanana. Unlike Museveni, Ravalomanana let donors hijack his policy agenda because it was in his interest to do so. Unlike his predecessors, Ravalomanana realized that Madagascar's exceptional biodiversity was an asset, a commodity that he could use to gain and retain donor interest along with the aid that usually comes with such interest.[104] For Nyerere, Tanzania's extraordinary natural endowments served to attract the aid he needed to finance his expensive socialist development policies. This created opportunities for donors interested in conservation to sensitize the Tanzanian government to the need to protect wildlife and, later, forests.

Where and when foreigners' and presidents' interests aligned with conservation norms, institutional innovations helped control deforestation. Conversely, where these interests fail to align, deforestation was not controlled. As discussed in Chapter 1, Madagascar's deforestation record has been, overall, better than Tanzania's, whose deforestation record is better than Uganda's. Madagascar may have had an additional advantage due to the concentration of environmental efforts in the forest sector. This was the case because most of the island's biodiversity (flora and fauna) is housed in its forests. At the same time, its extraordinary biodiversity was an incredible asset that Ravalomanana was quick to instrumentalize to advance his own political interests. This particular president's commitment to conservation, strong as it may have been, points to the fragility of the whole enterprise, however, because proper interest alignment that hinges on one leader's political calculations is ephemeral, especially where democratic elections are promoted. It is no surprise, thus, that, Ravalomanana's unconstitutional removal from power in 2009 ushered in a new era of uncontrolled deforestation.[105]

The injection of foreign assistance into Africa's environmental sectors has come at some costs to African governments. Conservation as a late twentieth-century ideology is a foreign import that Africans either do not buy into or, if they do, often cannot afford to fund given competing policy priorities. Consequently, aid-funded conservation has effectively expanded outsiders' decision-making powers and shrunk those of Africans. This has not necessarily been a bad thing for some African leaders. In fact, some see the situation as particularly advantageous, as was the case with Ravalomanana in the 2000s and Nyerere four decades earlier. In the end, though, conservationists have further weakened the link between those who govern and those who are governed. By locking African leaders and foreign donors into a situation of mutual dependency, aid-induced conservation has created incentives for African leaders to be accountable to foreign interests rather than their constituents, to legitimize their power based on their ability to attract foreign aid rather than deliver political goods, and to divert their policy priorities away from what most Africans would consider important (human welfare) and urgent (food, shelter, and health). In short, conservationists have widened the gap between African governments and African polities. As a result, and as I will discuss in Chapter 4, they cannot collaborate effectively to save the continent's forests. Under those circumstances, improvements in deforestation outcomes are a fortunate by-product, rather than the principal goal, of conservation politics. The multiplication of environmental institutions and projects that results generates opportunities for select individuals, foreign and national, to thrive materially and, in some cases, politically. Ultimately, these dynamics create incentives for key actors to maintain the status quo, making actual conservation goals and outcomes irrelevant. This, I argue, explains the persistence of deforestation in Africa.

NOTES

1. Horning, Nadia Rabesahala. "Strong Support for Weak Performance: Donor Competition in Madagascar." *African Affairs* 107.428 (2008): 431.
2. The main types of development assistance are bilateral (country to country) and multilateral (aid channeled through international financial institutions) (Moyo 2009; Moss 2007).
3. Addison, Tony, George Mavrotas, and Mark McGillivray, "Development Assistance and Development Finance: Evidence and Global Policy Agendas."
4. Dessy, Sylvain E., and Désiré Vencatachellum. "Debt Relief and Social Services Expenditure: The African Experience, 1989–2003." *African Development Review* 19.1 (2007): 200–16.

5. This section draws on a paper I presented at the International Studies Association annual meeting held in New York City in February 2009.
6. Schraeder, Peter J. "From Berlin 1884 to 1989: Foreign Assistance and French, American, and Japanese Competition in Francophone Africa." *Journal of Modern African Studies* 33.4 (1995): 539–67, 539.
7. The basic tenets of SAPs were: Privatization, fiscal discipline, and trade liberalization.
8. Knack and Rahman (2004), 17–18.
9. Mukulu, Andrew. "Uganda: Even 'Darlings' Can Get Fed Up." *New African*. September 2002: 23, and Cargill, Tom. "Uganda: Still the Donors' Darling." *The World Today* 60.12 (2004): 26.
10. "Down, Down, Up, and Maybe Down: Donor Fatigue in Uganda." *The Economist.* June 30, 2005: 44.
11. For a detailed discussion of aid inflows in Uganda, see Holmgren (1999).
12. Mukulu, Andrew. "Uganda: Even 'Darlings' Can Get Fed Up." *New African*. September 2002: 23.
13. Klare, M., and D. Volman. "The African Oil Rush and US National Security." *Third World Quarterly* 27.4 (2006): 609–28.
14. Analysts have conceptualized donor competition in a number of ways, including "donor proliferation," with newcomers or entrants (Schraeder 1995; Harford et al. 2009); "multiplication" of donor activities (Roodman 2006; Acharya et al. 2004), "aid bombardment" (Kimura et al. 2009), "donor fragmentation" (Knack and Rahman 2004), and "aid intensity" (O'Connell and Soludo 1998; Bräutigam 2000).
15. Acharya et al. (2004) report that the median number of official donors in recipient countries was 23 in 2000.
16. Mercer, Claire. "Reconceptualising State-Society Relations in Tanzania: Are NGOs 'Making a Difference'?" *Area* 31 (1999): 247–58.
17. Roodman, David. "Competitive Proliferation of Aid Projects: A Model." Center for Global Development Working Paper No. 89. Washington, DC, June 2006.
18. Ronsholt, Frans. "Donor Burdens and Donor Good Practices." *OECD Country Case Study Tanzania.* Web. 2002. www.aidharmonization.net, accessed February 12, 2009.
19. Jabweli, Okello, and Joyce Namutebi, "Africa: Museveni Slams Aid Conditions." *The New Vision.* August 7, 2002, author's emphasis.
20. Ibid.
21. Sautman, Barry, and Hairong Yan. "Friends and Interests: China's Distinctive Links with Africa." *African Studies Review* 50.3 (2007): 75–114.

22. Knack and Rahman (2004) refer to the latter phenomenon as "poaching" (4–6).
23. These negotiations are well captured in Peter Chappell's 1997 documentary, *Our Friends at the Bank*.
24. Myers, Norman et al. "Biodiversity Hotspots for Conservation Priorities." *Nature* 403.6772 (2000): 853–58.
25. This section draws on Horning (2008), especially pp. 413–20.
26. Harper, Janice. *Endangered Species: Health, Illness and Death among Madagascar's People of the Forest*. Durham: Carolina Academic Press. 2002.
27. Randrianjohary, Alain Pierre. Personal Interview. July 9, 2005.
28. For a critique of IUCN's 10% target, see Rodrigues et al. (2004).
29. Corson, Catherine Anne. *Mapping the Development Machine: The U.S. Agency for International Development's Biodiversity Conservation Agenda in Madagascar*. PhD Dissertation, University of California, Berkeley, Spring 2008.
30. "Madagascar, naturally!"
31. Barbault, Robert, and Jean-Patrick Le Duc. *Biodiversité, Science et Gouvernance: Actes de la Conférence Internationale Paris, 24–28 janvier 2005*. Paris: Muséum National d'Histoire Naturelle, 2005.
32. Horning, Nadia Rabesahala. "Strong Support for Weak Performance: Donor Competition in Madagascar." *African Affairs* 107.428 (2008): 405–31.
33. The first program of its kind in Africa, Madagascar's National Environmental Action Plan (NEAP) was set up in 1988 with World Bank support. This program was to help the Government of Madagascar (GOM) devise policies and carry out projects aimed at alleviating the island's environmental problems. It was given legal power when the National Assembly passed Law 90-033 in December 1990. Designed as a three-phase, fifteen-year program, NEAP's implementation began in 1991. NEAP contained six components, of which "protecting and managing the national heritage of biodiversity" was one. This program was carried out in three five-year phases known as EP1 (1991–1995), EP2 (1996–2002), and EP3 (2003–2008).
34. More recently a *Comité Conjoint* was also set up to ensure communication among key actors in the donor and NGO communities, all of whom come to the environmental table with compatible or competing agendas.
35. This is because forests host 90% of the island's biodiversity. This lack of distinction between wildlife conservation and forest protection is worth noting because it explains the concentration of conservation efforts on Madagascar's forests, which host most of the island's unique plant and animal species.

36. Schraeder, Peter. *African Politics and Society: A Mosaic in Transformation*. Boston: Bedford/St. Martins, 2000.
37. Levine, Arielle. "Convergence or Convenience? International Conservation NGOs and Development Assistance in Tanzania." *World Development* 30.6 (2002): 1043–55.
38. When Germany ruled Tanganyika from 1884 to 1919, the colonial government adopted a classic top-down approach to conservation and set aside areas of natural wealth (wildlife and forests), either for limited recreational use or for preservation. What initially motivated the commitment to establish conservation areas was Tanzania's spectacular fauna. When Britain took over, the colonial government maintained the protected areas the Germans had created. National parks were established in the 1930s, causing displacements among local people, with ensuing confusion and resentment. The brewing tension between dispossessed locals and the colonial government served the purposes of Tanganyika African National Union (TANU) nationalist leaders who, in the 1950s, exploited this friction to attract rural people to their anti-colonial struggle. Upon independence, however, Julius Nyerere's TANU government maintained protected areas and supported conservation initiatives.
39. Katila, Marko, Swedish International Development Cooperation Agency, Dept. for Natural Resources and the Environment et al. *Three Decades of Swedish Support to the Tanzanian Forestry Sector: Evaluation of the Period 1969–2002*. Stockholm: Swedish International Development Cooperation Agency, Dept. for Natural Resources and Environment, 2003.
40. Ibid., p. 366.
41. One of the consequences of this foreign push for conservation is that conservation projects are popularly called "*projects za mzungu*" or white man's projects (Songorwa 2009).
42. Alden Wily, Liz (2001), p. 6.
43. Levine, Arielle. "Convergence or Convenience? International Conservation NGOs and Development Assistance in Tanzania." *World Development* 30.6 (2002): 1043–55, author's emphasis.
44. Bonner, Raymond. *At the Hand of Man: Peril and Hope for Africa's Wildlife*. New York: Knopf, 1993.
45. Katila et al. (2003).
46. Ibid.
47. Jansen, E.G. "Does Aid Work? Reflections on a Natural Resources Programme in Tanzania." Christian Michelsen's Institute, 2009.
48. Katila et al. (2003), p. 16.
49. Ibid., p. 15.

50. Protected forests (14 million hectares) comprise 357 NFRs and 141 LAFRs. Nineteen million hectares fall outside forest reserves in either village lands or on land held by government in default of established local ownership (Alden Wily 2001, 6).
51. Mniwasa, Eugene, and Vincent Shauri. "Review of the Decentralization Process and Its Impact on Environmental and Natural Resources Management in Tanzania." Lawyers Environmental Action Team. 2001, 13.
52. Ibid., p. 11.
53. To further complicate the institutional picture, reforms in the forest sector have been underway since 2010. These reforms call for the creation of the Tanzania Forest Service (TFS) whose mandate would include "managing national natural forest reserves, national plantations and forest resources in general, and the enforcement of forestry legislation within TFS jurisdictions" (Harris et al. 2011, 19). FDB's functions and personnel would then become more limited.
54. Harris, Dan, Pilar Domingo, Cassian Sianga, Enock Chengullah, and Calyst Basil Kavishe. *The Political Economy of Social Accountability in Tanzania: Anti-logging Advocacy and the Mama Misitu Campaign*. London: Overseas Development Institute, 2011.
55. To give proper context to public's violent reaction to their president's decision, one must keep three important facts in mind: first, Uganda's forest cover diminished from 10.8 million hectares in 1890 to less than 5 million hectares in 1995, with no signs of deforestation abating. Second, Mabira is an important watershed forest on which Kampala's water supply depends. Third, this was not the first forest giveaway under Museveni's watch.
56. "Uganda Leader Defends Forest Plan." BBC. Web. April 13, 2007. http://news.bbc.co.uk/2/hi/africa/6551905.stm, accessed April 20, 2009.
57. This is widespread sentiment among defenders of the forest, but some remember Museveni being an articulate environmentalist. But his discourse changed around the 2006 election when he realized that a pro-forest stance was likely to alienate most of his voters, especially in the rural areas where the pressure for more agricultural land was mounting.
58. Personal communications, Kampala, Uganda 2006 and 2008.
59. Riots broke out after the president announced his decision, in 2007, to give large portions of Mabira forest to a sugar-processing company. Museveni subsequently changed his mind.
60. Mills, Greg, and Jonathan Oppenheimer. "Partners, Not Beggars: The Rich World Gives a Mild Endorsement to a New African Development Plan." *Time International*. July 8, 2002: 35.

61. Ringer, Greg. "Gorilla Tourism: Uganda Uses Tourism to Recover from Decades of Violent Conflict." *Alternatives Journal: Canadian Environmental Ideas and Action* 28.4 (2002): 16–19.
62. For a good discussion of the domestic and international factors behind governments' resistance to "go green," see Stuligross (1999).
63. Kapalaga, Isaac. Personal Interview. July 27, 2006.
64. Babetweera. Interview with Mohamed Bukenya. April 27, 2009, Balimunsi. Personal interview. July 26, 2006.
65. Onyango, Gershom. Personal Interview. July 27, 2006.
66. Oloka Onyango. Personal Interview. April 27, 2009.
67. Nsita. Personal Interview. April 28, 2009.
68. Kisawuzi, Thomas. Personal Interview. December 11, 2008.
69. Arumadri, Joel. *The Forest Revenue System and Government Expenditure on Forestry in Uganda*. Rome and Accra: Forestry Policy and Planning Division and Regional Office for Africa. 2001.
70. Ellyne, Mark J. "The Economic History of Uganda and Progress Under Its Structural Adjustment Programme." *The Uganda Journal* 42 (1995): 16–31.
71. World Resources Institute. Uganda, Protected Areas 2007. Web. 2007. http://www.wri.org/publication/uganda-gis-data#base, accessed June 11, 2011.
72. Kisawuzi, Thomas. Personal Interview. December 11, 2008.
73. The colonial government's increasing awareness of Ugandan forests' many values, coupled with threats to these forests, prompted British forestry officials to introduce a formal management system based on multiple forest uses, including forest reserves for production, conservation, or both; national parks for tourism; wildlife reserves for protection, etc.
74. Arumadri, Joel. *The Forest Revenue System and Government Expenditure on Forestry in Uganda*. Rome and Accra: Forestry Policy and Planning Division and Regional Office for Africa, 2001.
75. The other 70%, designated as "private lands" are privately owned and managed.
76. Turyahabwe, N., and A.Y. Banana. "An Overview of History and Development of Forest Policy and Legislation in Uganda." *International Forestry Review* 10.4 (2008): 641–56.
77. Hamilton, A.C. *Deforestation in Uganda*. Nairobi: Oxford University Press, 1987.
78. Since its creation, the Ministry of Environment has changed names several times, going from Ministry of Environment (ME) to Ministry of Waters, Land and Environment (MWLE). MWLE was then renamed Ministry of Water and Environment (MWE). Presumably, name changes reflect an effort to address emerging issues of contention specifically on land, development, and the environment (Nsita 2009).

79. Government of Uganda. National Forest Authority. www.nfa.org.ug, accessed August 8, 2011.
80. Government of Uganda. *Forest Sector Review* 2001, 84.
81. Kisawuzi, Thomas. Personal Interview. December 11, 2008.
82. Horning, Nadia Rabesahala. "Madagascar's Biodiversity Conservation Challenge: From Local- to National-level Dynamics." *Environmental Sciences* 5.2 (2008): 109–28.
83. Mukadasi. Personal Interview. May 5, 2009.
84. Ibid.
85. Tree plantations are a good investment because exotic trees mature in less than two decades and can be harvested to meet Uganda's huge demand for timber products.
86. Converting tropical forests into plantation forests or agricultural land is a means of accessing and privatizing land. Those who manage to do this, by controlling state-managed forests, become wealthy.
87. Bukenya, Mohamed. Personal Interview. May 7, 2009.
88. Ssali, Michael. "Kalangala Islanders Say Bidco Must Stop Destroying Forests." *Daily Monitor*. Web. June 17, 2008. www.monitor.co.ug, accessed July 30, 2010.
89. Kamugisha, J.R., and S. Cornelia. *The Consultative Process for the Promotion of National Forest and Related Land Use Programmes in Uganda in Support of Intergovernmental Panel on Forests (IPF) of the Commission for Sustainable Development of United Nations*, Ministry of Natural Resources, Kampala, 1996.
90. This is according to the 1964 National Parks Act.
91. Babetweera. Interview with Mohamed Bukenya. April 27, 2009.
92. NFA is charged with encouraging tree planting of public land, whereas SPGS focuses on private lands.
93. Jacovelli, Paul. Personal Interview. April 30, 2009.
94. Twinomuhangi, Leo. Personal Interview with Mohamed Bukenya. April 28, 2009.
95. Kasekende, L.A., and Atingi-Ego. "Uganda's Experience with Aid." *Journal of African Economies* 8.4 (1999): 617–49.
96. Wrong, Michela. *It's Our Turn to Eat: The Story of a Kenyan Whistle Blower*. New York: Harper, 2009.
97. Balimunsi. Personal Interview. July 26, 2006.
98. This was to create an industrial park but up to now, there are very few established industries that led to the declassification of the forest reserve.
99. 6500 hectares of forest on Bugala islands in Lake Victoria was given to BIDCO, a vegetable oil processing company, to establish a palm oil tree estate and oil refinery on the islands of Kalangala district.

100. Tumushabe G.W., R. Mwebaza, and R. Naluwairo. "Sustainably Utilizing Our National Heritage: Legal Implication of the Proposed Degazzetment of Butamira Forest Reserve." ACODE Policy Research Series, No. 4. 2001.
101. The reserve was declassified in 2001 to provide land for Kakira Sugar Works, provoking public outcry and legal battles.
102. Arguably, Andry Rajoelina has shown disregard for environmental conservation.
 One must keep in mind, however, that Rajaoelina's *Haute Autorité de la Transition* is a government only nominally. Effectively, Madagascar has not had a government since Ravalomanana left the country in March 2009.
103. Lancaster, Carol. *Aid to Africa: So Much to Do, So Little Done*. Chicago: University of Chicago Press, 1999.
104. Incidentally, it also gave Ravalomanana the opportunity to side with the conservation-oriented Anglo-Saxons (Americans and British, mostly), signaling to the French their monopoly on Madagascar's development and politics was a thing of the past.
105. Schuurman, Derek, and Porter P. Lowry II. "The Madagascar Rosewood Massacre." *Madagascar Conservation and Development* 4.2 (2009): 98–102.

Bibliography

Acharya, Arnab Kumar, De Lima, Ana Fuzzo, Mick Moore, and University of Sussex. Institute of Development Studies. *Aid Proliferation: How Responsible Are the Donors?* Brighton, Sussex, England: Institute of Development Studies, 2004.

Addison, Tony, George Mavrotas, and Mark McGillivray. "Development Assistance and Development Finance: Evidence and Global Policy Agendas," Working Papers RP2005/23, World Institute for Development Economic Research (UNU-WIDER), 2005.

Alden Wily, Liz. *Forest Management and Democracy in East and Southern Africa: Lessons from Tanzania*. London: International Institute for Environment and Development, 2001.

Anonymous. Personal Interview. April 30, 2009.

Arumadri, Joel. *The Forest Revenue System and Government Expenditure on Forestry in Uganda*. Rome and Accra: Forestry Policy and Planning Division and Regional Office for Africa, 2001.

Babetweera. Interview with Mohamed Bukenya. April 27, 2009.

Balimunsi. Personal Interview. July 26, 2006.

Barbault, Robert, and Jean-Patrick Le Duc. *Biodiversité, Science et Gouvernance: Actes de la Conférence Internationale Paris, 24–28 janvier 2005*. Paris: Muséum National d'Histoire Naturelle, 2005.

Bonner, Raymond. *At the Hand of Man: Peril and Hope for Africa's Wildlife.* New York: Knopf, 1993.
Bräutigam, Deborah. *Aid Dependence and Governance.* Stockholm: Almqvist & Wiksell International, 2000.
Bukenya, Mohamed. Personal Interview. May 7, 2009.
Cargill, Tom. "Uganda: Still the Donors' Darling." *The World Today* 60.12 (2004): 26.
Corson, Catherine Anne. *Mapping the Development Machine: The U.S. Agency for International Development's Biodiversity Conservation Agenda in Madagascar.* PhD Dissertation. University of California, Berkeley, Spring 2008.
Dessy, Sylvain E., and Désiré Vencatachellum. "Debt Relief and Social Services Expenditure: The African Experience, 1989–2003." *African Development Review* 19.1 (2007): 200–216.
"Down, Down, Up, and Maybe Down: Donor Fatigue in Uganda." *The Economist.* June 30, 2005: 44.
Ellyne, Mark J. "The Economic History of Uganda and Progress Under Its Structural Adjustment Programme." *The Uganda Journal* 42 (1995): 16–31.
Government of Uganda. National Forest Authority. Web. www.nfa.org.ug. Accessed August 8, 2011.
Hamilton, A.C. *Deforestation in Uganda.* Nairobi: Oxford University Press. 1987.
Harford, Tim, Bita Hadjimichael, and Michael Klein. "Aid Agency Competition: A Century of Entry, but No Exit." Web. http://siteresources.worldbank.org/. Accessed February 4, 2009.
Harper, Janice. *Endangered Species: Health, Illness and Death among Madagascar's People of the Forest.* Durham: Carolina Academic Press. 2002.
Harris, Dan, Pilar Domingo, Cassian Sianga, Enock Chengullah, and Calyst Basil Kavishe. *The Political Economy of Social Accountability in Tanzania: Anti-logging Advocacy and the Mama Misitu Campaign.* London: Overseas Development Institute, 2011.
Holmgren, Torgny. *Aid and Reform in Uganda Country Case Study.* Kampala, 1999.
Horning, Nadia Rabesahala. "Strong Support for Weak Performance: Donor Competition in Madagascar." *African Affairs* 107.428 (2008): 405–31.
———. "Madagascar's Biodiversity Conservation Challenge: From Local- to National-level Dynamics." *Environmental Sciences* 5.2 (2008): 109–28.
Hurst, Andrew. "State Forestry and Spatial Scale in the Development Discourses of Post-colonial Tanzania: 1961–1971." *The Geographical Journal* 169.4 (2003): 358–69.
Jacovelli, Paul. Personal Interview. April 30, 2009.
Jansen, E.G. "Does Aid Work? Reflections on a Natural Resources Programme in Tanzania." Christian Michelsen's Institute, 2009.

Kamugisha, J.R., and S. Cornelia. *The Consultative Process for the Promotion of National Forest and Related Land Use Programmes in Uganda in Support of Intergovernmental Panel on Forests (IPF) of the Commission for Sustainable Development of United Nations.* Ministry of Natural Resources, Kampala, 1996.

Kapalaga, Isaac. Personal Interview. July 27, 2006.

Kasekende, L.A., and Atingi-Ego. "Uganda's Experience with Aid." *Journal of African Economies* 8.4 (1999): 617–49.

Katila, Marko, Swedish International Development Cooperation Agency, Dept. for Natural Resources and the Environment, et al. *Three Decades of Swedish Support to the Tanzanian Forestry Sector: Evaluation of the Period 1969–2002.* Stockholm: Swedish International Development Cooperation Agency, Department for Natural Resources and Environment, 2003.

Kimura, Hidemi, Yasuyuki Sawada, and Yuko Mori. "Aid Proliferation and Economic Growth: A Cross-Country Analysis." Web. www.rieti.go.jp. Accessed February 12, 2009.

Kisawuzi, Thomas. Personal Interview. December 11, 2008.

Klare, M., and D. Volman. "The African Oil Rush and US National Security." *Third World Quarterly* 27.4 (2006): 609–28.

Knack, Stephen, and Aminur Rahman. *Donor Fragmentation and Bureaucratic Quality in Aid Recipients.* Washington: World Bank, Development Research Group, Public Services, 2004.

Kull, Christian A. "The Evolution of Conservation Efforts in Madagascar." *International Environmental Affairs* 8.1 (1996): 50–86.

Lancaster, Carol. *Aid to Africa: So Much to Do, So Little Done.* Chicago: University of Chicago Press, 1999.

Levine, Arielle. "Convergence or Convenience? International Conservation NGOs and Development Assistance in Tanzania." *World Development* 30.6 (2002): 1043–55.

Luttrell, Cecilia, and Innocent Pantaleo. "Budget Support, Aid Instruments, and the Environment: The Country Context. Tanzania Case Study. Final Report." Web. January 2008. http://www.odi.org.uk/resources/docs/3884.pdf. Accessed February 10, 2009.

Mercer, Claire. "Reconceptualising State-Society Relations in Tanzania: Are NGOs 'Making a Difference'?" *Area* 31 (1999): 247–58.

Mills, Greg, and Jonathan Oppenheimer. "Partners, Not Beggars: The Rich World Gives a Mild Endorsement to a New African Development Plan." *Time International.* July 8, 2002: 35.

Moss, Todd J. *African Development: Making Sense of the Issues and Actors.* Boulder: Lynne Rienner, 2007.

Moyo, Dambisa. *Dead Aid: Why Aid Is Not Working and How There Is a Better Way for Africa.* New York: Farrar, Straus and Giroux, 2009.

Mniwasa, Eugene, and Vincent Shauri. "Review of the Decentralization Process and Its Impact on Environmental and Natural Resources Management in Tanzania." Lawyers Environmental Action Team, 2001.
Mukadasi. Personal Interview. May 5, 2009.
Mukulu, Andrew. "Uganda: Even 'Darlings' Can Get Fed Up." *New African*. September (2002): 23.
Myers, N., R.A. Mittermeier, C.G. Mittermeier, G.A. Da Fonseca, and Kent, J. "Biodiversity Hotspots for Conservation Priorities." *Nature* 403.6772 (2000): 853–58.
Nash, Roderick. *Wilderness and the American Mind* (3rd ed.). New Haven: Yale University Press, 1982.
Nsita. Personal Interview. April 28, 2009.
O'Connell, Stephen A., and Charles Chukwuma Soludo. *Aid Intensity in Africa*. Oxford: CSAE, 1998.
Oloka-Onyango. Personal Interview. April 27, 2009.
Onyango, Gershom. Personal Interview. July 27, 2006.
Our Friends at the Bank. Dir. Peter Chappell. First Run/Icarus Films, 1997. DVD.
Randrianjohary, Alain Pierre. Personal Interview. July 9, 2005.
Republic of Uganda. *Forest Sector Review*. 2001.
Ringer, Greg. "Gorilla Tourism: Uganda Uses Tourism to Recover from Decades of Violent Conflict." *Alternatives Journal: Canadian Environmental Ideas and Action* 28.4 (2002): 16–19.
Rodrigues, A.S., S.J. Andelman, M.I. Bakarr, L. Boitani, T.M. Brooks, R.M. Cowling, L.D. Fishpool, G.A. Da Fonseca, K.J. Gaston, M. Hoffmann, J.S. Long, P.A. Marquet, J.D. Pilgrim, R.L. Pressey, J. Schipper, W. Sechrest, S.N. Stuart, L.G. Underhill, R.W. Waller, M.E. Watts, and X. Yan. "Effectiveness of the Global Protected Area Network in Representing Species Diversity." *Nature* 428.6983 (2004): 640–43.
Ronsholt, Frans. "Donor Burdens and Donor Good Practices." *OECD Country Case Study Tanzania* (2002). Web. www.aidharmonization.net. Accessed February 12, 2009.
Roodman, David. "Competitive Proliferation of Aid Projects: A Model," Center for Global Development Working Paper No. 89. Washington, DC, June 2006.
Sautman, Barry, and Hairong Yan. "Friends and Interests: China's Distinctive Links with Africa." *African Studies Review* 50.3 (2007): 75–114.
Schraeder, Peter. *African Politics and Society: A Mosaic in Transformation*. Boston: Bedford, 2000.
———. "From Berlin 1884 to 1989: Foreign Assistance and French, American, and Japanese Competition in Francophone Africa." *Journal of Modern African Studies* 33.4 (1995): 539–67.

Schuurman, Derek, and Porter P. Lowry II. "The Madagascar Rosewood Massacre" *Madagascar Conservation & Development* 4.2 (2009): 98–102.
Songorwa, Alex. Personal Interview. January 30, 2009.
Ssali, Michael. "Kalangala Islanders Say Bidco Must Stop Destroying Forests." *Daily Monitor*. Web. June 17, 2008. www.monitor.co.ug. Accessed July 30, 2010.
Stuligross, David. "The Political Economy of Environmental Regulation in India." *Pacific Affairs* 72.3 (1999): 392–406.
Tumushabe G.W., R. Mwebaza, and R. Naluwairo. "Sustainably Utilizing Our National Heritage: Legal Implication of the Proposed Degazzetment of Butamira Forest Reserve." ACODE Policy Research Series, No. 4, 2001.
Turyahabwe, N., and A.Y. Banana. "An Overview of History and Development of Forest Policy and Legislation in Uganda." *International Forestry Review* 10.4 (2008): 641–56.
Twinomuhangi, Leo. Personal Interview with Mohamed Bukenya. April 28, 2009. "Uganda Leader Defends Forest Plan." BBC. Web. April 13, 2007. http://news.bbc.co.uk/2/hi/africa/6551905.stm. Accessed April 20, 2009.
World Bank Group. *WDI Online*. Web. http://www.worldbank.org/wdiquery. Accessed July 23, 2010.
World Resources Institute. Uganda, Protected Areas 2007. Web. 2007. http://www.wri.org/publication/uganda-gis-data#base. Accessed June 11, 2011.
Wrong, Michela. *It's Our Turn to Eat: The Story of a Kenyan Whistle Blower*. New York: Harper, 2009.

CHAPTER 4

Across the Great Divide: Collaborative Forest Management

This book's central claim is that deforestation persists in Africa because policies and projects that aim to control the problem often ignore the limited and specific conditions under which the interests of key actors align in favor of conservation at multiple levels of decision-making. I have argued that a chronic disconnect between national- and local-level decision makers weakens anti-deforestation initiatives. The previous two chapters show that whereas deforestation policies assume environmental decision makers to be interdependent, in reality they operate in parallel institutional universes with distinct incentives to conserve forests or not. Because this disconnect fundamentally impedes interest alignment, it often leads to disappointing outcomes where and when conservation is attempted.

Since deforestation persists in the three countries under study, one might think that African governments have done little to bridge the gap between local and national environmental actors. This is not so. In fact, partnership between local communities and state agents is the fundamental principle behind community-based natural resource management (CBNRM) projects implemented in these (and other) countries since the 1990s. As an approach to resource management, CBNRM "integrates conservation and development goals by focusing on the needs, interests, knowledge, values, and capabilities of *local populations*."[1] Commonly thought of as a process of community empowerment, fundamentally CBNRM employs institutional innovation to align the interests of local and national actors and, by extension, raise the prospect of successful conservation.

Although some CBNRM experiences have been successful, the majority of CBNRM projects have yet to deliver positive, broad-scale conservation results on a consistent basis.[2] This chapter thus addresses the following question: Why do CBRNM projects succeed in controlling deforestation in some locales and not in others? Using interest alignment as a key explanatory variable, the chapter describes and explains variations in deforestation outcomes in specific sites across Madagascar, Tanzania, and Uganda where the CBNRM approach was used to combat this problem. Chapter 1 defined interest alignment as the convergence of goals vis-à-vis natural resources among key international, national, and local players. Looking at specific CBNRM sites, I show below that, as my theory predicts, deforestation was contained where interests aligned, and it persisted where interests failed to do so.[3] Specifically, positive outcomes were recorded in Madagascar's Arivonimamo region, negative outcomes were registered around Tanzania's Kitulang'halo Forest Reserve, and mixed results were achieved in Uganda's Mpigi District.

Explanations for CBRNM Success and Failure

Because of their lackluster record, CBRNM experiments have generated debates among scholars, practitioners, and policy makers regarding the reasons for their success and failure. Lamenting the fact that the literature on the subject has overly focused on reasons for failure, Measham and Lumbasi's review of this literature leads them to isolate four principal conditions under which CBNRM projects falter. Specifically, these projects fail when (1) they are initiated by outsiders and imposed on communities; (2) they do not provide adequate economic incentives to conserve resources; (3) local communities are deprived of autonomy because of higher authorities' interference; and (4) the costs of adopting CBNRM outweigh benefits to communities. While these are useful lessons, the authors argue that much can be learned from successful experiences such as the ones they encountered in Kenya and Australia. Comparing CBNRM projects in these two countries, they conclude that CBRNM projects initiated by communities rather than external actors (donors, state managers, researchers, etc.) are likely to succeed.[4] Thus, according to them, community ownership is a critical condition for CBNRM success. Measham and Lumbasi are correct to insist that much can be learned from successful cases, but both the factors for failure that they identify and the principal variable for success they come up with focus on one critical unit:

the community. Surprisingly, however, the authors neglect to define communities. If communities are a critical element of CBRNM success, is it wise to assume that there is a universal definition for them? Another reading of the CBNRM literature offers additional theoretical insights, one of which focuses on proper conceptualizations of communities.

This first school of thought, headed by Agrawal and Gibson, proposes that an important impediment to CBNRM success has to do with projects designed and executed using conventional definitions of "local communities" conceptualized as small spatial units, homogenous structures with members assumed to share interests and norms.[5] As an illustration, the Filipino government made this very mistake when it engineered "indigenous communities" to implement its 1993 Certificate of Ancestral Domain (CDAC) policy.[6] In many instances, such as in Kayasan on Palawan Island, CDAC communities did not reflect realities on the ground where competing interests, fluid migratory movements, a history of domination by migrants, hindered collective action capabilities, and local strategies of resource control (via exclusion of particular users) existed. As a result, CDAC's objective of controlling deforestation was unmet. Thus this school proposes that, to increase the chances of success, CBNRM projects should conceptualize "communities" as units that encompass multiple actors with diverse interests. Ultimately, successful communities devise institutions that reflect and accommodate diverse interests to structure their interactions around resource management.[7] The genius of these local institutions lies in the fact that they align key actors' interests in favor of conservation.

While this first school of thought focuses attention on proper conceptualizations of communities, a second one emphasizes culture. Those who champion cultural explanations contend that CBNRM projects are more likely to control deforestation when their design and execution are grounded in cultural understandings of the proper relationship between people and their natural environments. In this regard, the parallels between Analavelona forest in southern Madagascar (discussed in Chapter 2), and the sacred forests in Zimbabwe's Shona region are of note. In Zimbabwe, Byers, Cunliffe, and Hudak find that spiritual values embedded in Shona culture influence local people's behavior vis-à-vis forests and, thus, forest conservation.[8] As is the case in Analavelona, sacred forests in the Muzarabani area (northeastern Zimbabwe) are believed to host ancestral spirits that "would seek revenge on those who carry out unauthorized tree cutting."[9] I have argued elsewhere that, in reality, "sacredness" is a conceptual device used to control community members' behaviors. Fundamentally, local beliefs about the relationships between people and forests (as mediated by ancestral spirits) reflect a concern for survival: sacred forests must be conserved because humans derive material (such as timber and soil fertility) and nonmaterial benefits (such as preserving their cultural identity) from them. Thus cultural beliefs are fundamentally grounded in pragmatism.[10] Going back to the concept of interest alignment, the Zimbabwean case shows that

> [t]he sacred forests of Muzarabani contribute to livelihoods and quality of life at the local level, the district level, and the national level because of the many material and nonmaterial uses, values, and benefits they provide. The compatibility of many of these uses could allow a diverse group of stake-holders to *recognize their common interest in conserving* the Muzarabani dry forests, and *encourage them to cooperate to do so.*[11]

In this way, successful CBNRM projects are those that overcome collective action problems by devising institutions grounded in cultural beliefs about nature. In a similar vein, though going beyond "culture," Uphoff and Langholz argue that successful CBNRM projects, i.e., those that encourage resource-conserving behavior (RCB), balance legality, profitability (economic), and the cultural appropriateness of environmental decisions.[12]

A third CBNRM school of thought focuses on scale. Scale scholars argue that CBNRM projects falter when their design and execution overlook the fact that ecological systems involve multiple principles at multiple scales, notably spatial and temporal. As Sayer and Campbell point out, for example, "[i]n the real world, *different processes take place at different speeds*; some processes may be studied over short time frames while others may have to be studied over decades."[13] Likewise, many natural processes take place at different spatial scales. This is particularly clear when dealing with fugitive resources such as fish and wildlife, but it also happens with stationary ones, including forests, when taken in the context of the ecosystems of which they are part. For instance, forest ecosystems commonly straddle multiple administrative, even national boundaries.[14] In this regard, Herring cautions that "nature mocks administrative grids"[15] and points to the perils of focusing on a single level of management, including the local level, given that knowledge and resources are generated at multiple scales due to the attributes of the resource under management.

Put differently, scale scholars suggest that CBNRM projects do not deliver because administrative systems are seldom congruent with natural ones. Thus resource management systems should also incorporate multiple scales and principles of organization. Andersson and Ostrom's notion of polycentric governance captures this idea well:

> All human efforts to govern natural resources face the problem of creating rules that make sense for particular social, biophysical, and institutional context in which the resources exist. When policymakers create generalized rule systems that may not fit the local context well, the incentives of users to manage resources responsibly are considerably weakened. The polycentric approach studies conditions for interactive learning between local user groups and between these user groups and government officials. As such, it assesses the degree to which the governance process actually helps the actors to craft and adjust their own rules over time, thus increasing the likelihood of these rules being effective in regulating resource use.[16]

Central to the scale argument is the idea that institutional innovation requires careful consideration of the locus of authority (who has the right to make decisions?) and legitimacy (what and who is considered right, proper, and therefore acceptable?). Therefore, successfully managing a "local" resource requires considering larger ecological, social, political, and temporal processes.[17] In short, CBNRM projects whose designs ignore multi-scale processes are likely to fail, which jeopardizes environmental conservation.

This set of theories has advanced our understanding of CBNRM significantly. Each, however, has limitations for the cases at hand. As I detail below, success can happen whether or not a CBNRM project properly defines a specific community. Nor can shared cultural values, which is the product of growing together as a community, account for varying conservation outcomes where and when personal interests trump those of the greater community. Finally, while multi-scale governance holds more theoretical promise than the other two theories, in practice the theory falters in light of the fundamental fact that actors' interests drive their behaviors and, by extension, conservation outcomes.

As an alternative, I will show that interest alignment offers more analytical leverage by integrating key elements of the other theories. As a theoretical concept, interest alignment captures the fundamental fact that people define their interests in multiple ways (economically, culturally, politically, etc.), depending on the situations—involving time and place—in which they make resource decisions. Thus this theory is more robust than others because it captures the dynamic environments in which environmental decisions are made across space and time.

To demonstrate this, this chapter examines specific experiments with CBNRM in Madagascar, Tanzania, and Uganda after placing these experiments in their proper historical and institutional contexts. Doing so enables us to identify actors at multiple levels of decision-making, the interests that emerge from actors' interactions with one another and with the environment, and institutions devised to protect the various interests.

The Impetus for Decentralized Natural Resource Management in Africa

Paradoxically, decentralized resource management was an initiative driven by foreign actors keen to implement neo-liberal reforms, by African national actors eager to advance politically, and by local communities anxious to gain long denied decision-making powers in the environmental realm. Identifying these actors' motivations helps us understand why decentralization reforms were pushed, enacted, and implemented when they were introduced in the 1990s. At the same time, it helps us realize that for the various actors involved, fighting deforestation was not the chief goal of collaboration but a tangential one. It is important to note this to see why the legal frameworks put in place by the three countries to fight deforestation (see Chapter 3) have been ineffectual for the most part.

As the emblematic Berlin Wall fell in 1989, few African farmers could imagine that this event would somehow result in an unprecedented willingness on their governments' part, to give them a say in land and forest management in their respective locales. Nor, in fact, could African governments begin to conceive of sharing decision-making powers with those they governed. But the triumph of liberalism, symbolized by the wall's collapse, ushered in a period of power relations reconfiguration across Africa. Armed with an ideological monopoly, Western governments were quick to praise the virtues of neo-liberalism to their African (and other) counterparts. The targeted realms of reform were political (liberal democracy) and economic (free market capitalism). Although the tenets of liberal democracy (i.e., competition, participation, and freedom) were largely alien to African politics after decades of colonial and authoritarian rule, Africa's reliance on western aid and resulting debt burden left many African governments little choice but to reform their political and economic systems, or at least feign to do so.[18] On the economic front, the concept of pluralism by means of increased competition among economic actors (including private investors), though alien, was put into practice. In the political realm, African governments were expected to create environments in which power contenders could compete through free and fair democratic elections. Implementing these reforms secured debt relief and continued foreign assistance, hence African governments' eagerness to comply. But while liberal reforms increased the number of political actors in multiple governance realms, they did little to help to curb deforestation for several reasons.

Liberal reforms were carried out by means of structural adjustment programs (SAPs), competitive elections, and decentralization programs. In the African context, these developments affected natural resource management since the vast majority of Africans depended, and continue to depend, on forests for their livelihoods. Hobbled by decades of centralized resource governance by both colonial and post-colonial governments, African states faced a dire situation by the end of the 1980s: gross inefficiencies (resource waste), inequalities (in access and distribution of benefits), alienation of critical stakeholders (especially local communities) from the process of environmental decision-making, and unsustainable practices harmful to their resource capital were common outcomes. This situation was the driving force behind, or pretext for, donors' push for reform in multiple sectors, including the environment.

Additionally, the principles and putative goals of decentralized resource management were alluring to the donor community though not to African elites who were used to monopolizing political and economic power. Decentralization was associated with the re-distribution of decision-making power, enfranchisement, equity, justice, and expanded rights for local communities, all of which Westerners considered an improvement over existing African political values and practices. The goals of decentralization themselves were equally attractive to the extent that newly empowered local communities would be able to "manage their natural resources in an efficient, equitable, and sustainable way."[19]

Further, donors saw decentralized resource management as a way to advance and deepen democracy in Africa. Reaching this larger ideological goal was particularly urgent in Westerners' eyes, because African states were unitary, executive powers largely unrestricted, regimes authoritarian (in various ways), and political and economic power concentrated in the hands of small elite groups. All these features of African political systems were anathema to liberal democracy. Thus when the terms empowerment, enfranchisement, popular participation, government responsiveness, sharing rights and obligations, and accountability were associated with decentralized resource management, Western donors were eager to support the enterprise.

Africans' own political calculations also explain how readily neo-liberal reforms were adopted. African governments understood they would gain politically by committing to decentralization: by complying with western governments' and IFIs' reforms, African governments sought to continue benefiting from donor largesse. Another potential benefit was what can be termed the greening of governments' identities: appearing environmentally minded had the potential benefit of improving governments' image, increasing their legitimacy domestically and internationally and, again, attracting foreign support.[20] Reflecting on the experiences of the first decade of decentralized governance in South Asia and West Africa, Agrawal and Ribot note that "[g]overnments often perform acts of decentralization as theater pieces *to impress or appease international donors and NGOs* or domestic constituencies."[21] It mattered little that decentralization was more nominal than substantive: the crucial goal was to appear to reform. Local communities, for their part, had reason to embrace reform since they (erroneously) saw their involvement in resource management as a rare opportunity to expand, or restore, their rights to resources.[22]

Thus when decentralization was introduced to Africa, both domestic and foreign actors saw an opportunity to advance their interests, hence their eagerness to engage in the process. The irony of a top-down decentralization initiative was lost on everyone, which is why the various actors failed to anticipate the problems lying ahead.

Making CBNRM a Reality: Collaborative Forest Management in Madagascar, Tanzania, and Uganda

Where attempted, CBNRM projects needed to have a legal basis to gain traction. Consequently, the governments of Madagascar, Tanzania, and Uganda went through an elaborate process of building legal frameworks specifically for CBNRM projects. This section situates each CBNRM experiment in its institutional context, to assess whether the institutional setup per se influenced the experiments' outcomes. Put differently, did institutional setup facilitate interest alignment across the three countries? Based on Tanzania's unique political history of effective devolution of decision-making powers, one can assume that it is better positioned than the other two in terms of CBNRM. Has Tanzania had more success than Uganda in controlling deforestation by means of CBNRM, and has Uganda in turn been more successful than Madagascar? I turn to this question after discussing how each country set up the institutions needed to carry out CBNRM projects (Table 4.1).

Madagascar

The legal framework for CBNRM in Madagascar is *Loi 96-025*, known as *Loi Gelose* (for *Gestion Locale Sécurisée*, or secured local management), which passed on September 10, 1996. Article 1 of this text specifies the law's goal, namely, to allow for the effective participation of rural

Table 4.1 Models of CBNRM for forest management in the three countries

	Madagascar	Tanzania	Uganda
Overall Designation	GELOSE	PFM	PFM
Designation for CBNRM/Forest contracts	GCF	JFM	CFM
Eligible forest categories	All forests	NFRs	CFRs LFRs
Agreement name	*Contrat* GCF	JMA	CFMA
State actor, national level	MINENVEF/*Direction Générale des Eaux & Forêts (DGEF)*	Forest and Beekeeping Division	Forest Department
State actor, subnational level	*Direction Régionale des Eaux & Forêts (DREF)*	District forest service	NFA for CFRs DFS for LFRs
Community actors	CLB/COBA/VOI	VFC of Village Government	Local Community (LC1 level)
Legal framework	1996 *Loi* 96-025 1997 *Loi* 97-017 Décret 2001-122	1982 Local government act 1999 Village Land Act 2002 Forest Act (No. 14)	2001 Forest Policy (Section 15) 2001 National Forest Plan 2003 National Forestry and Treeplanting Act

populations in the sustainable conservation of renewable natural resource management. In 1997, Gelose was incorporated into the new forestry policy, *Loi 97-017*, which was followed four years later by enabling legislation, *Décret 2001-122*, to legalize forest management contracts, commonly called GCF.[23] These contracts bind local communities, called *Communautés Locales de Base* or COBAs, rural communes, and the central government (i.e., the Forest Service) to manage forest resources in collaboration with each other. COBAs are forest associations registered as nonprofits whose members join the COBA and enter GCF contracts on a voluntary basis. State-trained mediation professionals, called *médiateurs environnementaux*, coordinate contract negotiations and oversee their implementation. Under GCF contracts, a set of mutually agreed upon rules, called *dina*, regulate forest access and uses. GCF contracts are presented to local communities as opportunities to collaborate with the state on forest management and, importantly, share the benefits of forest protection or exploitation with the state.

The first Gelose contracts were set up in 1999 with about 30–40 contracts signed per year. Although setting up Gelose contracts involves a cumbersome, 22-step process, within five years the number of signed contracts had increased to 150 per year, by 2004 the total number of contracts effectively signed reaching 450. GCF contracts constituted more than 75% of all Gelose contracts.[24]

Tanzania

By contrast, and unique to Tanzania is the fact that "[t]he seeds were sown in the 1970s for rural empowerment through the structure of village government."[25] Tanzania's political history has been favorable to the devolution of resource management powers since early independence: to carry out Nyerere's *ujamaa* programs, 10,500 village governments were set up with legal status. These village governments form the basis for collaborative forest management, or CFM.[26]

Additionally, of the three countries, Tanzania's institutional set up for decentralized resource management is arguably the strongest. Three legal texts contain provisions that provide incentives for local communities to manage forest resources sustainably:

- the 1982 Local Government Act allows village communities to devise their own legally-binding and enforceable bylaws;

- the 1999 Village Land Act gives villages title deeds and the mandate to make decisions regarding resources sitting on village areas, including village land forest reserves; and
- the 2002 Forest Act, Article 14 ensures that the benefits derived from forest use and conservation are captured at the community level, thereby giving local communities incentives to manage forests sustainably.

There are two forms of CFM contracts in Tanzania, depending on the legal status of the forest subject to CBNRM: Community-Based Forest Management (CBFM) is the term used for village lands and general lands, and Joint Management (JFM) is for state-owned national forest reserves (NFRs). To the extent that communities enter into agreements with the local or the central government only under JFM, I focus on these contracts, which are comparable to GCF in Madagascar and CFM in Uganda, which I describe below. In 2006, nearly 12% of national and local government forests were under some form of JFM, with a total of 719 participant villages (about 40% of all villages participating in some form of Participatory Forest Management, or PFM). Of those, 149 had signed JFM agreements.[27] In 2008, these numbers were 871 and 155, respectively.[28] These numbers indicate a decrease in participation from less than 21% in 2006 to less than 18% in 2008.

While the institutional setup arguably gives Tanzania a comparative advantage, paradoxically the political context has not been conducive to effective decentralization. Hydén, for one, points out that despite institutional arrangements conducive to collective decision-making at multiple levels, a segment of the Tanzanian peasantry remained largely "uncaptured," as many resisted the state's expansion into their production space during the country's *ujamaa* experiment.[29] Even if one were to entertain the idea that the principles behind Nyerere's villagization policy were good, *ujamaa*'s execution eventually required a great deal of state coercion.[30] It also resulted in patronage politics whereby the governing party, TANU, distributed political favors in exchange for the aggressive implementation of the villagization policy in rural areas.[31]

The disastrous results that *ujamaa* produced in terms of economic production are well documented, but another realm was also adversely affected: peasant-state relations. My own interactions with rural dwellers in the Morogoro region in 2009 made it abundantly clear that district-level government agents were more interested in using their official positions to monopolize decision-making powers and extract rents from forests than sharing such powers with villagers. I discuss this phenomenon in greater detail in my description of the Kitulang'halo case. Considering this historical context, CBNRM initiatives seem like déjà vu all over again, and it is hardly a mystery that another experiment with peasant-state collaboration has yielded disappointing results. So, although the institutional setup could give Tanzania an edge over the other two countries, the political culture necessary to implement CBNRM successfully is largely absent there.

Uganda

In Uganda, CFM agreements resulted from the 1999 forest sector reform, which ushered in a series of institutional initiatives relating to forest management. The institutional framework for decentralized forest management consists of:

- the 2001 Uganda Forest Policy (UFP);
- the 2001 National Forest Plan; and
- the 2003 National Forestry and Tree Planting Act, which contains provisions for establishing community forests.

To facilitate decentralized forest management, a Forestry Sector Support Department (FSSD) was created within the Ministry of Water and Environment's Directorate of Environment Affairs. FSSD's mission is "to effectively coordinate, guide and supervise Uganda's forest sector" with the main goal of achieving social welfare by way of sustainable forest management.[32] As well, the centralized Forestry Department was abolished and replaced by the National Forestry Authority (NFA) in 2003, as discussed in Chapter 3.

Uganda's decentralized forest management takes three forms: CFMAs (Collaborative Forest Management Agreements), CFAs (Community Forests Agreements), and PFs (Private Forests). Under CFMAs, communities enter into agreements with the government to manage classified forests. These communities register as legal entities to convert forested communal lands into community forests whose management in principle benefits the community as a whole. In PFs local community members either manage their own trees on private land or participate in the management of private natural forests, forest plantations, or forests officially owned by indigenous groups. As such, they do not require collaboration with the state, although private owners are free to work with foresters if they wish. As explained in Chapter 2, Uganda's forest estate is organized into Central Forest Reserves (CFRs), Local Forest Reserves (LFRs), and Private Reserves (PRs). With CFRs co-management involves communities and NFA representatives. With LFRs communities' partners are District Forest Services (DFS) representatives who operate at the district level.[33] Unlike in Madagascar, no specially trained facilitators (*médiateurs environnementaux*) take part in the negotiations. Yet neither NFA nor DFS employees are equipped to initiate and negotiate CFMAs.[34]

The Ugandan government began to experiment with PFM prior to institutionalizing CFM. As early as 1993, the approach was applied across select districts—notably in Bwindi Impenetrable National Park— and, in 1996, the CFM model was applied to other national parks.[35] In this early experimentation period, FD held consultations with various actors, including communities adjacent to the various forests. In 1998, it officially launched CFM pilot activities.[36] Although the Ugandan CFM process contains fewer steps than Madagascar's *Gelose* (9 versus 22, respectively), the number of signed agreements was substantially smaller: from 1998 to 2011, only 27 contracts had been signed and 30 applications had been approved by NFA.[37]

Like in Tanzania, Uganda's decentralization initiatives did not automatically create a political environment where shared forest management responsibilities and benefits could be realized on the ground. Despite an impressive array of initiatives and legal texts, local governments could not effectively combat the forces of centralized control, which a variety of mechanisms such as re-classifying forests kept intact.[38] In fact, Uganda remains infamous for oscillating between centralized and decentralized resource management and has done little to effectively bridge the gap between local communities and government agents.[39] Beck attributes the persistence of centralized control to an institutional culture of central planning that challenges local communities' participation in decision-making.

Thus setting up institutions that enable collaboration across various levels of environmental decision-making is necessary. However, institutions effectively change people's behavior only where the political context allows them to. While one would expect Tanzania's CBNRM initiatives to blossom "naturally," due to its unique history of devolution of political powers, Madagascar had more success in bringing about collaborative management between local communities and the state. Madagascar also did better than Uganda where considerable investments were made to set up the right institutions and where the state experiments with CBNRM even before it was formalized. Therefore, institutions are necessary, but they are not sufficient for conservation by means of CBNRM. Put differently, institutions can facilitate interest alignment, but they cannot be assumed to achieve this condition regardless of political context.

How Interest Alignment Impacts Conservation Outcomes: Evidence from the Ground

Although the three countries' political contexts have not been conducive to shared decision-making, some CBNRM experiments have served forest conservation well, others less so, and still other less so. I explain these outcomes in three CBNRM locales—Arivonimamo (Madagascar), Kitulang'halo (Tanzania), and Mpigi (Uganda)—by examining the extent to which actors' interests aligned or failed to align in each case.

Case 1: The Tapia Forest and Silkworms of Arivonimamo, Madagascar

In 2000, the Swiss NGO HELVETAS Swiss Intercooperation put Madagascar's decentralized policy into practice by setting up a community-based forest management project in Arivonimamo, a rural community located outside the capital city of Antananarivo. The project received funding from *Coopération Suisse*, Switzerland's development agency. Through this project, Swiss Intercooperation supported various COBAs' efforts to alleviate pressures on community forests and also conserve an endemic tree species, called *tapia*, which hosts a particular silkworm vital to the local silk industry.

Each key actor had strong incentives to participate in this project. For its part, Swiss Intercooperation's main goal was captured in its mission statement: "to advance rural people's living standards by improving people-environment relations, thereby securing the sustainable use of natural resources and helping rural communities develop their decision-making capacities at various levels."[40] Arivonimamo communities, for their part, felt the ill effects of bush fires and forest overharvesting and wanted to correct the problem. They also had limited capacity to start the GCF process, come up with bylaws, or carry out a forest management plan that would allow them to benefit from the forests. Finally, the state had a stake in this project because it could potentially rely on local communities to carry out conservation activities (set up and enforce rules, monitor compliance, sanction rule breakers, and resolve disputes when they occur), thus saving on conservation costs; at the same time, the communal governments could benefits from taxing the communities' revenues.

With Swiss Intercooperation's help, Arivonimamo COBAs turned their negative situation around and, within five years, reported real ecological, economic, financial, and socio-political improvements. The ecological rewards included a well-preserved *tapia* forest, controlled bush fires, and silkworm regeneration (the silkworm population was declining at the time the project started). The economic benefits were improvements in livelihoods thanks to the revival of the local silk industry and improved water supply for paddy rice cultivation. Positive outcomes were also reached with the emergence of a local leadership and with improved social capital, due to cooperation and the development of trust, within COBAs and between COBAs and *communes*. Another significant social benefit that the communities received was reduced marginalization of their poorest households. A final benefit that COBAs derived from the project was access to foreign funding.[41]

Such an experience speaks well to the advantages of state-community partnerships in forest management. But what actually contributed to the project's success? First, some community members displayed a willingness to improve a situation they deemed worrisome but not beyond repair. Second, an outside partner, the foreign NGO, identified these communities as ripe for the type of intervention the NGO was willing and able to make. In particular, the NGO staff was primarily interested in these communities' needs as communities identified them. Third, the project built on an existing industry rather than creating new income-generating activities for communities. Given the existing national and international silk markets, reviving the local silk industry presented practically no risks. Fourth, the NGO staff looked at communities not as beneficiaries, but as development and conservation partners. Finally, both the NGO and communities readily seized co-management opportunities that the decentralization policy framework offered.

In short, under these conditions the interests of all stakeholders—international, domestic, and local—aligned nicely. The Swiss government desired to support both development and conservation; the Malagasy government hoped to demonstrate the effectiveness of its decentralization policy; the Swiss NGO looked to demonstrate the effectiveness of its development approaches; the communal government stood to benefit financially from successful partnerships with COBAs; and the COBAs turned local communities into development actors (not mere beneficiaries) and successful forest managers. In this case, the outside actor to the GCF process (outside to the community and the state) played a critical role for interest alignment. This is not surprising, in the case of Swiss Intercooperation whose projects are governed by five basic principles, one of which is explicitly "alignment and coordination." This NGO's commitment to honor the needs of rural communities, defend the interests of its development partners (including rural communities), facilitate communication among development actors, and help the most vulnerable members of rural communities is a critical factor behind this experiment's success.

Heartening as this case may be, the fact remains that positive conservation outcomes were reached only under limited and the specific conditions outlined above—just as the remarkable conservation of Analavelona sacred forest (discussed in Chapter 2) had more to do with interest alignment than conservation policies and projects per se. There, Bara communities set up institutions that reflected local knowledge of their resource environment and in tune with local cultural beliefs and social norms, which supports cultural explanations for CBNRM projects success. Again, when actors' interests align, however these interests emerge, deforestation can be controlled.

Case 2: Kitulang'halo National Forest Reserve, Tanzania

Kitulang'halo forest is located southeast of the Uluguru Mountains, near a road that connects Morogoro town to Dar es Salaam. It is part of the Eastern Arc Mountains Forests, which are world renowned for their biodiversity and water catchment significance. Due to their special value, these mountains were placed under the strictest protection status in the early 1900s. A combination of increased human pressures and failed state-led forest management resulted in a series of co-management experiments in the late 1990s, funded by the government of Tanzania, Danida (Danish aid agency), Finnida (Finnish aid agency), Norad (Norwegian aid agency), and the World Bank.[42] By 2006, nearly half of all of all Tanzania's JFM agreements were signed in the Morogoro region alone.

One of the Kitulang'halo JFM communities, Maseyu, is included in this study's sample. In Maseyu, villagers' main management partner is the central government, represented by FBD's Regional Catchment Forest, which is based in Morogoro. The government's interest, at least putatively, is to conserve this important water catchment forest. Due to the ecological and economic importance of this forest, interested parties also include Sokoine University of Agriculture (SUA) whose faculty and students use the forest for research. Additionally, private businesses and individuals exploit the forest for tourism, logging, and charcoal production. Finally, foreign NGOs and donors want to conserve the entire Eastern Arch Mountains range.

In sharp contrast to the Malagasy case, actors' interests did not align in favor of conserving Kitulang'halo forest in Maseyu, Tanzania. As an indication, Pfliegner reports that several years into Maseyu's JFM initiative, no Joint Management Agreement (JMA)—the legal backbone of collaborative management—was signed despite clear governmental guidelines to this effect.[43] She also reports that Maseyu's Village Forest Committee (VFC), which was set up as FBD's counterpart, went "dormant" within six years of starting the JFM process.[44] Why did villagers' enthusiasm for this project wane? To put it bluntly, the state failed to hold up its end of the bargain. FBD never came up with the money and field equipment that it promised Maseyu's VFC members in compensation for their monitoring activities.

This begs the question: if the state was interested in conserving this area, why did this collaborative project ultimately fail? The main answer is that state actors had multiple, conflicting interests around Kitulang'halo forest, some of which were incompatible with forest conservation. On multiple occasions, survey respondents said that members of the local and regional government were "in cahoots" with charcoal and timber producers who harvested illegally from the forest. Although my research assistant and I could not verify these allegations, it was evident from walking from hamlet to hamlet, speaking to villagers and SUA faculty, and traveling along the Morogoro-Dar es Salaam road that plenty of timber and charcoal came out of Kitulang'halo.

Opportunities to exploit the forest (illegally) for profit create incentives that undermine forest conservation. This is true for both state representatives and members of the local government and is reflected in FBD staff's reluctance to follow through with the JFM process. It is also reflected in the relationship between villagers and those in charge of managing the forest. In a nutshell, the relationship is based on mutual distrust: villagers view everyone in charge of managing the forest (including VFC members) as corrupt and greedy, and FBD staff view villagers as incapable of forest management, which they consider a science. Convinced that farmers are below them, state representatives simply refuse to view them as partners or co-managers. Thus, the better, more profitable alternative is to continue engaging in resource capture, often to the detriment of villagers' welfare. In this regard, a Maseyu farmer's words are telling: "We need people of faith to take charge. These people [everyone associated with the state] have no fear of God. As a result, they steal with impunity." Pfliegner and Moshi expressed farmers' sentiment of helplessness and alienation slightly differently: "Villagers feel that the representatives of the forest administration and village leaders have put a committee [VFC] into place without leaving the villagers with the means to control them... nobody is controlling what they are taking out of the forest."[45]

Thus, despite the fact that Tanzania's institutional framework is among the best for collaborative forest management and there has been plenty of support (especially financial) for JFM initiatives, deforestation persists. This is not to suggest that JFM forests have experienced no improvements, especially compared to forests that have remained under exclusive state management.[46] But conservation outcomes have simply not been commensurate with CBNRM investments, primarily because actors' interests did not align with conservation goals at the outset.

Case 3: The Mpigi District Forest Estate, Uganda

Located near Lake Victoria, in the south-central part of Uganda, Mpigi District's forest estate is made up of CFRs, communal forests, private forests, and at least one sacred forest. The forest estate covers about 36,000 hectares, and Mpigi was a pilot district for the 1993 decentralization experiments mentioned above. In a 2007 study, Banana et al. investigated the reasons for variable effectiveness of decentralized forest management across nine sample forests. The forests selected for the study represent all legal categories. They were sampled throughout three phases of the country's tumultuous decentralization process: before 1993, in 1994–1995, and after 1995, then forest conditions were classified as "rapidly degrading," "degrading," "improving," and "stable."[47]

To identify factors that positively affect forest conditions, it is useful to focus on the Mpanga Strict Nature Reserve ("stable"), the Namungo Private Forest ("stable"), and the Kizzikibbi Forest Reserve whose conditions went from "degrading" to "improving." For Mpanga forest, the authors identify EU funding and high monitoring and enforcement capabilities as key factors behind successful conservation. They note, for instance, that this forest alone was granted seven forest guards while the rest of the forest estate, i.e., eight forests, shared fifteen forest guards. As a result, minimal community involvement was noted in this particular case, which makes it less than ideal for assessing co-management efforts. The case indicates, however, that high financial investments (by means of foreign assistance) can help deforestation.

Paradoxically, the private forest of Namungo better helps understand the merits of collaborative management in that the forest owner, Mr. Namungo, works closely with local government authorities and neighboring communities to strike a balance between exploitation and conservation. It is important to note, however, that Mr. Namungo is "conservation minded" and has the financial means and legitimacy to monitor harvesting levels and enforce forest rules as a sub-county chief of the Buganda kingdom. Nevertheless, this is a private forest whose management success relies on the owner's willingness to cooperate with local communities and state authorities, on the one hand, and his personal values, which favor conservation, on the other hand.

Finally, in Kizzikibbi Forest Reserve forest conditions went from "degraded" to "improving" due primarily to communities', local councilors' and the DFO's awareness that forest resources were disappearing. This collective awareness resulted in agreed upon conservation measures that were collectively executed, resulting in improvements in forest conditions. This positive outcome was possible because all who had a stake in forest conservation had the opportunity to participate in decision-making, notably regarding harvesting rules for commercial fuelwood (charcoal and firewood) and timber.

What we learn from the positive conservation outcomes for these three Mpigi District forests confirms what we learned from Madagascar, namely that conservation requires recognition–on the part of various forest managers at different decision-making levels–that forest degradation is overall more costly than beneficial. It also requires mobilizing financial and human resources (i.e., forest guards) to carry out monitoring and rule enforcement activities. In Arivonimamo (Madagascar) and Mpanga (Uganda), external funding from *Coopération Suisse* and the European Union, respectively, was necessary to mobilize the resources needed to discourage overharvesting. The funding need not come from outside actors, however. In Uganda, Mr. Namungo self-financed monitoring activities and reduced the cost of monitoring by involving local councilors and forest users from surrounding communities in management decisions.

Thus interests aligned when managing partners recognized the nefarious effects of forest degradation (put differently, a crisis point was reached), when they shared decision-making power regarding rules regulating resource access and uses, and when financial and human resources were mobilized to carry out monitoring and enforcement activities, thereby discouraging non-compliance. Where these conditions were met, conservation was possible.[48]

Conclusion

Studies of CBNRM experiments throughout the developing world consistently deliver a bleak message: if they are not in some state of disrepair, they have failed.[49] These three countries' experiences are no exception. As this chapter has shown, achieving forest conservation by way of CBNRM is more challenging than one would think. We have seen that success was achieved in Madagascar, but not in Tanzania. Results were mixed in Uganda. What explains these divergent outcomes?

Proponents of the community attributes theory would predict project failure where the local community was misconstrued as small, spatially bound, homogeneous, and made up of members with common interests. Of the three cases discussed in this chapter, Madagascar had success in Arivonimamo's *tapia* forest. In the context of GCF contracts, local communities, or COBAs, are legally defined as associations comprising "group[s] of *people with common objectives*" whose "inhabitant[s] resid[e] *within the limits of the territory* of the basic community."[50] In this case, local communities were "misdefined" exactly as Agrawal and Gibson caution against. And yet the CBNRM project succeeded. This particular project's COBAs had a common interest, saving the local economy, and a shared goal of restoring the silkworms' natural environment through forest conservation.

These communities were also spatially defined since they lived where *tapia* trees grow and where silkworms can thrive, i.e., on a specific territory of Madagascar's highlands. Thus success allows for some of the "wrong" community characteristics to be present, which suggests that community attributes alone cannot fully predict outcomes. The Ugandan case makes this point abundantly clear. Kizzikibbi, a CFR, went from "degraded" to "improving" even though no clear definition, legal or other, exists for local communities in the context of CFM. A review of scholarly articles on CBNRM experiments in Uganda yielded eleven terms for "local community."[51] One article's abstract, in fact, contained three of the terms to refer to the same unit![52] This indicates that success can happen regardless of how community is defined and operationalized in the context of a specific CBNRM project. Thus "community attributes," as a variable, has limited explanatory power.

Cultural explanations offer a second possibility. Recall that those who claim that culture matters argue that successful CBNRM projects build upon institutions grounded in cultural beliefs about nature. Although this proposition seems reasonable, it is difficult to see how culture explains success vs. failure across cases since CBNRM sites are selected on the basis of local communities' proximity to forests, and thus, presumably local cultural beliefs exist wherever CBNRM is attempted. Of course, it is true that local beliefs about forests are not equally represented across space and time. For instance, migratory flows can influence or even change local beliefs about nature.

This was the case in Andranomaintso, near Zombitse National Parc in Madagascar (see Chapter 2). There, economic interests trumped Bara values about the initially sacred forest shortly after immigrants settled in the area. But if we consider the opposite outcomes of CBNRM projects described in this chapter, cultural beliefs about the forest were present in both Arivonimamo (Madagascar) and Maseyu (Tanzania). What made the difference in these cases was not the existence of cultural beliefs per se, but the interests that those representing the communities (COBAs in Arivonimamo and VFC in Maseyu) defended as government officials' interlocutors. In Maseyu, members of the VCF were members of the community who nonetheless abandoned their community's interests to pursue personal gain. Although VCF members were products of the local culture, their personal interests trumped those of the greater community. Because this did not happen in Arivonimamo, interests converged in favor of forest conservation. Thus interest alignment accounts for these drastically different outcomes better than cultural explanations.

Unlike explanations based on community attributes and culture, those focused on scale may have more explanatory power. These posit that projects which integrate multiple scales of governance are more likely to succeed than those that do not. By design, CBNRM projects adhere to the principles of polycentric governance by connecting actors within and across multiple levels by means of institutional innovation. Arivonimamo's COBAs collaborate among themselves and with outsiders (foresters and the Swiss NGO) to manage the *tapia* forest. Likewise, forest-adjacent communities near Kizzikibbi forest have collaborated with Ugandan foresters from multiple administrative levels to come up with a sound management plan for this particular forest. The same is true of Namungo forest: Mr. Namungo worked closely with surrounding communities and LC1-level foresters to secure his forest's sustainability.

Clearly, collaborative management yielded positive results in these cases, suggesting that the theory of governance scale is helpful. If integrating multiple governance scales were sufficient, however, all CBNRM projects would succeed since all are based on the very principle of multilevel collaborative management. Yet, as we saw in Maseyu (Tanzania), the CBNRM approach failed to stop deforestation. This, I argue, is because the scale argument does not adequately capture interest alignment. As we saw previously, at each level of governance interests exist whereby those who have power to control forest access (with associated benefits) do not easily relinquish it to other actors. Near Maseyu, for instance, the local forest committees abandoned local communities and joined forces with corrupt foresters to capture the financial benefits of illegal harvesting. Sometimes these interests are so entrenched that no institutional innovation can overcome the free rider's problem, thereby hampering collective action. So, while multi-scale governance is theoretically sound, unlike interest alignment this variable cannot fully answer the basic question of why some CBNRM projects succeed while others fail.

Indeed, interest alignment holds more theoretical leverage than many of its alternatives. The three cases examined have shown that where key actors' interests aligned, co-management resulted in effective forest conservation. Where interests misaligned, co-management yielded disappointing results. This begs the question: what is so difficult about aligning interests?

Four principal reasons emerge from the CBNRM experiments described in this chapter: first, the principle of decentralized forest governance was, by and large, a foreign idea. In the three locales examined in this chapter, CBNRM projects were designed and executed in ways that privileged conservation defined mainly by Westerners. Where local communities did not see eye to eye with conservation "cowboys," local communities became effectively disempowered and collaboration did not yield conservation.[53]

Second, there was no tradition and thus practice of collaborative governance between the state and local communities, even in Tanzania where Nyerere's *ujamaa* experiments created a hierarchy of decision-making powers linking all administrative levels, from the national to the village. Decades of centralized government under colonial rule, first, and authoritarian rule, later, precluded the emergence of a political culture of local community participation that could meet the expectations of CBNRM projects. Under these adverse circumstances, interest alignment could happen only under exceptional conditions.

Third, rather than building on existing institutions, the process of decentralization relied on new ones, creating new official hierarchies of decision-making and reconfiguring power relations especially at the local level. This process of power reconfiguration required adaptation, which delayed involved parties' responsiveness. Whereas local elites, notably at the national level, were quick to respond to foreigners' expectations, at the village level resource users took longer to respond mostly due to lack of information regarding the costs and benefits of decentralization. Under these circumstances, interest alignment was extraordinarily difficult to achieve.

Finally, rather than building from the ground up, on the basis of successful experiments at the local level, decentralization was paradoxically initiated at and carried out, as a blueprint, from the top.[54] As a result, decentralized resource management has, overall, brought about modest positive change in terms of aligning the interests of environmental actors in ways that have effectively helped forest conservation. Consequently, forest conservation has eluded conservationists.

Notes

1. Uphoff, Norman. "Community-Based Natural Resource Management: Connecting Micro and Macro Processes, and People With Their Environments." International Workshop on Community-Based Natural Resource Management Proceedings, World Bank, Washington, DC, 1998· 15
2. Dressler, W., B. Büscher, M. Schoon, D. Brockington, T. Hayes, C. Kull, J. McCarthy, and K. Shrestha, "From Hope to Crisis and Back Again? A Critical History of the Global CBNRM Narrative." *Environmental Conservation* 37.1 (2010): 5–15; Measham, Thomas G., and Jared A. Lumbasi. "Success Factors for Community-Based Natural Resource Management (CBNRM): Lessons from Kenya and Australia." *Environmental Management* 52.3 (2013): 649–659.

3. In the three countries, as elsewhere in Africa and the rest of the non-Western world, efforts to connect environmental actors across levels of decision-making were carried out by way of projects conceived and implemented in the larger context of decentralization policies carried out in the 1990s. African governments' efforts to decentralize governance received substantial support from western actors, including governments, international financial institutions, and conservation NGOs mainly because the principles guiding them were in line with liberal democratic ideals, the main one being endowing the people (*demos*) with political power.
4. Measham and Lumbasi (2013), 658.
5. Agrawal and Gibson (2001). *Communities and the Environment*.
6. McDermott, Melanie Hughes. "Invoking Community: Indigenous People and Ancestral Domain in Palawan, the Philippines," in Agrawal and Gibson (2001), 32–62.
7. Agrawal and Gibson (2001), 7–15. Here institutions are defined as rules and norms that govern resource users' behaviors.
8. Byers, Bruce A., Robert N. Cunliffe, and Andrew T. Hudak. "Linking the Conservation of Culture and Nature: A Case Study of Sacred Forests in Zimbabwe." *Human Ecology* 29.2 (2001): 187–218.
9. Byers et al. (2001), 192.
10. Horning, Nadia R. (2008), 131.
11. Byers et al. (2001), 213, authors' emphasis.
12. Uphoff and Langholz (1998).
13. Sayer, Jeffrey, and Bruce Campbell. *The Science of Sustainable Development: Local Livelihoods and the Global Environment*. Cambridge University Press (2004), 80, authors' emphasis.
14. Maasai land in East Africa is a case in point: because Kenya's and Tanzania's state borders cut through this ecological and social ecosystem, what is "local" (community x) is also national (countries x, y) and even regional (East African plains).
15. Herring, Ronald J. "Authority and Scale in Political Ecology: Some Cautions on Localism." Geisler, Charles C., John Schelhas, and Eva Wollenberg. *Biological Diversity: Balancing Interests Through Adaptive Collaborative Management*. New York: CRC Press, 2001, 188.
16. Andersson, Krister P., and Elinor Ostrom. "Analyzing Decentralized Resource Regimes from a Polycentric Perspective." *Policy Sciences* 41.1 (2008): 78.
17. In the context of tropical Latin America, Collins (1986) observes that smallholder farmers base their environmental decisions on opportunities and constraints that higher-level decision makers create for them regarding "land tenure, credit policies, titling, and other institutional factors [that] condition the resource management strategies of the producers who work the land," 1.

18. Van de Walle, Nicolas. *African Economies and the Politics of Permanent Crisis, 1979–1999.* Cambridge University Press (2001), 162–163.
19. Blaikie, Piers. "Is Small Really Beautiful? Community-Based Natural Resource Management in Malawi and Botswana." *World Development* 34.11 (2006), 1942.
20. President Ravalomanana of Madagascar, whose political strategies are discussed in Chapter 3, is a clear example of this type of calculating individual.
21. Agrawal, Arun, and Jesse Ribot. "Accountability in Decentralization: A Framework with South Asian and West African Cases." *The Journal of Developing Areas* 33.4 (Summer 1999), 2, emphasis added.
22. Beck, Peter A. "Conservation, Development and Collaboration: Analyzing Institutional Incentives for Participatory Conservation in Uganda." PhD Diss., Indiana University, 2000.
23. GCF stands for *Gestion Contractualisée des Forêts*, or contractual forest management.
24. Collas de Chatelperron (2007), pp. 45–53.
25. Blomley et al. (2010), p. 128.
26. Personal interview with Tom Blomley on 1 July 2009 in Dar Es Salaam.
27. CBFM takes place on village land; the central government's involvement is minimal, and the costs and benefits of management go to the owner (private individuals or groups). JFM, like GCF in Madagascar, allows communities to enter into agreements with the central or local government. Responsibilities for and benefits of management are shared. See Government of Tanzania. Forestry and Beekeeping Division "Participatory Forest Management in Tanzania: Facts and Figures," July 2006 available at http://www.tzonline.org/pdf/pfmstatus.pdf, accessed August 15, 2012.
28. Mbwambo et al. (2012), p. 98.
29. Hydén, Göran (1980).
30. Bernstein (1981), p. 45.
31. Hydén (1980), pp. 108–109.
32. Government of Uganda http://www.mwe.go.ug/index.php?option=com_content&view=article&id=116&Itemid=128, accessed August 12, 2012.
33. For various forest classifications and government institutions in charge of their management, see Chapter 2, especially Fig. 2.4.
34. Jagger (2010), pp. 107–108.
35. Turyahabwe and Banana (2008), p. 652.
36. Turyahabwe et al. (2006).
37. Turyahabwe et al. (n.d.), p. 53.
38. Ribot et al. (2006).
39. Beck (2000), pp. 67–71.

40. "*le souci majeur [est] de faire progresser le mieux-vivre de la population en améliorant les rapports Homme-Environnement, garantissant la durabilité de l'exploitation des ressources naturelles et le renforçant de l'emprise des communautés rurales dans les prises de décisions à différents niveaux à travers les projets.*" Translation: the main concern is to advance people's welfare by improving their relationship with the environment. Doing so secures the sustainable use of natural resources, and it integrates rural communities into the decision-making process across various levels through projects.
41. Randrianarisoa et al. (2010), pp. 249–250.
42. Blomley and Ramadhani (2006).
43. Pfliegner (2010), p. 89.
44. Ibid., p. 206.
45. Pfliegner and Moshi (2010), p. 19.
46. According to Blomley and colleagues, overall the quality of JFM forests has improved due to reduced disturbance and uncontrolled activity. The same cannot be said of non- JFM forests and CBFM sites.
47. Banana et al. (2007), p. 441.
48. One could argue that sharing decision-making power was not a necessary condition in Mpanga Strict Nature Reserve, where communities where minimally involved, robust financial and human resources served to compensate for this institutional shortcoming. It suggests that, compared to Namungo and Arivonimamo forests, Mpanga might be more vulnerable to overexploitation, especially if outside support ended.
49. Measham and Lumbasi (2013) and Dressler et al. (2010).
50. Pollini and Lassoie (2011), pp. 5–6, author's emphasis.
51. The terms were: "local communities," "local community organizations," "local organizations," "local actors," "farmers," "village households," "local user groups," "villages adjacent to forests," "forest-adjacent communities," "LC1," and "village local councils."
52. Turyahabwe et al. (2006).
53. Dressler et al. (2010), p. 11.
54. Measham and Lumbasi (2013), 651.

Bibliography

Agrawal, Arun, and Clark C. Gibson, eds. *Communities and the Environment: Ethnicity, Gender and the State in Community-Based Conservation.* New Brunswick: Rutgers University Press, 2001.

Agrawal, Arun, and Jesse Ribot. "Accountability in Decentralization: A Framework with South Asian and West African Cases." *The Journal of Developing Areas* 33.4 (Summer 1999): 473–502.

Andersson, Krister P., and Elinor Ostrom. "Analyzing Decentralized Resource Regimes from a Polycentric Perspective." *Policy Sciences* 41.1 (2008): 71–93.

Banana, Abwoli Y., Nathan D. Vogt, Joseph Bahati, and William Gombya-Ssembajjwe. "Decentralized Governance and Ecological Health: Why Local Institutions Fail to Moderate Deforestation in Mpigi District of Uganda." *Scientific Research and Essay* 2.10 (2007): 434–445.

Beck, Peter A. "Conservation, Development and Collaboration: Analyzing Institutional Incentives for Participatory Conservation in Uganda." PhD Diss., Indiana University, 2000.

Bernstein, Henry. "Notes on State and Peasantry: the Tanzanian Case." *Review of African Political Economy* 8.21 (1981): 44–62.

Blaikie, Piers. "Is Small Really Beautiful? Community-Based Natural Resource Management in Malawi and Botswana." *World Development* 34.11 (2006): 1942–1957.

Blomley, Tom, Hadija Ramadhani, Yassin Mkwizu, and Adreas Böhringer, "Hidden Harvest: Unlocking the Economic Potential of Community-Based Forest Management in Tanzania." in German, Laura A., Alain Karsenty, and Anne-Marie Tiani, eds. *Governing Africa's Forests in a Globalized World*. London: Earthscan, 2010.

Blomley, Tom, Kerstin Pfliegner, Jaconia Isango, Eliakimu Zahabu, Antje Ahrends, and Neil Burgess. "Seeing the Wood for the Trees: An Assessment of the Impact of Participatory Forest Management on Forest Condition in Tanzania." *Oryx* 42.3 (2008): 380–391.

Blomley, Tom, and Hadija Ramadhani. "Going to Scale with Participatory Forest Management: Early Lessons from Tanzania 1." *International Forestry Review* 8.1 (2006): 93–100.

Byers, Bruce A., Robert N. Cunliffe, and Andrew T. Hudak. "Linking the conservation of culture and nature: a case study of sacred forests in Zimbabwe." *Human Ecology* 29.2 (2001): 187–218.

Chatelperron, Collas de. "L'état des lieux du transfert de gestion à fin 2003." *Le transfert de gestion à Madagascar, dix ans d'efforts: Tanteza*. Antananarivo: CIRAD, 2007: 47–54.

Collins, Jane L. "Smallholder Settlement of Tropical South America: the Social Causes of Ecological Destruction." *Human Organization* 45.1 (1986): 1–10.

Dressler, W., B. Büscher, M. Schoon, D. Brockington, T. Hayes, C. Kull, J. McCarthy, and K Shrestha. "From Hope to Crisis and Back Again? A Critical History of the Global CBNRM Narrative." *Environmental Conservation* 37.1 (2010): 5–15.

Government of Tanzania. Forestry and Beekeeping Division "Participatory Forest Management in Tanzania: Facts and Figures", July 2006 Available at http://www.tzonline.org/pdf/pfmstatus.pdf. Accessed August 15, 2012.

Government of Uganda. http://www.mwe.go.ug/index.php?option=com_content&view=article&id=116&Itemid=128. Accessed August 12, 2012.

Herring, Ronald J. "Authority and Scale in Political Ecology: Some Cautions on Localism," in Geisler, Charles C., John Schelhas, and Eva Wollenberg, eds. *Biological Diversity: Balancing Interests Through Adaptive Collaborative Management*. New York: CRC Press, 2001: 187–204.

Horning, Nadia R. "Behind Sacredness in Madagascar: Rules, Local Interests and Forest Conservation in Bara Country," in Sheridan, Michael J. and Celia Nyamweru, eds. *African Sacred Groves: Ecological Dynamics and Social Change*. Oxford: James Currey, 2008.

———. "The Cost of Ignoring Rules: Forest Conservation and Rural Livelihood Outcomes in Madagascar." *Forests, Trees and Livelihoods* 15.2 (2005): 149–166.

Hydén, Göran. *Beyond Ujamaa in Tanzania: Underdevelopment and an Uncaptured Peasantry*. Berkeley: University of California Press, 1980.

Jagger, Pamela. "Forest Sector Reforms, Livelihoods and Sustainability in Western Uganda," in German, Laura A., Alain Karsenty, and Anne-Marie Tiani, eds. *Governing Africa's Forests in a Globalized World*. London: Earthscan, 2010: 103–125.

Mbwambo, L., T. Eid, R. E. Malimbwi, E. Zahabu, G. C. Kajembe, and E. Luoga. "Impact of Decentralised Forest Management on Forest Resource Conditions in Tanzania." *Forests, Trees and Livelihoods* 21.2 (2012): 97–113.

McDermott, Melanie Hughes. "Invoking Community: Indigenous People and Ancestral Domain in Palawan, the Philippines," in Agrawal, Arun, and Clark C. Gibson, eds. *Communities and the Environment: Ethnicity, Gender and the State in Community-Based Conservation*. New Brunswick: Rutgers University Press, 2001: 32–62.

Measham, Thomas G., and Jared A. Lumbasi. "Success Factors for Community-Based Natural Resource Management (CBNRM): Lessons from Kenya and Australia." *Environmental Management* 52.3 (2013): 649–659.

Pfliegner, Kerstin. "The Impacts of Joint Forest Management on Forest Condition, Livelihoods and Governance: Case Studies from Morogoro Region in Tanzania." PhD Diss., University of East Anglia, 2010.

Pfliegner, Kerstin and Ernest Moshi. "Is Joint Forest Management Viable in Protection Forest Reserves? Experiences from Morogoro Region." *The Arc Journal*, Issue 21 (2010) Available at http://www.tfcg.org/downloads/Arc-Journal-21.pdf. Accessed August 15, 2012.

Pollini, Jacques, and James P. Lassoie. "Trapping Farmer Communities Within Global Environmental Regimes: The Case of the GELOSE Legislation in Madagascar." *Society & Natural Resources* 24.8 (2011): 814–830.

Randrianarisoa, Aimée, Estelle Raharinaivosoa, and Annette Kolff, "Decentralized Forest Resource Management in the Highlands of Madagascar: The Cases of Arivonimamo and Merikanjaka," in German, Laura A., Alain Karsenty, and Anne-Marie Tiani, eds. *Governing Africa's Forests in a Globalized World*. Earthscan, 2010: 249–50.

Ribot, Jesse C., Arun Agrawal, and Anne M. Larson. "Recentralizing while Decentralizing: How National Governments Reappropriate Forest Resources." *World Development* 34.11 (2006): 1864–1886.
Sayer, Jeffrey, and Bruce Campbell. *The Science of Sustainable Development: Local Livelihoods and the Global Environment.* Cambridge: Cambridge University Press, 2004.
Turyahabwe, Nelson, and Abwoli Y. Banana. "An Overview of History and Development of Forest Policy and Legislation in Uganda." *International Forestry Review* 10.4 (2008): 641–656.
Turyahabwe, N., C. J. Geldenhuys, S. Watts, and J. Obua. "Local Organisations and Decentralised Forest Management in Uganda: Roles, Challenges and Policy Implications." *International Forestry Review.* 9.2 (2006): 581–596.
Turyahabwe, Nelson, Jacob Godfrey Agea, Mnason Twejeyo, and Susan Balaba Tumwebaze. "Collaborative Forest Management in Uganda: Benefits, Implementation Challenges and Future Directions." n.d. Available at http://cdn.intechopen.com/pdfs-wm/35230.pdf. Accessed September 16, 2014.
Uphoff, Norman. "Community-Based Natural Resource Management: Connecting Micro and Macro Processes, and People with Their Environments." International Workshop on Community-Based Natural Resource Management Proceedings, World Bank, Washington, DC. 1998.
Uphoff, Norman, and Jeff Langholz. "Incentives for Avoiding the Tragedy of the Commons." *Environmental Conservation.* 25.3 (1998): 251–261.
Van de Walle, Nicolas. *African Economies and the Politics of Permanent Crisis, 1979–1999.* Cambridge: Cambridge University Press, 2001: 162–163.

CHAPTER 5

Epilogue

We are very fond of blaming the poor for destroying the environment. But often it is the powerful, including governments, that are responsible.
Wangari Maathai

Wangari Maathai will likely be remembered as an environmental activist who inspired fellow Kenyans to plant trees. Her "little thing," she once said, "is planting trees." In reality, she did more than a little thing, and she did more than plant trees. Instead, she sowed the seed of democratic governance in a country where most people simply had no say in how their society should be governed. By giving people a voice in governance, she unveiled the political nature of deforestation. This is one of the most important contributions that her activism has made.

Just as Wangari Maathai's activism went beyond fighting deforestation, this book is not solely about deforestation. Rather, it is about the political forces behind continued deforestation despite efforts to control it. I have argued in the preceding chapters that deforestation continues to vex activists, politicians, scholars, and ordinary citizens not because it has been ignored, but because it has been poorly understood. Against common explanations relating to economics, demographics, institutional shortcomings, and the global system of trade, aid, and debt, etc., I have examined deforestation through the prism of politics, focusing on how key decision-makers' interests form, how these interests align or misalign regarding forest conservation at critical levels of decision-making, and how the institutions that result from decision-makers' interactions effectively control, or fail to control, people's behavior vis-à-vis forest resources. In short, to tame deforestation key actors' interests must align simultaneously at the national and local levels for institutions to be effective tools of conservation. Thus what best explains the puzzle of persistent deforestation in light of efforts to control it is the failure to identify the specific and limited conditions under which forest conservation is likely.

THE PURPOSE OF THIS BOOK

This book has detailed the process of interest formation and institutional development at two distinct levels of environmental decision-making: the local and the national. It has done this in three African countries experiencing deforestation to varying degrees: Madagascar, Tanzania, and Uganda. Three prevailing assumptions about forest conservation were put to the test, namely that (1) state-sanctioned rules deter deforestation at the local level; (2) foreign aid encourages conservation at the national level; and (3) the national and local levels of decision-making work in a symbiotic manner whereby outcomes at one level affect decisions at the other in ways that encourage conservation behavior. However, for reasons explained earlier and summarized below, these operating assumptions beg to be revisited.

ASSUMPTION ONE: STATE-SANCTIONED RULES DETER DEFORESTATION AT THE LOCAL LEVEL

To what extent do state-sanctioned regulations deter deforestation at the local level? In fact, what rules apply at this level, and what motivates compliance and non-compliance with these rules to explain variable conservation outcomes across communities of forest users? Given that the effectiveness of rules is contingent upon users' willingness to conform with them, Chapter 2 explored the compliance calculus that farmers perform as they contemplate conserving or exploiting forest resources.

Two principal findings emerged from this chapter. First, the rules that apply at the local levels are hybrids of formal legislation and community-devised rules. In no communities encountered throughout Madagascar, Uganda, and Tanzania was it the case that formal legislation applied single-handedly. Instead, communities absorb elements of formal legislation they deem likely to complement their own local institutions within their respective social and natural environments. Second, farmers' compliance with conservation rules is motivated by three important factors: (1) the perceived legitimacy of rules and of those who enforce them; (2) the quality of rule enforcement (are rules enforced consistently and in predictable fashion?); and (3) the extent of social cohesion as measured by local leaders' legitimacy.

A systematic examination of local-level conservation scenarios reveals that forest conservation is most likely where and when key actors' interests properly align to create incentives for forest users to comply with conservation rules. Interests align where and when local circumstances allow formal legislation and local rules and norms to be complementary. More often than not, this complementarity is not spontaneous. Instead, it results from the deliberate and careful absorption of "external" (formal) rules into the local institutional fabric. Thus, to assume that conservation will happen where and when formal legislation is enacted is facile and misleading.

ASSUMPTION TWO: FOREIGN AID ENCOURAGES CONSERVATION AT THE NATIONAL LEVEL

To tackle the second conservation assumption, Chapter 3 turned to environmental politics at the national level, where environmental policies are negotiated and enacted. At this level interest alignment is also critical, the key players are domestic (African governments dominated by the executive) as well as international (donors and conservation NGOs), and the operating assumption is that foreign assistance is necessary to build or reinforce African states' institutional capacities. What typically results from key players' interactions at the national level is an impressive array of environmental institutions put in place ostensibly to fight deforestation and other forms of environmental degradation.

On the surface, the institutional proliferation these interactions produce reflects governments' commitment to conservation, which foreign actors push by financing institutional innovation. But a careful examination of processes at play suggests a different reality, one in which African governments and donors depend on each other to advance interests hardly limited to conservation. On the one hand, African executives capitalize on their countries' extraordinary natural assets and foreigners' urge to conserve them to attract foreign aid and expand their clientelistic networks to stay in power. Donors and conservation NGOs, for their part, utilize conservation funding to infiltrate domestic politics and bend African governments' policy agendas in favor of their own visions of political and economic progress.

How the three presidents discussed in Chapter 3 maneuvered environmental politics resulted in three distinct conservation outcomes in Madagascar, Tanzania, and Uganda. Particularly symptomatic of conservation politics gone awry is the case of Uganda whose impressive institutional proliferation, far from controlling deforestation, exacerbated it. Lest Uganda is cast aside as an exception, Madagascar and Tanzania's lackluster conservation performance despite institutional proliferation must serve as a reminder that institutional activity in the environmental sector cannot be equated with conservation commitments. That Madagascar has done better than Tanzania, which has done better than Uganda is, it bears pointing out, all relative. The reality is, in all three countries conservation outcomes have not been commensurate with institutional investments, far from it in fact. Thus, the notion that foreign aid helps forest conservation rests on little more than naiveté.

The debilitating effects of environmental politics on African political systems must not be underestimated. Indeed, how environmental institutions are negotiated at the national level shapes politics in three important ways. First, government commitment to environmental protection hinges on securing foreign aid in exchange for compliance with donors' visions of what constitutes development. This compromises Africans' ability to make decisions free of external influence and interference. Put differently, it erodes African sovereignty and perpetuates state weakness.

Second, donors can push through their conservation agendas only with African governments' acquiescence and support. Thus, they depend on African decision makers to advance their own interests. This creates a situation of mutual dependence that alienates ordinary Africans from the political process, thereby widening the gap between those who govern and those who are governed. That is, it widens the gap between African leaders and their polities. Put differently, foreign interference perverts African social contracts.

Finally, African leaders take advantage of foreign aid injections to expand rent-seeking opportunities. In doing so, they consolidate their political power (with all accompanying material privileges). The political outcomes that result from manipulating conservation aid clash with the putative goals of conservation policies, namely public welfare, of which environmental conservation is part. African politicians pursue their political agendas by enacting environmentally friendly legislation, adopting environmental policies, devising strategies (supposedly to meet environmental goals), sanctioning conservation programs and projects, and creating new institutions, all largely funded by foreigners. The multiplication of environmental institutions and projects that results generates opportunities for select individuals, foreign and national, to pursue personal interests ranging from material and professional to political. Ultimately, these dynamics create incentives for key actors to maintain the status quo, making actual conservation goals and outcomes irrelevant, at best. In sum, conservation politics thwarts progress.

Assumption Three: The National and Local Levels of Decision-Making Work Symbiotically

The third "truth" driving conservation politics in Africa is that local and national levels work in a symbiotic fashion whereby conservation outcomes at the local level drive decisions at the national level, and vice versa. This symbiotic relationship is assumed to be conducive to conservation. In reality, these two levels work in tandem, connecting only sporadically. As discussed in Chapter 4, more commonly observed is a chronic disconnect between the two levels of environmental decision-making. Far from facilitating interest alignment, this disconnect hinders it. As a result, decentralized forest management has scarcely been achieved, as evidenced by the high number of failed CBRNM projects.

By examining factors behind these projects' mixed record in the three countries included in this study, it becomes clear that interest alignment does not happen by the stroke of a presidential pen. Decentralized resource management can help interest alignment and forest conservation, but only under specific conditions related to implementing CBNRM-like projects in the right environment. In particular, to succeed CBNRM initiatives must target communities that are ready and willing to incorporate outside institutions into their own local institutional landscapes because they see this strategy as advancing their interests. Not all local communities have reached this stage of institutional development. Nor, in fact, are most equipped to open their local institutional environment to outside institutions. Because this prerequisite is consistently overlooked, attempts to build bridges between the national and local levels often fail.

The three "truths" guiding Africa's environmental policies must be treated as illusions if forest conservation is to be achieved on the continent. This, however, is not likely to happen because conservation myths are the very foundation blocks upon which conservation politics have rested for decades. As such they have served the interests of the most powerful conservation actors, both foreign and domestic, who conveniently blame deforestation on the decisions and actions of local farmers—"the poor"—to escape proper scrutiny and avoid change.

Beyond Madagascar, Tanzania, and Uganda

Can interest alignment and misalignment explain persistent deforestation beyond the three cases included in this study? It is critical to address this question because deforestation is going unabated in various parts of the world, albeit not everywhere, and its costs are tremendous: biodiversity loss, climate change, food insecurity, loss of cultural identities, diseases, and conflicts all result from the loss of forest habitats. In Africa, both the Democratic Republic of Congo, a critical area where a significant share of the Congo Basin forests are located, and Cameroon are examples. Other parts of the continent are affected as well: Burundi in the Great Lakes region, Kenya in East Africa, Mauritania and Niger in the Sahel, Ethiopia and Somalia in the Horn, Comoros in the Indian Ocean, Nigeria, Togo, Benin, and Ghana in West Africa, and Zambia, Zimbabwe, and Botswana in Southern Africa. No corner of the continent is spared. That said, deforestation is not an African phenomenon.[1] Most notorious are the examples of the Brazilian Amazon and Mexico's Chiapas, but also Indonesia and Malaysia in Southeast Asia, and Sri Lanka in South Asia.[2]

Because these regions are different ecologically, culturally, geographically, politically, economically, demographically, etc., one would not expect them to face similar challenges. Yet deforestation afflicts them all. The juxtaposition of these two realities suggests that the politics driving deforestation are similar across vastly different areas. Andrew Hurrell's analysis of the politics of Amazonian deforestation, for instance, makes it amply clear that local, national, and international actors' interests drive deforestation in Brazil. Not unlike Africa, Brazil's deforestation problems persist in the midst of a diverse set of vested interests.[3] Similarly, Peter Dauvergne argues that "the process that leads to deforestation in Indonesia cannot be fully understood without examining how

Indonesian politics and the attitudes of decision makers, with support from the international system, shape and drive the various factors which contribute to deforestation."[4]

As an analytical tool, interest alignment transcends geographical, cultural, and ecological borders because it rests on what comprises all political systems: power players, interests, and institutions.

Beyond Deforestation

As a theoretical framework, interest alignment has shown some utility, notably in Stephen Walt's work on alliance formation in times of war or, to remain in Africa, Kim Yi Dionne's study of HIV/AIDS interventions. Walt's interest is in explaining and predicting alliance strategies—balancing vs. bandwagoning—with implications for world security.[5] Dionne, for her part, sheds light on the ineffectiveness of HIV/AIDS interventions in Africa by pointing to the misalignment of donors' and beneficiaries' policy priorities.[6] Despite its utility, this framework has not been widely applied to the study of social and political issues, including resource governance. This book fills this gap by showing how interest alignment (or misalignment) shapes institutions that create incentives for key players to conserve resources or not.

The framework could, in fact, extend its utility to explaining and predicting other public "bads" affecting Africa and other parts of the world. Those include the brain drain that hurts Africa's capacity to deal with its problems using its own resources; conflicts such as the ones currently ravaging eastern DRC, Syria, and Yemen; human trafficking of the sort Europe is increasingly experiencing; global drug trafficking that is wrecking havoc in multiple societies; or piracy that disrupts global trade, etc.

These public bads have one thing in common: key players who stand to gain from maintaining them. In this regard, Ken Menkhaus's analysis of the advent of warlordism is useful: the purpose of wars, Menkhaus claims, is no longer to win but to "create and maintain environments of lawlessness and violence from which certain groups and individuals profiteer."[7] As is the case with deforestation, the current issues mentioned here create, and also result from, situations where individual advancement trumps the public good and where institutions put in place to fight these problems are rendered ineffectual not by the absence of institutions per se, but by the lack of institutionalism.

Moving Forward?

On April 28, 2015, the government of Madagascar made permanent the status of forty-eight new protected areas. No doubt this initiative was taken to signal the new government's intention to get back on track with conservation after a disastrous four-year hiatus of lawlessness that stripped the island of its most precious wood species at the hands of unscrupulous international buyers.[8] Encouraging as the decision may be to conservationists, a key question was, once again, ignored: How many of these new permanent protected areas are cases of aligned interests at the three critical levels of environmental decision-making? As seen throughout this book, answering this very question is the critical first step toward raising the prospect of conserving these areas. Failure lurks when conservation efforts target locales where local communities' interests may not align with those of the state. Skipping this first step compromises the chances of adopting adequate conservation measures later on. And it perpetuates a situation in which political expediency trumps conservation.

Proceeding incrementally, using local conservation interest as a criterion for selecting protected areas would allow the state to invest its scarce resources more wisely simply because it would secure interest alignment. The notion of proceeding incrementally—from the bottom up—no doubt will leave many skeptical, even agitated, since science has long determined the choice of protected areas. The skeptics' view is understandable: once biodiversity is gone, it is gone forever. Therefore, it is risky to intervene only where and when local interests align with those of the state, leaving the fate of critical areas to local actors' readiness. But is it reasonable to expect conservation to happen, i.e., for local interests to align with those of outside players, by the stroke of a legal pen? In fact, what in the history of Africa's protected areas gives reason to assume that local interests will change once the state declares that a forest has official protected status? If this is a good strategy, why is there still deforestation in and around protected areas the world over?[9]

It is common for conservation practitioners to advocate increasing awareness about the importance of conserving natural resources at the community level. Such awareness building has been attempted by means of enriching primary school curricula with environmental conservation, sending foresters and other conservation agents out to village communities, and broadcasting messages about conservation through various media outlets and even churches. In principle, these efforts are commendable. In practice, however, they require a tremendous investment in resources that are notoriously scarce in Africa: human and financial capital as well as political will. Besides overestimating state capacity, this strategy assumes that local communities are not aware of the danger that environmental degradation presents to their livelihoods. Most of them are. Finally, it assumes that these communities have the power to repel outsiders who come into their local territories to extract resources, often against locals' better judgment.

Local resource users are tuned to their natural environment and even if they lack "scientific knowledge," they are capable of recognizing a situation of disequilibrium. And it is this awareness that something is out of balance, that a crisis point has been reached, that prompts conservation interest and action. Because their survival depends on sound resource management, these communities are veritable conservation catalysts. By capitalizing on situations where local communities are interested in conserving resources, whatever their motivations may be, outside players could find receptive partners in them. We saw in previous chapters that local communities have superior monitoring capabilities. They happen to be where the resources are located and so, they have real power to steer local users' behaviors toward conservation. The benefits of conservation that would accrue over time in these catalyst communities could inspire surrounding communities to follow suit. And so, even though it may be risky to leave conservation to local actors' readiness, the reality is that this option may be the only viable one.

Aligning interests is challenging and it does not guarantee conservation success. Why pursue it, then? The answer to this question is that interest alignment can be achieved under the right conditions. When achieved, it significantly raises the prospect of protecting the environment. Thus, Africa's conservation efforts must not be seen as doomed. Currently, several restoration projects are happening in Africa in reaction to the deforestation's detrimental effects. To combat desertification, twenty African nations are collaborating to plant trees from Senegal to Djibouti, covering 11 countries over 4800 miles for a projected total of 45,000 sq. miles.[10] Although the media have described this initiative as involving African governments and international financial partners, the fact that Senegalese citizens are the ones actively planting trees opens up the opportunity for interests to align and for such an ambitious project to succeed.[11] The key players in this project stand to benefit from its success in varied ways. The most important fact is that local communities see it in *their* interest to plant trees and maintain forests. Because this is the case, the key condition of interest alignment is met. Granted, this is a case of forest generation and not forest conservation per se, the fact is that forests are being established in the Saharan desert and that local communities are benefitting from this development in material and social ways. For this reason, they are willing to invest in the forests' maintenance with the support of national- and international-level players. Thanks to initiatives such as this one and several others (e.g. the restoration of Lake Chad spearheaded by Nigeria[12]), we know that the potential for positive change exists, which gives reason for hope.

Notes

1. Food and Agriculture Organization of the United Nations. "Managing Forests for the Future." http://www.fao.org/docrep/014/am859e/am859e08.pdf, accessed May 26, 2015.
2. Schiffman, Richard. "Amazon Deforestation Soars After a Decade of Stability." http://www.newscientist.com/article/dn27056-amazon-deforestation-soars-after-a-decade-of-stability.html, accessed May 11, 2015.
3. Hurrell, Andrew. "The Politics of Amazonian Deforestation." *Journal of Latin American Studies* 23.01 (1991): 197–215.
4. Dauvergne, Peter. "The Politics of Deforestation in Indonesia." *Pacific Affairs* 66.4 (Winter 1993–1994): 498.
5. Walt, Stephen M. *The Origins of Alliance*. Cornell University Press, 1990.
6. Dionne, Kim Yi. "Local Demand for a Global Intervention: Policy Priorities in the Time of AIDS." *World Development* 40.12 (2012): 2474.
7. Menkhaus, Ken. "Warlordism and the War on Terrorism." *Foreign Policy in Focus* 26 (2001).
8. Environmental Investigation Agency (EAI). "Illegal Logging and Trade of Madagascar's Precious Wood." https://www.youtube.com/watch?v=q-7gaSpcyAXI, accessed April 28, 2015. See also Schuurman, Derek, and Porter P. Lowry II. "The Madagascar Rosewood Massacre." *Madagascar Conservation & Development* 4.2 (2009): 98–102.
9. Patel, Erik R. "Logging of Rare Rosewood and Palissandre (Dalbergia spp.) Within Marojejy National Park, Madagascar." *Madagascar Conservation & Development* 2.1 (2007): 12–13.
10. British Broadcasting Corporation. Web. http://www.bbc.com/news/10344622, accessed December 28, 2017.
11. *The Guardian*. Web. https://www.theguardian.com/environment/2012/jul/12/senegal-great-green-wall, accessed December 28, 2017.

12. *Premium Times.* Web. https://www.premiumtimesng.com/news/more-news/253690-nigeria-host-conference-restoration-lake-chad.html, accessed January 2, 2018.

Bibliography

British Broadcasting Corporation. Web. http://www.bbc.com/news/10344622. Accessed December 28, 2017.

Dauvergne, Peter. "The Politics of Deforestation in Indonesia." *Pacific Affairs* 66.4 (Winter 1993–1994): 497–518.

Environmental Investigation Agency (EAI). "Illegal Logging and Trade of Madagascar's Precious Wood." https://www.youtube.com/watch?v=q7gaSpcyAXI. Accessed April 28, 2015.

Food and Agriculture Organization of the United Nations. "Managing Forests for the Future." http://www.fao.org/docrep/014/am859e/am859e08.pdf. Accessed May 26, 2015.

Hurrell, Andrew. "The Politics of Amazonian Deforestation." *Journal of Latin American Studies* 23.01 (1991): 197–215.

Menkhaus, Ken. "Warlordism and the War on Terrorism." *Foreign Policy in Focus* 26 (2001).

Patel, Erik R. "Logging of Rare Rosewood and Palissandre (*Dalbergia* spp.) within Marojejy National Park, Madagascar." *Madagascar Conservation & Development* 2.1 (2007): 11–16.

Premium Times. Web. https://www.premiumtimesng.com/news/more-news/253690-nigeria-host-conference-restoration-lake-chad.html. Accessed January 2, 2018.

Schiffman, Richard. "Amazon Deforestation Soars After a Decade of Stability" http://www.newscientist.com/article/dn27056-amazon-deforestation-soars-after-a-decade-of-stability.html. Accessed May 11, 2015.

Schuurman, Derek, and Porter P. Lowry II. "The Madagascar Rosewood Massacre." *Madagascar Conservation & Development* 4.2 (2009): 98–102.

The Guardian. Web. https://www.theguardian.com/environment/2012/jul/12/senegal-great-green-wall. Accessed December 28, 2017.

Walt, Stephen M. *The Origins of Alliance.* Cornell University Press, 1990.

Index

A
African Development Bank, 6, 110
African Union, 1
Agrawal, Arun, 17, 137, 142, 154
Aid to Africa
 aid competition, 96–99
 overview, 93
 reasons for receiving, 94–96
Amani Nature Reserve, 47
ANAE *(Association Nationale d'Actions Environmentales)*, 104
Analavelona Sacred Forest, 45–51, 53–54, 56–59, 61–62, 66, 70, 73, 82, 137, 150
Andranoheza, 51
Andranomaintso, 51–58, 61
 Analavelona and, 53, 57–58, 61–62
 deforestation outcomes and, 56–57
 forest products, 48-52
 residents, 62–66, 84n7, 85n26
 Zombitse National Park, 54–56, 82, 155
ANGAP *(Association Nationale pour la Gestion des Aires Protégées)*, 55, 104, 120
Angola, 16 –17

Anti-poverty policies and strategies (PRSP), 94

B
Bara Zafimanely family, 68, 70, 73
Beijing Consensus, 98
Bhattarai, Madhusudan, 16–17
Bricolage, 22
Buganda Kingdom, 8, 111, 153
Buggala Island, 115, 119–120
Burundi, 7, 15–16, 170

C
Cabo Verde, 16–17
Cameroon, 6, 15–17, 170
Campbell, Bruce, 138
CBFF (Congo Basin Forest Fund), 6
CBFM (Community-Based Forest Management), 145, 159n27, 160n46
CBNRM (Community-Based Natural Resource Management), 26, 135–140, 142–148, 150, 152, 154–157, 169

interest alignment, 148–154
Kitulang'halo forest, 150–152
Madagascar, 143–144
overview, 135–136
success and failure, 136–140
Tanzania, 144–146
Tapia forest, 148–150
Uganda, 146–148
CCM *(Chama Cha Mapinduzi)*, 105
CFM (Collaborative Forest Management), 144–147, 155
CFMA (Collaborative Forest Management Agreements), 146–147
CFRs (Central Forest Reserves), 112–114, 120, 147, 152, 155
Cheru, Fantu, 7
China, 96, 98
Civil war, 109–110
CLB. *See* COBAs
Cleaver, Frances, 22
Climate change, 5, 10–11, 170
COBAs *(Communautés Locales de Base)*, 144, 148–150, 154–156
COMIFAC (Central Africa Forests Commission), 6
Congo Basin, 6–8, 13
Convention on Biological Diversity (CBD), 9
Côte d'Ivoire, 16

D
DD *(Direction des Eaux et Forêts)*, 103
DEA (Directorate of Environmental Affairs), 119
Death, Carl, 19
DEF *(Direction des Eaux et Forêts)*, 103, 120
Deforestation
in African context, 7–13
African politics and, 18–20
complexities of, 14–23

global commons, 20–23
tropical, 15–18
Democratic Republic of Congo, 16, 109, 170
Denmark, 97
DFS (District Forest Services), 118–119, 147
Dionne, Kim Yi, 171
DMH *(Dinan'ny Mpanao Hatsaka)*, 55–56, 62, 64, 86n26
Dunn, Kevin C., 7

E
E&F *(Eaux et Forêts)*, 52, 54–56, 58–59, 62–66, 69–73, 82
EKC (Environmental Kuznets Curve), 17
England, 97, 105
Englebert, Pierre, 7
Environmental politics, national level
aid to Africa, 93–99; aid competition, 96–99; reasons, 94–96
institutional proliferation, 113–121
overview, 91–93
protection of resources, 99–113; Madagascar, 100–104; Tanzania, 105–108; Uganda, 109–113
Equatorial Guinea, 6, 15–16
European Union, 11, 110, 153–154

F
Fanjakana, 50–51, 53, 57–62, 70, 85n24, 85n25
FD (Forest Department), 111–112, 114–115, 147
FID (Forestry Inspectorate Division), 119
FLEGT (Forest Law Enforcement, Governance, and Trade), 9–11
Fokonolona, 64–65, 86n26

INDEX

Fokontany, 71
Forsyth, Tim, 13
FRs (Forest Reserves), 111
FTM (national geographic institute), 103

G
Gabon, 6, 16
Gambia, 16
GCF (contract-based forest management), 144–145, 148, 150, 154
GELOSE *(Gestion Locale Sécurisée)*, 26, 104
Germany, 98, 102, 105, 126n38
Gibson, Clark C., 18, 20, 137, 154
Global North and South, 13
Governing the Commons (Ostrom), 21
GTZ *(Deutsche Gesellschaft für Technische Zusammenarbeit)*, 98

H
Hammig, Michael, 16–17

I
Iarindrano and Ihera forests, 47, 66–73
IFIs (International Financial Institutions), 97, 102, 107, 111, 142
IFRI/SANREM project, 47, 74, 174
India, 96
Industrialization, 8, 93, 96, 109–110, 119
Institutional investments, 4, 25, 91–92, 100–102, 111, 113–114, 121, 168
Institutionalism, 21–22
Interest alignment, 23–24

International Union for Conservation of Nature (IUCN), 102
IUCN (International Union for Conservation of Nature), 102, 106

J
JFM (Joint Forest Management), 145, 150–152, 159n27, 160n46

K
Kakira Sugar Works, 130n101
Kalangala District, 115, 129n99
Kamosa (*Chef de Cantonnement, Sakraha*), 59, 62, 71–72
Kampala, 109, 114, 127n55
Kanju, 22
Kasyoha-Kitomi forest reserve, 118–119
Kayasan, 137
Kenya, 7, 15–16, 18, 136, 170
Kerry, John, 2
KFW *(Kreditanstalt für Wiederaufbau)*, 98
Kibale, 111, 116–117
Kisawuzi, Thomas, 110, 113
Kitulang'halo Forest Reserve, 47, 136, 146, 148, 150–152
Kizzikibbi Forest Reserves, 153, 155–156
Knack, Stephen, 94
Kremen, Clair, 23
Kyoto Protocol, 24

L
LAFRs (Local Authority Forest Reserves), 107, 127n50
LCI, 156

LCs (Local Councils), 118
Lesotho, 16
LFRs (Local Forest Reserves), 112, 118, 147
Liberia, 18
Local level, resources and
  Analavelona and Zombitse, 48–66
  forest dependence, 47–48
  leader's legitimacy and social cohesion, 77–78
  lessons from Madagascar, 73–74
  overview, 43–45
  rule enforcement and enforcers, 75–77
  rule legitimacy, 74–75
  study of, 45–47
  Ugandan farmers, 79–80
LOGA (Local Government Authority), 107

M
MAAIF (Ministry of Agriclture, Animal Industry, and Fisheries), 119
Madagascar. *See also* ANGAP
  ANAE *(Association Nationale d'Actions Environmentales)*, 104
  CBNRM and, 143–144
  DD *(Direction des Eaux et Forêts)*, 103
  DEF *(Direction des Eaux et Forêts)*, 103, 120
  GCF (contract-based forest management), 144–145, 148, 150, 154
  GELOSE *(Gestion Locale Sécurisée)*, 26, 104
  ONE *(Office National de l'Environnement)*, 104
  protection of resources, 100–104
  SMB *(Secrétariat Multi-Bailleurs)*, 104

MANAPA (Madagascar National Parks). *See* ANGAP
Mauritius, 16, 170
Mbatu, Richard S., 13
MDGs (Millennium Development Goals), 5
ME (Ministry of Environment), 112, 128n78
MEMD (Ministry of Energy and Mineral Development), 118
Menkhaus, Ken, 171
MITI (Ministry of Tourism, Trade, and Industry), 118
MLG (Ministry of Local Government), 118
Mount Kilimanjaro, 107
Mpanga Strict Nature Reserve, 153–154, 160n48
Museveni, Yoweri, 93, 96, 98–100, 109–112, 115–116, 120–122, 127n55, 127n59. *See also* Uganda
MWE (Ministry of Water and Environment), 119, 128n78

N
Namungo Private Forest, 153–154, 156, 160n48
NCAA (Ngorongoro Conservation Area Authority), 107
NEAP (National Environmental Action Plan), 103–104, 125n33
Nelson, Fred, 19
NEMA (National Environmental Management Authority), 112, 120
NFA (National Forest Authority), 79, 112–118, 146–147
NFRs (National Forest Reserves), 107, 127n50, 145
Nigeria, 17–18, 170, 174
Nongovernmental organizations (NGOs), 150

Norway, 6, 13, 97
Nyerere, Julius, 78, 93, 97, 100, 105–106, 121–123, 126n38, 144–145

O

Olopade, Dayo, 22
Olson, Mancur, 23
ONE *(Office National de l'Environnement)*, 104
Onyango, Oloka, 110
Ostrom, Elinor, 20–21, 139

P

PAs. *See* Protected areas
PCE (Policy Committee on Environment), 112
Peluso, Nancy, 20
PFE (Permanent Forest Estate), 111–112, 116–117
PFM (Participatory Forest Management), 26, 145, 147
Poaching, 110
Poteete, Amy, 19
PRC (People's Republic of China). *See* China
Protected areas, 45, 71, 100, 102, 104, 106, 111, 116, 120, 126n38, 172
PRSP. *See* Anti-poverty policies and strategies

R

Rahman, Aminur, 94
Rajoelina, Andry, 1, 130n102
Ravalomanana, Marc, 1, 93, 100–104, 106, 121–123
REDD+ (Reducing Emission from Deforestation and Forest Degradation), 9–13. *See also* United Nations
Reforestation, 10, 117
Rule enforcement and reform, 75–77
Rule legitmacy, 74–75
Rwanda, 7, 15–17, 109

S

SAPs (structural adjustment programs), 94, 99, 111–112, 141
Sayer, Jeffrey, 138
SDGs (Sustainable Development Goals), 5
Seychelles, 16
SFD (Scientific and Forest Department), 111
Sierra Leone, 18–19
Silk industry, 148–149
SMB *(Secrétariat Multi-Bailleurs)*, 104
Smouts, Marie-Claude, 12
South Sudan, 7, 94
Squatters, 116
Sudan, 98, 109
Swaziland, 16
Sweden, 97, 107

T

Tanzania
  CBFM (Community-Based Forest Management), 145, 159n27, 160n46
  CBNRM and, 144–146
  CCM *(Chama Cha Mapinduzi)*, 105
  JFM (Joint Forest Management), 145, 150–152, 159n27, 160n46
  Kitulang'halo Forest Reserve, 136
  LAFRs (Local Authority Forest Reserves), 107, 127n50

LOGA (Local Government Authority), 107
NCAA (Ngorongoro Conservation Area Authority), 107
NFRs (National Forest Reserves), 107, 127n50, 145
protection of resources, 105–108
TANAPA (Tanzania National Parks), 107
TANU (Tanganyika African National Union), 105, 126n38, 145
Thompson, Mary C., 12
Toliara, 49, 51–53, 63, 65, 72

U
Uganda
  CBNRM and, 146–148
  CFM and, 144–147, 155
  civil war, 109–110
  DEA (Directorate of Environmental Affairs), 119
  FID (Forestry Inspectorate Division), 119
  FRs (Forest Reserves), 111
  FSSD (Forestry Sector Support Department), 119, 146
  LCs (Local Councils), 118
  LFRs (Local Forest Reserves), 112, 118, 147
  MAAIF (Ministry of Agriclture, Animal Industry, and Fisheries), 119
  ME (Ministry of Environment), 112, 128n78
  MEMD (Ministry of Energy and Mineral Development), 118
  MITI (Ministry of Tourism, Trade, and Industry), 118
  MLG (Ministry of Local Government), 118
  MWE (Ministry of Water and Environment), 119, 128n78
  NEMA (National Environmental Management Authority), 112, 120
  NFA (National Forest Authority), 79, 112–118, 146–147
  PCE (Policy Committee on Environment), 112
  PFE (Permanent Forest Estate), 111–112, 116–117
  protection of resources, 109–113
  SFD (Scientific and Forest Department), 111
  UWA (Uganda Wildlife Authority), 79, 112–113, 116–118
Ujamaa program, 78, 105, 144–145, 157
United Nations
  Conference on Environment and Development (1992), 10
  Development Program (UNDP), 10, 110
  Food and Agriculture Organization (FAO), 7, 10
  UNFCCC, 10, 110. *See also* REDD+
United States, 6, 102
USAID (United States Agency for International Development), 98, 110, 120

V
Vazaha, 62, 70
VFC (Village Forest Committee), 151–152, 155

W
Washington Consensus, 94
Wily, Alden, 106

World Bank, 5, 16, 99, 107, 110, 150
World Wildlife Fund (WWF), 52, 55–56, 62–66, 71, 85n26

Z
Zambia, 18
Zimbabwe, 18, 137–138
Zombitse National Park, 46, 48–49
   background on, 51–52
   conservationism and, 82
   deforestation and, 56–57
   economic interests and, 155
   forest rules, 54–56
   illegal uses of, 62–63, 65–66
   WWF and, 71

The manufacturer's authorised representative in the EU is Springer Nature Customer Service Centre GmbH, Europaplatz 3, 69115 Heidelberg, Germany. If you have any concerns regarding our products, please contact ProductSafety@springernature.com

Printed and bound by CPI Group (UK) Ltd, Croydon, CR0 4YY

23/03/2026

02076672-0001